SPOTLIGHT™ on MUSIC

Authors

Judy Bond

René Boyer

Margaret Campbelle-Holman

Emily Crocker

Marilyn C. Davidson

Robert de Frece

Virginia Ebinger

Mary Goetze

Betsy M. Henderson

John Jacobson

Michael Jothen

Chris Judah-Lauder

Carol King

Vincent P. Lawrence

Ellen McCullough-Brabson

Janet McMillion

Nancy L. T. Miller

Ivy Rawlins

Susan Snyder

Gilberto D. Soto

Kodály Contributing Consultant

Sr. Lorna Zemke

HAL•LEONARD®

Macmillan McGraw-Hill

i

ACKNOWLEDGMENTS

Creative Direction and Delivery: The Quarasan Group, Inc.

From the Top—On National Radio! selections are adapted from the nationally distributed public radio program, *From the Top.* CEOs/Executive Producers: Jennifer Hurley-Wales and Gerald Slavet. Authors: Ann Gregg and Joanne Robinson. © 2000, 2001, 2002, 2003 From the Top, Inc.

The Broadway Junior® logo and MTI® logo are trademarks of Music Theatre International. All rights reserved.

Grateful acknowledgment is given to the following authors, composers and publishers. Every effort has been made to trace the ownership of all copyrighted material and to secure the necessary permissions to reprint these selections. In the case of some selections for which acknowledgment is not given, extensive research has failed to locate the copyright holders.

Songs and Speech Pieces

A la puerta de cielo (At the Gates of Heaven), from BIRCHARD MUSIC SERIES, BOOK 5. Adapted by Augustus D. Zanzig. Copyright © 1962 (Renewed) by Birch Tree Group Ltd. International Copyright Secured. All Rights Reserved.

Allundé, Alluia, Words and Music by Margaret Campbelle Holman. Used by Permission.

Ame fure (Rain), Japanese Folk Song collected and transcribed by Kathy Sorensen. © 1991 Kathy B. Sorensen. All Rights Reserved.

America, My Homeland, Words and Music by Robert de Frece and Shirley Funk. Used by Permission.

Arroyito serrano (Mountain Stream), Words and Music by Carlos Gustavino. Copyright © 2002 by BMG Music Publishing Argentina SA and SADAIC Latin Copyrights, Inc. All Rights for BMG Music Publishing Argentina SA in the U.S. Administered by BMG Songs, Inc. International Copyright Secured. All Rights Reserved.

At the Hop, Words and Music by Arthur Singer, John Madara and David White. Copyright © 1957 (Renewed) by Arc Music Corporation (BMI) and Six Continents Music Publishing, Inc. (BMI). All Rights Administered by Arc Music Corporation (BMI). International Copyright Secured. All Rights Reserved. Used by Permission.

Bamboo, Words and Music by Dave Van Ronk. © 1962 (Renewed) PEPA-MAR MUSIC CORP. All Rights. Administered by WB MUSIC CORP. All Rights Reserved. Used by Permission.

Bamboo Flute, Chinese Fishing Song collected and transcribed by Kathy Sorensen. © 1991 Kathy B. Sorensen. All Rights Reserved.

Big Bunch, a Little Bunch, by John W. Work. Copyright © 1945 (Renewed) by Templeton Publishing, a division of Shawnee Press, Inc. (ASCAP). International Copyright Secured. All Rights Reserved. Reprinted by Permission.

Boogie Woogie Ghost, The, Words and Music by Nadine Pelgar. Copyright © 1973 (Renewed 2001) by Scholastic, Inc. International Copyright Secured. All Rights Reserved.

Circle of Song, Words and Music by Emily Crocker. Copyright © 2000 by HAL LEONARD CORPORATION. International Copyright Secured. All Rights Reserved.

December Nights, December Lights, Words and Music by Emily Crocker. Copyright © 2000 by MUSIC EXPRESS, LLC. International Copyright Secured. All Rights Reserved.

Don't Let the Music Stop, Words Adapted from Walt Whitman and Arthur O'Shaughnessy. Additional Words and Music by Eugene Butler. Copyright © 1978 by Heritage Music Press (a division of The Lorenz Corporation). International Copyright Secured. All Rights Reserved.

Down at the Twist And Shout, Words and Music by Mary Chapin Carpenter. © 1990 EMI APRIL MUSIC INC. and GETAREALJOB MUSIC. All Rights Controlled and Administered by EMI APRIL MUSIC INC. All Rights Reserved. International Copyright Secured. Used by Permission.

E nānā kākou i nā manu (Let's Watch the Birds), Words and Music by Herbert Mahelona and Stacey Naki. Copyright © 1999 by Plymouth Music Co., Inc. International Copyright Secured. All Rights Reserved.

El manisero (Peanut Vendor), English Words by Marion Sunshine and L. Wolfe Gilbert. Music and Spanish Words by Moises Simons. Copyright © 1928, 1929, 1931 by Edward B. Marks Music Company. Copyright Renewed. International Copyright Secured. All Rights Reserved. Used by Permission.

Follow Your Dream, Words and Music by Mary Donnelly. Copyright © 1990 by Alfred Publishing Co., Inc. International Copyright Secured. All Rights Reserved.

Grandma's Feather Bed, Words and Music by Jim Connor. Copyright © 1973; Renewed 2001 Cherry River Music Co. (BMI) and Dimensional Songs Of The Knoll (BMI). Worldwide Rights for Dimensional Songs Of The Knoll Administered by Cherry River Music Co. International Copyright Secured. All Rights Reserved.

Happiness, from YOU'RE A GOOD MAN, CHARLIE BROWN. Words and Music by Clark Gesner. © 1965 JEREMY MUSIC INC. © Renewed 1993 MPL MUSIC PUBLISHING, INC. All Rights Reserved.

Happy Talk, from SOUTH PACIFIC. Lyrics by Oscar Hammerstein II. Music by Richard Rodgers. Copyright © 1949 by Richard Rodgers and Oscar Hammerstein II. Copyright Renewed. WILLIAMSON MUSIC owner of publication and allied rights throughout the world. International Copyright Secured. All Rights Reserved.

Hey, Look Me Over, from WILDCAT. Music by Cy Coleman. Lyrics by Carolyn Leigh. © 1960, 1961 (Renewed 1988, 1989) NOTABLE MUSIC CO., INC. and EMI CARWIN CATALOG INC. All Rights on behalf of NOTABLE MUSIC CO., INC. Administered by WB MUSIC CORP. Print Rights on behalf of EMI CARWIN CATALOG INC. Administered by WARNER BROS. PUBLICATIONS U.S. INC. All Rights Reserved.

Hine Ma Tov (How Good It Is), Words from Psalm 133:1. Music by Allen E. Naplan Copyright © by Boosey & Hawkes Co., Inc. International Copyright Secured. All Rights Reserved. Used by Permission.

Hitori, Japanese Folksong. Arranged by Mary Donnelly and George Strid. Copyright © 2000 by HAL LEONARD CORPORATION. International Copyright Secured. All Rights Reserved.

I Heard a Mockingbird, Words and Music by Carol King and Rebecca Treadway. Copyright © by Carol King and Rebecca Treadway. International Copyright Secured. All Rights Reserved.

I'll Rise When the Rooster Crows, Appalachian Folk Song. Music by Uncle Dave Macon. Copyright © 1983 by Butterside Music. International Copyright Secured. All Rights Reserved.

It's the Hard-Knock Life, from MTI's Broadway Junior Broadway for Kids ANNIE Junior. Music by Charles Strouse. Lyrics by Martin Charnin. Music and Lyrics Copyright © 1977, 1978 by Edwin H. Morris & Co, a Division of MPL Communications, Inc. and Charles Strouse. All Rights Reserved. Used by Permission.

I Think I'm Gonna Like It Here, from MTI's Broadway Junior Broadway for Kids ANNIE Junior. Music by Charles Strouse. Lyrics by Martin Charnin. Music and Lyrics Copyright © 1977, 1978 by Edwin H. Morris & Co, a Division of MPL Communications, Inc. and Charles Strouse. All Rights Reserved. Used by Permission.

I Will Be Your Friend, from *I Will Be Your Friend: Songs and Activities for Young Peacemakers.* Words and Music by Guy Davis. Copyright © 2002 by MEDICINE HAND MUSIC/Administrator: Royalty Tracking Music (BMI). International Copyright Secured. All Rights Reserved.

Just One Planet, Words and Music by Sarah Stevens and Catherine Marchese. Copyright © 2001 by SARAH STEVENS and CATHERINE MARCHESE. International Copyright Secured. All Rights Reserved.

La otra España (The Other Spain), Words and Music by Juan C. Calderon. Copyright© by ED. MUSICALES POLYGRAM S.A./DISCORAMA. All rights administered in the United States and Canada by UNIVERSAL – POLYGRAM INTERNATIONAL PUBLISHING, INC. International Copyright Secured. All Rights Reserved.

La sanjuanerita (The Girl From San Juan), Words and Music by L. y M. Guadalupe Hernández. Copyright © 1980 by the World Association of Girl Guides and Girl Scouts. All Rights Reserved.

continued on page 409

A

The McGraw·Hill Companies

 **Macmillan/McGraw-Hill**

Published by Macmillan/McGraw-Hill, of McGraw-Hill Education, a division of The McGraw-Hill Companies, Inc., Two Penn Plaza, New York, New York 10121.

ISBN: 978-0-02-296701-7
MHID: 0-02-296701-X

2 3 4 5 6 7 8 9 DOW 16 15 14 13 12 11 10

Printed in the United States of America

SPOTLIGHT on MUSIC

CONTRIBUTORS

Consultants

Brian Burnett,
Movement

Stephen Gabriel,
Technology

Magali Iglesias,
English Language Learners

Roberta Newcomer,
Special Learners/Assessment

Frank Rodríguez,
English Language Learners

Jacque Schrader,
Movement

Kathy B. Sorensen,
International Phonetic
Alphabet

Patti Windes-Bridges,
Listening Maps

Linda Worsley,
Listening/Singable
English Translations

Sr. Lorna Zemke,
Kodály Contributing
Consultant

Recordings

Executive Producer: John Higgins
Senior Music Editor/Producer: Emily Crocker
Senior Recording Producer: Mark Brymer
Recording Producers: Steve Millikan, Andy Waterman
Associate Recording Producers: Alan Billingsley, Darrell Bledsoe, Stacy Carson, Rosanna Eckert, John Egan, Chad Evans, Darlene Koldenhoven, Chris Koszuta, Don Markese, Matthew McGregor, Steve Potts, Edwin Schupman, Michael Spresser, Frank Stegall, David Vartanian, Mike Wilson, Ted Wilson
Project/Mastering Engineer: Mark Aspinall; Post-Production Engineer: Don Sternecker
Selected recordings by Buryl Red, Executive Producer; Michael Rafter, Senior Recording Producer; Bryan Louiselle and Buddy Skipper, Recording Producers; Lori Casteel and Mick Rossi, Associate Recording Producers; Jonathan Duckett, Supervising Engineer

Contributing Writers

Allison Abucewicz, Sharon Berndt, Rhona Brink, Ann Burbridge, Debbie Heim Daniel, Katherine Domingo, Kari Gilbertson, Janet Graham, Hilree Hamilton, Linda Harley, Judy Henneberger, Carol Huffman, Bernie Hynson, Jr., Sheila A. Kerley, Elizabeth Kipperman, Ellen Mendelsohn, Cristi Cary Miller, Leigh Ann Mock, Patricia O'Rourke, Barbara Resch, Soojin Kim Ritterling, Isabel Romero, Carl B. Schmidt, Debra Shearer, Ellen Mundy Shuler, Rebecca Treadway, Carol Wheeler, Sheila Woodward

Multicultural Consultants

William Anderson, Chet-Yeng Loong, Edwin Schupman, Kathy B. Sorensen, Gilberto D. Soto, Judith Cook Tucker, Dennis Waring

In the Spotlight Consultant

Willa Dunleavy

Multicultural Advisors

Brad Ahawanrathe Bonaparte (Mohawk), Emmanuel Akakpo (Ewe), Earlene Albano (Hawaiian), Luana Au (Maori), Bryan Ayakawa (Japanese), Ruby Beeston (Mandarin), Latif Bolat (Turkish), Estella Christensen (Spanish), Oussama Davis (Arabic), Mia Delguardo (Minahasa), Nolutho Ndengane Diko (Xhosa), Angela Fields (Hopi, Chemehuevi), Gary Fields (Lakota, Cree), Gilad Harel (Hebrew), Josephine Hetarihon (Bahasa Indonesian, Minahasa, and Maluko dialect), Judy Hirt-Manheimer (Hebrew), Rose Jakub (Navajo), Elizabeth Jarema (Fijian), Rita Jensen (Swedish), Malou Jewett (Visayan), Alejandro Jimenez (Hispanic), Chris Jones (Hungarian), Wendy Jyang Shamo (Mandarin), Amir Kalay (Hebrew), Michael Katsan (Greek), Silvi Madarajan (Tamil), Georgia Magpie (Comanche), Nona Mardi (Malay), Aida Mattingly (Tagalog), Mike Kanathohare McDonald (Mohawk), Vasana de Mel (Sinhala), Marion Miller (Czech), Etsuko Miskin (Japanese), Mogens Mogenson (Danish), Kenny Tahawisoren Perkins (Mohawk), Pradeep Nayyar (Punjabi, Hindi), Renu Nayyar (Punjabi), Mfanego Ngwenya (Zulu), Wil Numkena (Hopi), Samuel Owuru (Akan), Nina Padukone (Konkani), Hung Yong Park (Korean), James Parker (Finnish), Jose Pereira (Konkani), Berrit Price (Norwegian), John Rainer (Taos Pueblo, Creek), Lillian Rainer (Taos Pueblo, Creek, Apache), Arnold Richardson (Haliwa-Saponi), Ken Runnacles (German), Trudy Shenk (German), Ron Singer (Navajo), Ernest Siva (Cahuilla, Serrano [Maringa']), Bonnie Slade (Swedish), Cristina Sorrentino (Portuguese), Diane Thram (Xhosa), Elena Todorov (Bulgarian), Zlatina Todorov (Russian), Tom Toronto (Lao, Thai), Rebecca Wilberg (French, Italian), Sheila Woodward (Zulu), Keith Yackeyonny (Comanche)

Contents

In the Spotlight . . . . **A**

Spotlight on Concepts 1

Unit 1 Music for Everyone **2**
Body Percussion ■ $\frac{4}{4}$ meter ■ Melodic Contour
■ Rhythm Patterns ■ ♩, ♫, ♩, and ♩ ■ *Do Re Mi So La*
■ Phrases ■ Expression

Unit 2 Musical Messages, Musical Journeys **42**
Three and Four Sounds to a Beat ■ Tonal Center ■ Low *La*
■ Low *Sol* ■ ♫♫, ♪♫ and ♫ ■ Contrasting Sections

Unit 3 Happy Go Lucky! **82**
Three Equal Sounds to a Beat ■ Melodic Contour ■ *Fa* ■ $\frac{6}{8}$ ■ $\frac{2}{2}$
■ Dynamics ■ I-V Harmony ■ ♫♪, ♩♪ and ♩.

Unit 4 Musical Discoveries **122**
Octave Leaps ■ High *Do* ■ Pitch Syllables ■ ♪♩ ♪ ■ I-IV-V
■ Pentatonic Melody ■ Triads ■ Descants

Unit 5 One Musical Planet **162**
Beats in Groups of Three ■ Major or Minor ■ Melodic Phrases
■ Tempo ■ ♩ ♪ ■ *Ti* ■ $\frac{3}{4}$

Unit 6 A Time to Dream, A Time to Sing **202**
Expression ■ AB Form ■ Augmentation and Diminution
■ Three-Part Harmony ■ Homophonic Texture
■ Ornamentation ■ Minor ■ Theme and Variations

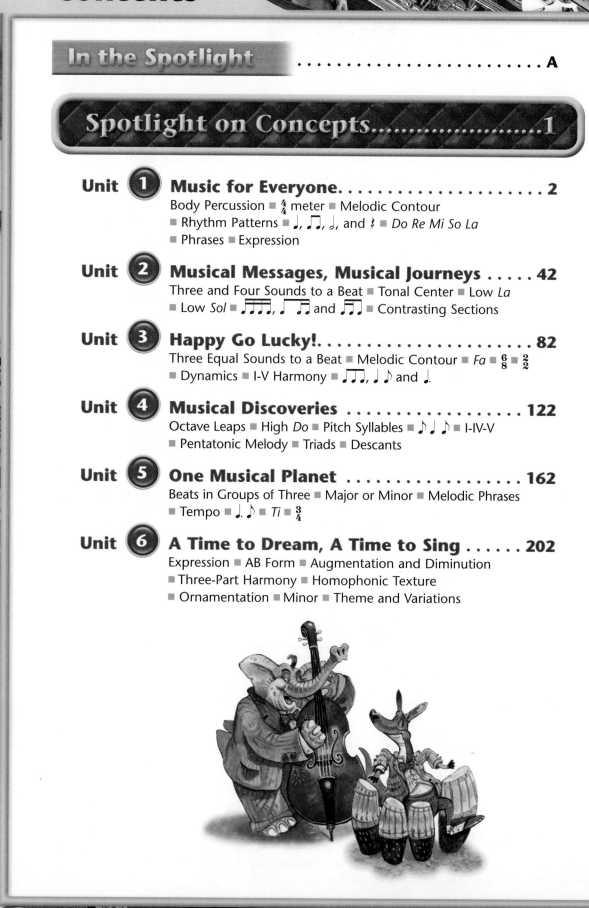

Spotlight on Music Reading..........241

Unit **1** **Concepts: More Music Reading** 242
Basic Rhythms; *Do Re Mi; So;* Pentatonic Melodies

Unit **2** **Concepts: More Music Reading** 248
Low *So;* Low *La;* Tonal Center; Sixteenth Notes

Unit **3** **Concepts: More Music Reading** 256
$\frac{6}{8}$ $\left(\frac{2}{}\right)$ meter; Unequal Rhythms; *Fa*

Unit **4** **Concepts: More Music Reading** 264
Syncopation; High *Do;* Leap from *Do* to High *Do*

Unit **5** **Concepts: More Music Reading** 272
$\frac{3}{4}$ meter; *Ti;* The Major Scale; Chords

Unit **6** **Concepts: More Music Reading** 280
Major and Minor

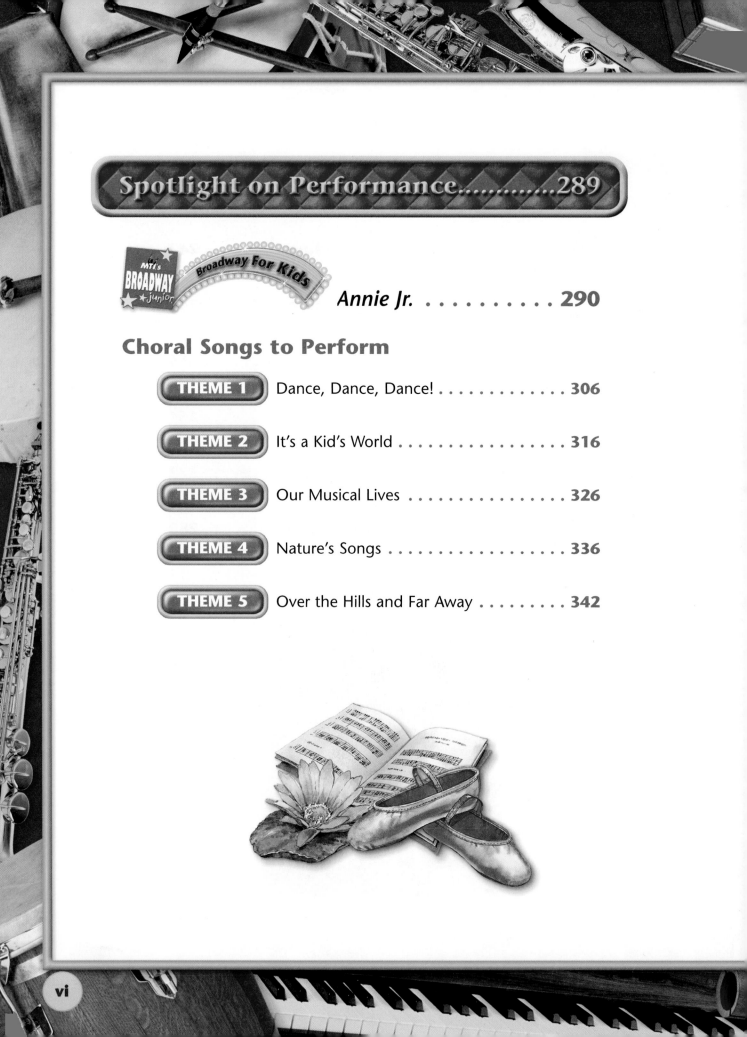

Spotlight on Performance............289

Broadway For Kids

Annie Jr. 290

Choral Songs to Perform

THEME 1 Dance, Dance, Dance! 306

THEME 2 It's a Kid's World 316

THEME 3 Our Musical Lives 326

THEME 4 Nature's Songs 336

THEME 5 Over the Hills and Far Away 342

Spotlight on Celebrations............353

PATRIOTIC 354

AUTUMN 362

WINTER 372

SPRING 390

SUMMER 396

Playing the Recorder 398

Glossary of Instruments 399

Glossary of Terms 405

Indexes 411

In the Spotlight

Let's sing the songs of America!
Let's play the tunes of people and places,
old and new, grand and small.
Let's sing the songs of the cities and states,
the beach and the prairie,
the skies and the seas.
Beat the drum! Sound the trumpet!
Step into the light!
Let's sing the songs of America!

Step into the Spotlight

**Spotlight CD
Track 1**

Words and Music by John Jacobson,
Emily Crocker, and John Higgins

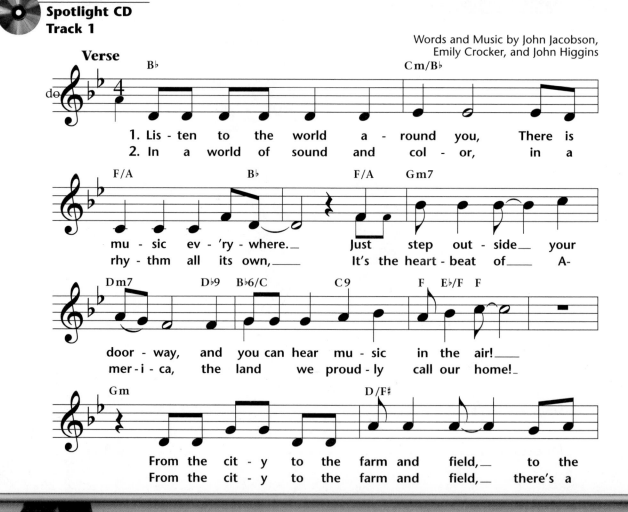

Verse

B♭   Cm/B♭

1. Lis - ten   to   the   world   a - round   you,   There is
2. In   a   world   of   sound   and   col - or,   in   a

F/A   B♭   F/A   Gm7

mu - sic   ev - 'ry - where.___   Just   step   out - side___   your
rhy - thm   all   its   own,___   It's the heart - beat of___   A-

Dm7   D♭9   B♭6/C   C9   F   E♭/F   F

door - way,   and   you can hear   mu - sic   in the   air!___
mer - i - ca,   the   land   we proud - ly   call our   home!_

Gm   D/F♯

From   the   cit - y   to   the   farm and   field,___   to the
From   the   cit - y   to   the   farm and   field,___   there's a

A

rush - ing   riv - er   free,___   there's mus - ic   all   a-
hope that's shin - ing   bright.__   So   sing   out strong, A-

round   us,   there's mu - sic   in   you and   me!___ }
mer - i - ca,   and   step   in - to   the   light!__ }

Come on and

step   in - to   the   spot   -   light!___   Come on and

step   in - to   the   spot   -   light!   Let   it   shine,   shine,

shine   on   our   mus - ic   and our   song.__   Come on and

step   in - to   the   spot   -   light!___   Come on and

step   in - to   the   spot   -   light!   Let   it

shine!   Let   it   shine on   ev - 'ry - one!__

B

The songs of America are rich and varied.
They remind us of where we are,
where we have been,
where we are going,
and sometimes
where we long to be.

SHENANDOAH

Spotlight CD
Track 4

Traditional Sea Chanty

1. Oh, Shen - an - doah,____ I long to hear you.
2. Oh, Shen - an - doah,____ I'm bound to leave you.
3. 'Tis sev'n long years____ since last I saw you.

A - way,_____ you roll - ing riv - er.
A - way,_____ you roll - ing riv - er.
A - way,_____ you roll - ing riv - er.

Oh, Shen - an - doah,____ I long to hear you.
Oh, Shen - an - doah,____ I'll not de - ceive you.
'Tis sev'n long years____ since last I saw you.

A - way,_____ I'm bound a - way
A - way,_____ I'm bound a - way
A - way,_____ I'm bound a - way

'cross the wide Mis - sour - i.
'cross the wide Mis - sour - i.
'cross the wide Mis - sour - i.

In the Spotlight

The songs of America remind us of our favorite places, whether "On Top of Old Smokey," "Down by the Riverside," or having lots of fun at Grandma's house!

Spotlight CD
Track 7

Words and Music by Jim Conner

Verse

When I was a lit-tle-bit-ty boy
Af-ter sup-per we'd sit a-round the fire, the

just up off-a-the floor,
old folks-'d spit and chew,

We used to go down to
Pa would talk a-bout the

Grand-ma's house ev-'ry month end or so,
farm and the war and Gramy'd sing a bal-lad or two.

We'd have
I'd

chick-en pie and coun-try ham and
sit and lis-ten and watch the fire till the

home-made but-ter on the bread,
cob-webs filled my head,

But the best thing of all a-bout
Next thing I'd know I'd

Grand - ma's house was her great big feath-er bed.
wake up in the morn-in' in the mid-dle of the old feath-er bed.

Refrain

It was nine feet tall and six feet wide,

soft as a down-y chick. It was made from the feath-ers of

for - ty 'lev - en geese took a whole bolt of cloth for the

tick. It - 'd hold eight kids an' four hound dogs and a

pig-gy we stole from the shed. We did-n't get much sleep but we

had a lot of fun on Grand-ma's feath-er - bed.

In the Spotlight

When we sing the songs of America, we demonstrate our pride in being an American.

Through our songs, we declare that we are proud to live in a land where we have the right to wave our flag, voice our opinion, and be who we want to be.

There is a light in my heart.

It is the song of America.

Let's sing the songs of America!

Patriotic Medley

**Spotlight CD
Track 10**

Words by George M. Cohan,
Woody Guthrie, and Katharine Lee Bates.

You're a Grand Old Flag

You're a Grand Old Flag, you're a high flyin' flag.
And forever in peace may you wave.
You're the emblem of the land I love,
The home of the free and the brave.
Ev'ry heart beats true
for the red, white, and blue,
Where there's never a boast or brag.
But should auld acquaintance be forgot,
Keep your eye on the grand old flag.

This Land Is Your Land

This land is your land, this land is my land
From California to the New York Island.
From the redwood forest
to the Gulf Stream waters,
This land was made for you and me.
As I was walking that ribbon of highway,
I saw above me that endless skyway.
I saw below me that golden valley.
This land was made for you and me.

America, the Beautiful

America! America! God shed His grace on thee.
And crown thy good with brotherhood,
From sea to shining sea!

H

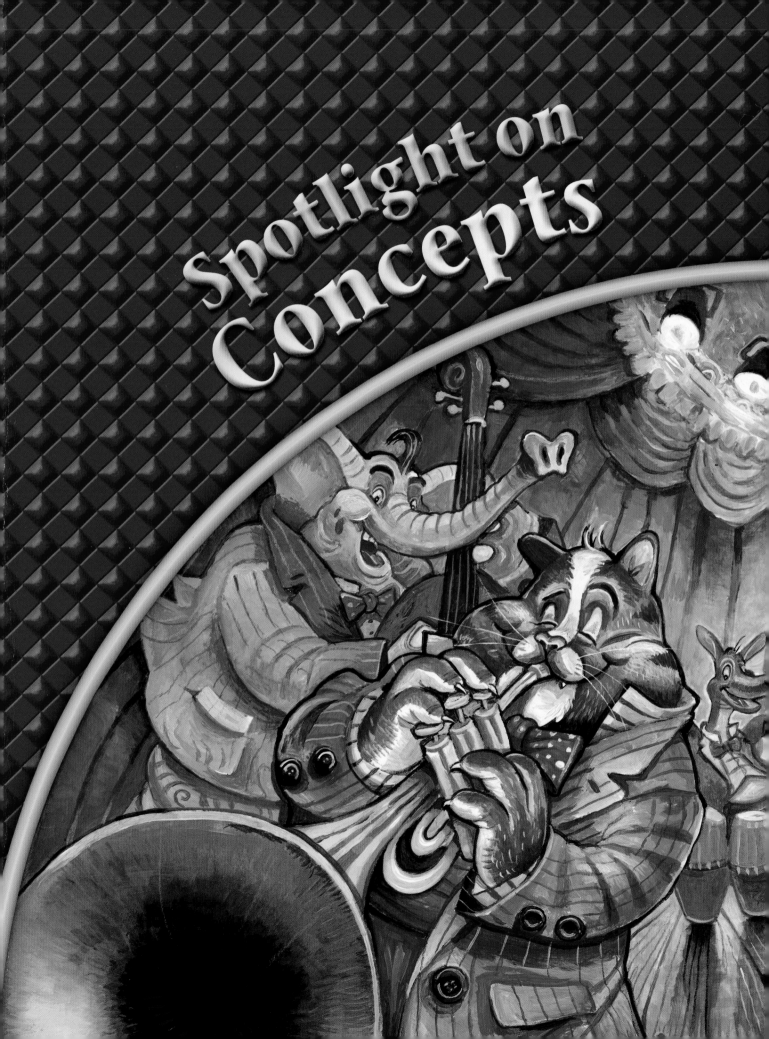

Spotlight on
Concepts

Spotlight on
Concepts

Spotlight on Concepts

Unit **1** **Music for Everyone**. 2
Body Percussion ▪ $\frac{4}{4}$ meter ▪ Melodic Contour
▪ Rhythm Patterns ▪ ♩, ♫, ♩, and 𝄽 ▪ *Do Re Mi So La*
▪ Phrases ▪ Expression

Unit **2** **Musical Messages, Musical Journeys** 42
Three and Four Sounds to a Beat ▪ Tonal Center ▪ Low *La*
▪ Low *So* ▪ , and ▪ Contrasting Sections

Unit **3** **Happy Go Lucky!**. 82
Three Equal Sounds to a Beat ▪ Melodic Contour ▪ *Fa* $\frac{6}{8}$ ▪ $\frac{2}{2}$
▪ Dynamics ▪ I-V Harmony ▪ , ♩ ♪ and ♩.

Unit **4** **Musical Discoveries** 122
Octave Leaps ▪ High *Do* ▪ Pitch Syllables ▪ ♪ ♩ ♪ ▪ I-IV-V
▪ Pentatonic Melody ▪ Triads ▪ Descants

Unit **5** **One Musical Planet** 162
Beats in Groups of Three ▪ Major or Minor ▪ Melodic Phrases
▪ Tempo ▪ ♩. ♪ ▪ *Ti* ▪ $\frac{3}{4}$

Unit **6** **A Time to Dream, A Time to Sing** 202
Expression ▪ AB Form ▪ Augmentation and Diminution
▪ Three-Part Harmony ▪ Homophonic Texture
▪ Ornamentation ▪ Minor
▪ Theme and Variations

Music for Everyone

Music is for everyone. No matter who you are, where you are from, or what you like, music has something for you! In Unit 1 you will sing, play, listen, and create music that you can enjoy and share with others.

Coming Attractions

Move to a folk song from Spain.

Listen to and sing a Native American lullaby.

Sing a fun rock and roll song.

Music can express messages
of happiness, hope, and friendship.
"Something for Me, Something for You"
is a song about how a little sharing between friends
can make a big difference. What can you do to make
a difference in someone's life?

Something for ME, Something for YOU

CD 1:1

Words and Music by J.D. Steele, Larry Long, Brian C. Herron and Nate Underwood

Refrain

Some-thing for me,____ some-thing for you,____ you show love for me,____ I show love for you.____ If we take time to see____ what this world could be____ we could live peace-ful-ly,____ we all could be free.

Verse (Rap)

1. I'm the voice of the future
   The next in charge
   So this world's up to us to
   Protect from harm
   It's about love and peace and
   Respecting each other
   You shouldn't judge somebody
   Just because of their color
   Yo!
   We're all a little different
   Something unique
   But these same differences
   Make the world complete
   Whether boy or girl –
   Put-downs is wack!
   We need to show each other
      support
   Instead of all that
   Fightin' just ain't the answer
   We need to talk
   And get past all the hate
   So we can see it resolved
   And, adults, understand that
   We learn from you
   Everything in this world that
   A person should do
   Peace works for everybody
   Meaning me and you
   And we can make Dr. King's
   Dream really come true
   Take time, spread love
   And believe in you
   And together we can learn to
   Put love to use

   Refrain

2. Sometimes I get sad at what
   I hear on the news
   Or when I see kids getting
   Into fights at school
   I know all are equal
   That means we're all one
   Not saying there aren't
      differences
   That we need to love
   We gotta learn patience
   And know what's right
   We might disagree
   But we don't have to fight
   Respect is respect and we
   Need to show it
   That's why we came together
   On this song
   So you could know it
   Since we're the future
   We're telling you now
   All the racism and hatred
   We're shutting it down
   We live and we learn
   And we share with one another
   And smile at the new things
   That we discover
   And it's all from the heart
   Meaning nothing but love
   And we're gonna make better
   What was given to us
   It don't matter if you're out
      of town
   Or live on my street
   Just try to be a friend to
   Whoever you meet
   And make peace!

   Refrain

LESSON 1

CONCEPT
METER

SKILLS
SING, LISTEN, DESCRIBE

LINKS
FINE ART, MOVEMENT

Taking the Pulse of Music

When you put a finger on your wrist, you can feel the steady beat of your pulse. Music also has a steady pulse. It is called **beat**. Beats in music are felt in groups of strong and weak beats.

Listen for the strong and weak beats in "My Town, My World."
Sing the song.

MY TOWN, MY WORLD

CD 1:4

Words and Music by
John Jacobson and John Higgins

I'm on - ly one per-son, an in-di-vid - u-al.

You've got your own life, too.__ The feel-ing's nat-u-ral, But

our lives are con-nect - ed with ev-'ry boy and girl.__ We're a

fam-i-ly, a neigh-bor-hood, a coun-try and a world.__

My town,_ my world!_ My town,_ my world!_

My street_and my neigh-bor-hood,_ I know each mile holds

some-thing good!_ My town,_ my world!_ My town,_ my world!_

Heart to heart__ and face to face,_ each a part_ of the hu-man race,_

tak-ing care_ of our spe-cial place,_ my town, my

world! Yes,_ world! My town, my world!__

Group the Beat

Which pattern below shows the beat groupings for "My Town, My World"?

Meter signatures, such as $\frac{2}{4}$, $\frac{3}{4}$, and $\frac{4}{4}$ are found at the beginning of songs. The top number shows the number of beats in each group or measure. The bottom number shows which note gets the beat.

Identify the meter signature in "My Town, My World."

$\frac{2}{4}$ can also be written like this: $\frac{2}{4}$

$\frac{4}{4}$ can also be written like this: $\frac{4}{4}$

Art Gallery

Child with a Dove

Pablo Picasso (1881–1973) created this drawing in 1901. The dove is a symbol for peace.

THINK! Read the words of "My Town, My World." What do Picasso's painting and this song have in common?

Listen to "Hush, Little Baby."

Bobby McFerrin and Yo-Yo Ma ▶

 LISTENING CD 1:7

Hush, Little Baby American folk song

The song has three verses and is a **duet** performed by Yo–Yo Ma and Bobby McFerrin. In a duet, two musicians play or sing together. **Describe** how McFerrin uses his voice when he is not singing words.

Practice the movements below.

PAT (1 beat)   CROSS (1 beat)   CLAP (1 beat)   THUMBS UP (2 beats)

Perform the movements in this order each time you hear the interludes between verses in "Hush, Little Baby." **Move** to the beat.

1	PAT	PAT	CROSS	CROSS
2	PAT	PAT	CROSS	CROSS
3	PAT	CLAP	PAT	CLAP
4	THUMBS UP		THUMBS UP	

Shape Up and Ship Out!

CONCEPT
MELODY
SKILLS
SING, DESCRIBE,
COMPARE
LINKS
SOCIAL STUDIES,
CULTURES

Just as waves in the ocean rise and fall, the **pitch** of "Somos el barco" also goes up and down. Pitch is the highness and lowness of a sound.

Sing the song.

We Are the Boat

CD 1:8

Words and Music by Lorre Wyatt
Arranged by Estaire Godinez

Move your hand up and down with the shape of the **melody**.
A melody is a series of pitches that moves upward, downward,
or stays the same.

The Contour Connection

Imagine you are hiking along a mountain trail. You will go up and down many times. In music, the ups and downs of a melody are known as **contour**.

"A la puerta del cielo" is a folk song from Spain.

Sing the song. **Identify** where the melody moves up and where the melody moves down.

MAP
FRANCE
PORTUGAL
SPAIN
MOROCCO   ALGERIA

A la puerta del cielo

At the Gate of Heaven

CD 1:12

Spanish Folk Song
English Version by MMH

F   C7

Spanish: A   la   puer - ta   del   cie - lo   ven - den   za - pa - tos,
Pronunciation: a   la   pwer   ta   ðel   sye   lo   ßen   den   sa   pa   tos
English: At   the   gate   of   Heav'n   they   are   sell - ing   *za - pa - tos,*

F   C7

Pa - ra   los   an - ge - li - tos   que an - dan   des - cal - zos.
pa   ɾa   los   aŋg   xe   li   tos   kean   dan   des   kai   sos
For   the   lit - tle   an - gels who   go   walk - ing   bare - foot.

D7   Gm   C7   F   C7

Duér - me - te,   ni - ño,   duér - me - te,   ni - ño,
dweɾ   me   te   ni   nyo   dweɾ   me   te   ni   nyo
Slum - ber   my   ba - by,   slum - ber   my   ba - by,

F   Bb   F   C7   F

Duér - me - te,   ni - ño,   a - rru,   a - rru.
dweɾ   me   te   ni   nyo   a   ɾu   a   ɾu
slum - ber   my   ba - by,   a - rru,   a - rru.

12

Compare these contour lines with each line of the song. Which contour line appears twice in the song?

🔘 **LISTENING**   CD 1:16

English horn

Adagio from *Concierto de Aranjuez* (excerpt) by Joaquín Rodrigo

This recording features guitar and English horn with orchestra.

Listen for the English horn playing the melody in "Adagio" from *Concierto de Aranjuez*. Trace the contour of the melody in the air with your hand as you listen again.

Meet the Musician

Joaquín Rodrigo (1901–1999), composer, was born in Valencia, Spain. At age three he was blinded by an illness, yet he still learned to play the piano and violin. He wrote over sixty songs and many choral and instrumental works. Rodrigo said his blindness led him to music. "I remember the song of the crickets, the pounding of the waves, the sound of the organ, and the church bells in my hometown."

CD-ROM

Use *Orchestral Instruments* **CD-ROM** to learn more about the English horn and other instruments of the orchestra.

Rhythm, Round, Fun!

CONCEPT
RHYTHM
SKILLS
READ, PLAY, SING
LINKS
LANGUAGE ARTS,
SOCIAL STUDIES

This speech piece is about traveling the globe. If you could go anywhere on the planet, where would you go?

Read "A Journey."

CD 1:17

Speech Piece by MMH

1 2 3

4/4 Let's go on a jour-ney. Where shall we go?

Pick some plac-es on the plan-et. There's so much to know.

Tra-vel to the con-tin-ents. There's so much to see.

Get your lug-gage load-ed up. Come with me!

All music has sounds and silences of different lengths. These sounds and silences, organized around beat, make up the **rhythm** of a piece. Look at the rhythm symbols below.

♩	**quarter note**	one sound to a beat
♫	two **eighth notes**	two sounds to a beat
♪	**half note**	sound lasting two beats
𝄽	**quarter rest**	silence the length of a beat

Identify some of these rhythms in "A Journey."

Play these rhythm patterns on percussion instruments as you perform "A Journey" again.

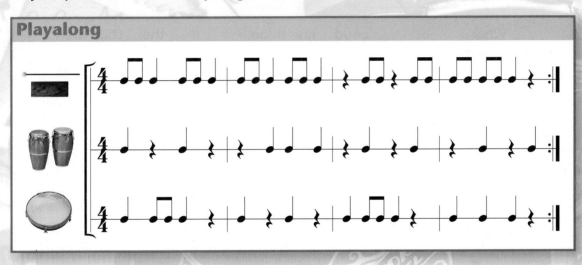

Playalong

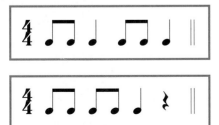

THINK! **Compare** these two rhythm patterns. If you substitute the first pattern for the first measure of "A Journey," would it work? Why or why not?

Canon and Round

When two or more voices perform the same melody but start at different times it is called a **round**. Singing a round is fun! The music can go on as long as the singers wish.

Sing the melody of "Peace Round." Then sing it as a round with the class.

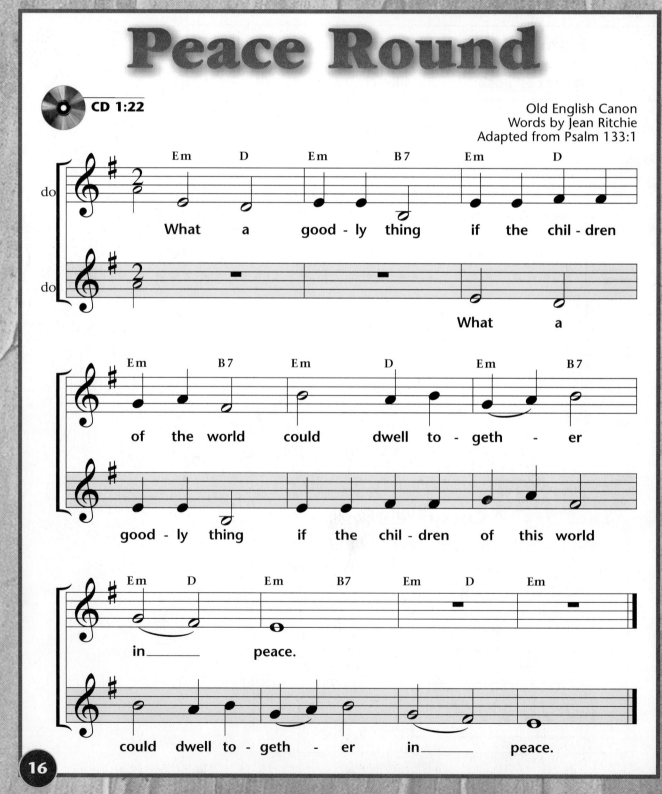

Peace Round

CD 1:22

Old English Canon
Words by Jean Ritchie
Adapted from Psalm 133:1

What a good-ly thing if the chil-dren

What a

of the world could dwell to-geth - er

good-ly thing if the chil-dren of this world

in_____ peace.

could dwell to-geth - er in_____ peace.

A round is a type of **canon**. Canon can have a melody performed in different ways at the same time.

Listen to *Canon in D*. **Compare** it to "Peace Round."

🔘 **LISTENING** CD 1:26

Canon in D by Johann Pachelbel

Canon in D was written almost three hundred years ago for string instruments. This recording features percussion instruments.

Meet the Musician

Brian Slawson (b. 1957) plays percussion for many different styles of music. He has played with such musicians as blues guitarist Stevie Ray Vaughan and the conductor and composer Leonard Bernstein. Brian studied at The Juilliard School of Music in New York City. He paid for his school by playing marimba on the streets of the city!

Read these rhythm patterns using body percussion.

Perform each pattern above four times as you listen to *Canon in D* again. Then start with pattern 8 and go backwards, reading each pattern four times.

LESSON 4

CONCEPT
MELODY

SKILLS
SING, LISTEN, DESCRIBE

LINKS
FINE ART, CULTURES

Melodies Take Shape

Almost everywhere in the world, people have quiet songs they sing to comfort babies and put them to sleep. These songs are called **lullabies**. "Bu-Vah" is a lullaby of the Hopi, a Native American tribe in Arizona.

Sing the song. Trace the melody with your finger as you sing.

BU-VAH

Sleep

CD 1:27

Hopi Lullaby
As sung by Tsung–ayah

Hopi: Bu - u Va - ah_____ ah Bu va - ah Ba va - ah____
Pronunciation: bu va a bu va bu va

su bü ba veh - e - e_____ eh Bu va - ah Bu va - ah____
su bü ba vɛ e ɛ bu va bu va

Ko - kyang oh yaht u - u_____ u Bu va - ah Bu va - ah____
ko kyang ho yat ʊ ʊ bu va bu va

nah i kwe o Kyang u - u - u Bu va - ah Bu va - ah____
na i kwe o kyang ʊ ʊ bu va bu va

Bu va - ah Bu va - ah____ Bu va - ah
bu va bu va bu va

Listen to an original recording of "Bu-Vah."

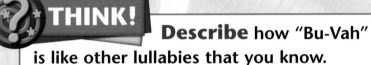

LISTENING CD 1:30

Bu-Vah Hopi Lullaby

This recording features "Bu-Vah" sung by Tsung–ayah, a Hopi singer.

? THINK! **Describe** how "Bu-Vah" is like other lullabies that you know.

Learn About Hopi Culture

The Hopi are a unique Native American tribe living in the northeast of Arizona. They trace their roots in North America all the way back to A.D. 500. The Hopi people created many unique methods of farming to adapt to the dry climate of the southwestern region of North America. Farming is a way of life for the Hopi. A Hopi farmer once said, "This is not about growing vegetables; it is about growing kids."

Art Gallery

This plaque with traditional Hopi designs was made of wicker by Hopi women in Arizona.

Shape That Melody

The shape, or contour, of a melody is formed when pitches move up, down, or repeat.

"Li'l 'Liza Jane" is a folk song from the eastern United States. **Sing** the song.

CD 2:1

Li'l 'Liza Jane

American Dance-Game Song

Verse

Leader

1. There's a gal in Bal - ti - more, Li'l 'Li - za Jane,
2. Come, my love, and mar - ry me, Li'l 'Li - za Jane,
3. If you'll come and be my own, Li'l 'Li - za Jane,
4. We'll have chick - ens 'round our door, Li'l 'Li - za Jane,

Leader

She's the one that I a - dore, Li'l 'Li - za Jane.
I will take good care of thee, Li'l 'Li - za Jane.
We'll eat ham and sweet corn pone, Li'l 'Li - za Jane.
Brus - sels car - pet on our floor, Li'l 'Li - za Jane.

Refrain

All

O E - li - za, Li'l 'Li - za Jane,

O E - li - za, Li'l 'Li - za Jane.

The first and third time you sing the words "Li'l 'Liza Jane," the melody is shaped liked this.

Li'l
    'Li-   Jane
       za

MIDI

Use "Li'l 'Liza Jane" from **Spotlight on MIDI** for more practice with identifying the contour of a melody.

The second and fourth times you sing those words, the melody is shaped like this.

Li'l 'Li-
   za
     Jane

The melody for the verse of "Li'l 'Liza Jane" uses five different pitches: **do re mi so la**. This set of five pitches is called a **pentatonic scale**.

do re mi so la

Name the pitch syllables in each pattern below. Use the pentatonic scale above as a guide.

The **tonal center** of a song is the home tone, or the pitch around which the melody is centered. The tonal center of "Li'l 'Liza Jane" is *do*. **Identify** *do* each time it occurs in "Li'l 'Liza Jane."

Phrases for the Morning

CONCEPT
FORM

SKILLS
SING, ANALYZE,
LISTEN

LINKS
SOCIAL STUDIES,
CULTURES

A paragraph is made up of sentences. Music has sentences, too. A musical sentence is called a **phrase**. A phrase is a short section of a song, or other piece of music, that is a complete musical thought.

The melody of "Morning Has Broken" is Gaelic, originally from the Isle of Man in the British Isles.

Sing "Morning Has Broken."
Identify each phrase of the song.

Morning Has Broken

CD 2:4

Traditional Gaelic Melody
Words by Eleanor Farjeon

1. Morn-ing has bro - ken   Like the first morn - ing,
2. Sweet the rain's new   fall   Sun - lit from heav - en,

Black-bird has spo - ken   Like the first bird.____
Like the first dew - fall   On the first grass.____

Praise for the sing - ing!   Praise for the morn - ing!
Praise for the sweet - ness   Of the wet gar - den,

Praise for them, spring - ing   Fresh from the world!____
Sprung in com - plete - ness   Where His feet pass.____

Listen to another recording of "Morning Has Broken."

🔘 **LISTENING** **CD 2:7**

Morning Has Broken traditional Gaelic melody

This recording of "Morning Has Broken" features the singer Art Garfunkel.

Listen closely for all of the instruments in the recording.

violin

Meet the Musician

Arthur "Art" Garfunkel (b. 1941), singer, was born in Forest Hills, New York. He began recording his own songs at the age of four. By the age of 11, he was performing in school talent shows with his friend, Paul Simon. Today he is best known for being part of the folk duo they formed, Simon & Garfunkel. They won five Grammy awards together, as well as many other awards for their famous song, "Bridge Over Troubled Water."

cello

piano

Phrases from South Africa

Global Voices

"Vinqo" is a song of the Zulu people, who live in South Africa. The Zulu and Xhosa people live in the same part of South Africa.

🔊 **LISTENING** CD 2:8

Vinqo Zulu Song from South Africa

The singers of "Vinqo" are Xhosa children. The words of the song are nonsense, but fun for the children to sing. Listen for the tongue clicks when the children are singing. This is part of the way they pronounce words in their language.

Listen to "Vinqo." **Move** to it as you listen again.

Zulu woman performing a traditional dance

The Zulu people are known for their beautiful beadwork. They send each other messages with these beads.

A Xhosa dancer in South Africa

Follow the translation of "Vinqo" below as you listen to the song again.

Vinqo

VERSE

Uph' unyoko? Vinqo!

Usal' ekhaya. Vinqo!

Usaleleni? Vinqo!

Ulunyw' imbengolo. Vinqo!

Imlume kuphi? Vinqo!

Emlenzeni Vinqo!

REFRAIN (sung twice)
Sawubona khanda lentulo

Ngomcwabosi ngomphothulo nkomo

Zobuy' emasisweni. Vinqo!

VERSE

Where is Granny?

She stayed home.

Why did she stay home?

She was bitten by a donkey.

Where was she bitten?

On her leg.

REFRAIN (sung twice)
Hello, head of the lizard!

Pound the maize into flour.

The cattle will be returned from where they were lent.

What's the Form?

Just like sentences make up a paragraph, phrases make up **form** in music. The structure, or plan, of a piece of music is called form.

Use lowercase letters to outline the form of the phrases in music. The first phrase is **a**.
The next phrase will be **a** if it is the same, **b** if it is different.
The musical outline of "Vinqo" is **a a a a a a a b b**.

Listen to "Vinqo" again, following the form.

The Music of Running Water

CONCEPT
TONE COLOR

SKILLS
SING, PLAY, READ

LINKS
SOCIAL STUDIES,
LANGUAGE ARTS

"**A**me fure" is a song from Japan that describes the sound of rain. **Sing** the song.

MAP
RUSSIA
CHINA
NORTH KOREA
JAPAN
SOUTH KOREA

Ame fure
Rain

CD 2:9

Collected and Transcribed by
Kathy B. Sorensen
English Words by Linda Worsley

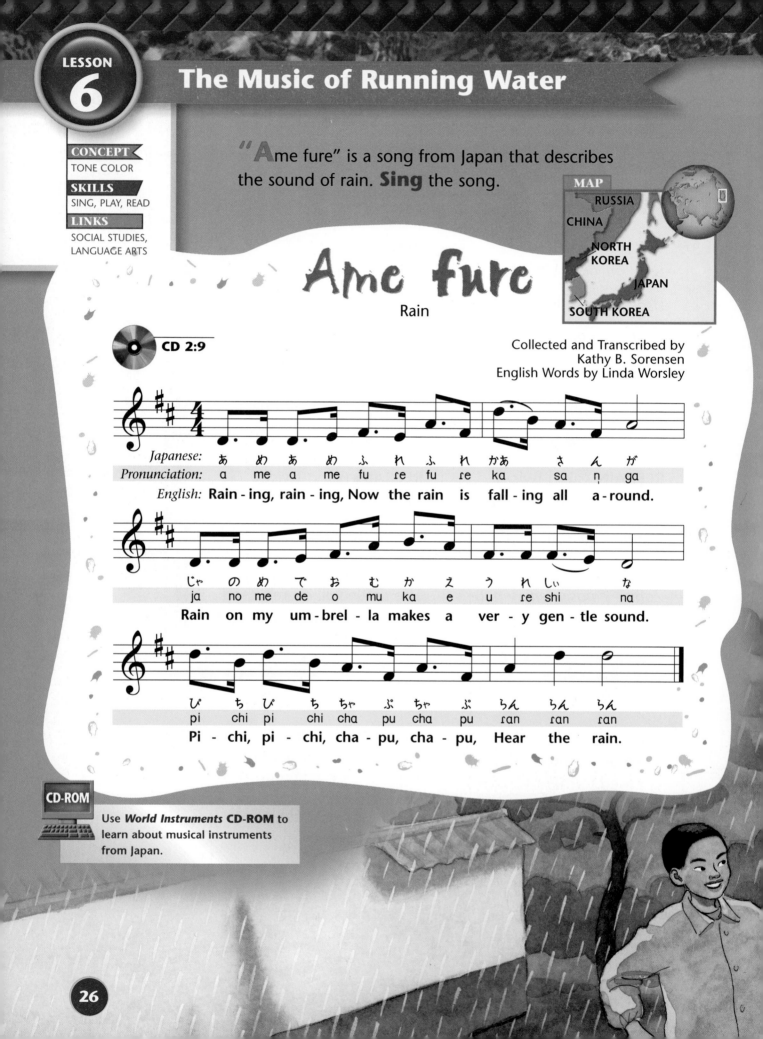

Japanese: あめあめふれふれかあさんが
Pronunciation: a me a me fu ɾe fu ɾe ka sa n̩ ga
English: **Rain - ing, rain - ing, Now the rain is fall - ing all a - round.**

じゃのめでおむかえうれしいな
ja no me de o mu ka e u ɾe shi na
Rain on my um - brel - la makes a ver - y gen - tle sound.

ぴちぴちちゃぷちゃぷらんらんらん
pi chi pi chi cha pu cha pu ɾan ɾan ɾan
Pi - chi, pi - chi, cha - pu, cha - pu, Hear the rain.

CD-ROM

Use *World Instruments* **CD-ROM** to learn about musical instruments from Japan.

Play these rhythm patterns on percussion instruments as you sing "Ame fure."

Read this haiku about rain. Haiku is a form of poetry originally from Japan that has exactly seventeen syllables.

Rain Haiku

Rain drenches pale leaves
dark wood railing, road beyond.
I feel like singing.

—M.A. Mohanraj

THINK! What kind of body percussion could you perform that would sound like rain? **Perform** your body percussion while a partner reads the haiku above.

Listening for Water

Water has many different sounds. You hear it when rain falls. You hear it as a stream rushes by. You even hear it as it drops over a waterfall.

 **LISTENING** CD 2:13

Miniwanka (or The Moments of Water)
by R. Murray Schafer

The Canadian composer R. Murray Schafer (b. 1933) wrote "Miniwanka (or The Moments of Water)" to capture the sounds of water. He used different words for water from the languages of the Native American peoples of the American Northwest and Western Canada. In addition to "Miniwanka," he has written many works for orchestra, chorus, and musical theater, as well as multimedia pieces on computer. Besides being a composer, Schafer is also known as an educator, environmentalist, literary scholar, and a visual artist.

Listen to "Miniwanka" for how the singers change the **tone color** of their voices to create the sound of a rain shower. Tone color is the term used to describe the sound of an instrument or voice.

Follow the listening map below as you listen to the beginning of "Miniwanka" again.

Listening Map for Miniwanka (or The Moments of Water)

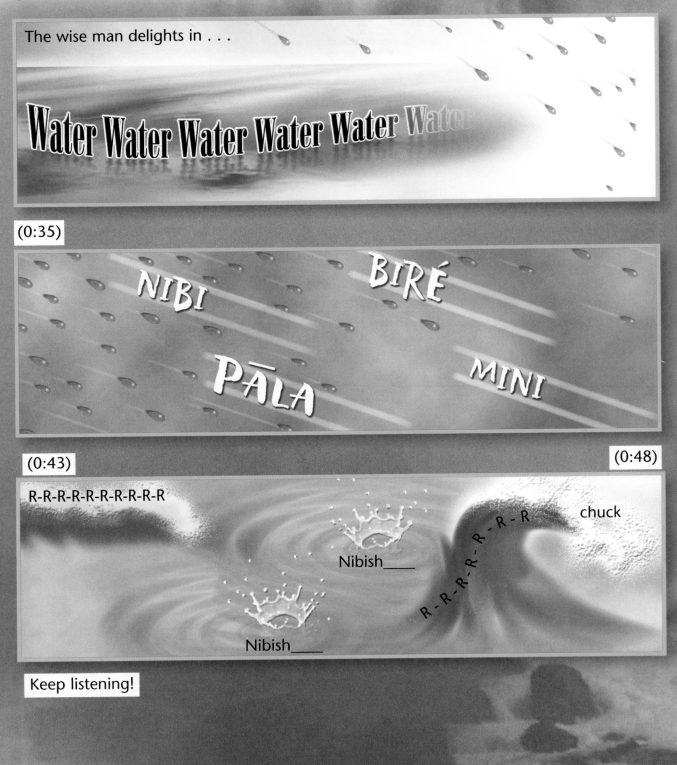

The wise man delights in . . .

Water Water Water Water Water Water

(0:35)

NIBI

BIRÉ

PĀLA

MINI

(0:43)   (0:48)

R-R-R-R-R-R-R-R-R-R

Nibish____

R - R - R - R - R - R

chuck

Nibish____

Keep listening!

CONCEPT
MELODY

SKILLS
SING, DESCRIBE, PLAY

LINKS
DANCE

Sing "Octopus's Garden." How might you move to show the beat and shape of the melody?

Octopus's Garden

CD 2:14

Verse

Words and Music by Richard Starkey

1. I'd like to be___ un - der the sea___
   He'd let us in___ knows where we've been__

2. We would be warm_ be - low the storm_
   Rest - ing our head_ on the sea - bed__

1. in {an/his} Oct - o - pus - 's Gar - den in the shade.
2. in our lit - tle hide - a - way__ be - neath the sea.
   in an Oct - o - pus - 's Gar - den near a cave.

I'd ask my friends to come and see_____
We would sing and dance a - round_____

an Oct - o - pus - 's Gar - den with me._____
be - cause we know we can't be found.

30

Refrain

I'd like to be____ un-der the sea____ in an

1.,2. Oct - o - pus -'s Gar - den in the shade.
3. Oct - o - pus -'s Gar - den with you.

3. We would shout____ and swim a-bout____ the cor - al____that

lies be-neath the waves.__ Oh, what joy____ for

ev'-ry girl and boy____ know-ing____they're hap-py and they're

safe. We would be so hap-py__ you and me;__

____ no one there to tell us what to do.____

Fun with a Canon

"Old Abram Brown" is from a song collection called *Friday Afternoons*. This collection was written for students to have fun songs to sing on a Friday afternoon.

Sing the song. Then sing it again as a canon.

Old Abram Brown

CD 2:17

Music by Benjamin Britten
Words by Walter de la Mare

1
Old A - bram Brown is dead and gone,

2
You'll nev - er see him more.

3
He used to wear a long brown coat

4
That but - toned down be - fore.

Move in Canon

Moving to show the shape of a melody is fun! Form three groups. **Perform** these movements in canon, as you sing "Old Abram Brown."

1 Crouch down for six beats.

2 Leap up on the word "more."

3 Slowly return to the starting position.

THINK! What are other ways you can move to show the shape of the melody of "Old Abram Brown"?

Play these parts on mallet instruments while the class sings the song.

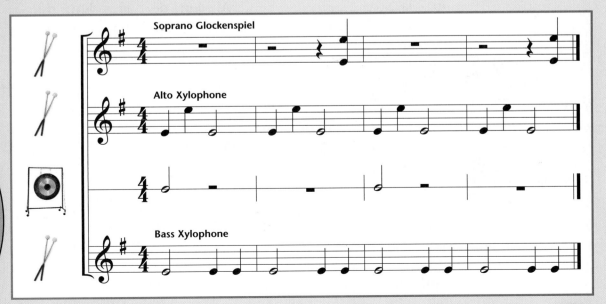

LESSON 8

CONCEPT
MELODY

SKILLS
SING, READ, COMPOSE

LINKS
SOCIAL STUDIES, FINE ART

Melodies for the Night and Day

Sometimes it is a mystery how a song comes to us from a far-off country. The melody for "Allundé, Alluia" was an old harvest song from Nigeria, West Africa. People loved it so much it was sung in other parts of Africa, and the words changed. Now it has new life as a lullaby. Mothers sing their children to sleep with this song.

Sing "Allundé, Alluia." The melody uses the pitches of the pentatonic scale. **Read** the refrain using pitch syllables. Then sing the refrain in canon.

Allundé, Alluia

CD 2:20
Refrain
Gently Rocking

Melody based on a Nigerian Harvest Song
As sung and arranged by
Margaret Campbelle-Holman

Al - lun - dé, al - lun - dé._____ Al - lun - dé, al -
Pronunciation: a lʊn de a lʊn de   a lʊn de a

lu - ia._____ Al - lun - dé, al - lun - dé._____
lu ya   a lʊn de a lʊn de

3rd time go to Coda   *End canon*

Al - lun - dé, al - lu - ia._____
a lʊn de a lu ya

Verse
mf

1. Jé   pu   wah   yé_____   yé_____   ku - sah,
   ʒe   pu   wa   ye   ye   ku   sa
2. Man - dé   a - qua - qua   a - qua - qua   man - dé,
   man   de   a   kwa   kwa   a   kwa   kwa   man   de

Loving Embrace
Keith Mallett (b. 1948) created
this painting in 1993. It shows
a mother holding her child.

MAP

AFRICA

NIGERIA

Ai - yai - yai yé_____ al - lun - dé.____
aì yaì yaì ye   a   lʊn de

p (for D.S.—*pp*)

Ai - yai - yai yé_____ ai - yai - yé____ al - lun - dé._____
aì yaì yaì ye   aì yaì ye   a   lʊn de

1.   *to Refrain* 2. *D.S. to 3rd ending* 3.   *to Refrain and Coda*

Coda

Al - lun - dé,   al - lu - ia.____
a   lʊn de   a   lu   ya

p   *pp*

Al - lun - dé,   al - lu - ia.____
a   lʊn de   a   lu   ya

Unit 1 Music for Everyone   35

Crow and Sing!

Roosters really do crow when the sun comes up in the morning. You could even call them a farmer's alarm clock!

Sing "I'll Rise When the Rooster Crows."

I'll Rise When the Rooster Crows

CD 2:24

Appalachian Folk Song
As Sung by Uncle Dave Macon

I'll rise when the roos - ter crows.

I'll rise when the roos - ter crows.

I'm go - ing down south where the sun shines hot,

Down where the sug - ar - cane grows.

Something Worth Repeating

One kind of accompaniment is called an **ostinato**.

Ostinato is an Italian word that means stubborn.
In music, an ostinato is stubborn because it repeats
itself over and over!

Perform the ostinati below to accompany
"I'll Rise When the Rooster Crows."

Create an Ostinato

Create your own ostinato. Fill two measures in ²₄
Use these rhythms: ♩, ♫, ♩, and 𝄽
Play your ostinato on a percussion instrument as you
sing "I'll Rise When the Rooster Crows."

Spotlight Your Success!

REVIEW

1 How many beats per measure are there in music in $\frac{2}{4}$ meter?

   a. 1   **b.** 3   **c.** 2   **d.** 4

2 Which pitches are in a pentatonic scale?

   a. *do re mi fa so la*

   b. *do re mi fa so*

   c. *do re mi so la*

   d. *do mi fa so*

3 What is the pitch around which a melody is centered?

   a. central pitch

   b. tonal center

   c. ostinato

   d. pitch syllable

READ AND LISTEN

1 **Read** these rhythms. Then listen. Which rhythm pattern do you hear?

   a.

   b.

   c.

2 **Read** these melody patterns using pitch syllables. Then **listen.** Which pattern do you hear?

a.

b.

c.

THINK!

1 What do you have to think about to be successful in singing a round?

2 **Describe** the ways that a roller coaster is similar to the contour of a melody.

3 Tell in your own words the meaning of the lyrics of "Something for Me, Something for You."

4 **Write** about your favorite song from this unit. What do you enjoy about it? How would you describe it to a friend?

CREATE AND PERFORM

1 Use ♩, ♩, ♫, and 𝄽 to fill four measures in ²⁄₄ meter.

2 **Create** a melody by choosing pitches for your rhythm. Use pitches from the pentatonic scale in the key of C. End your melody on C.

3 **Sing** your melody using pitch syllables. Then play it on a mallet instrument.

4 **Perform** your melody for a friend.

Meet the Musician
ON NATIONAL RADIO!

Name: Abraham Feder
Age: 16
Instrument: Cello
Hometown: Chicago, Illinois

When Abraham Feder was two years old, all he wanted to do was to play his older brother's cello. "I'd ask my mom to let me play it, but every day she would say to me, 'Abe, don't touch your brother's cello!'"

Abe would not give up. Although his mother had told him not to touch his brother's cello, she never said he couldn't touch the bow. That gave Abe a great idea!

"I dragged out my father's 12-string guitar and grabbed my brother's cello bow," recalls Abe. "Then I sat on my bucket of stuffed bunnies, turned the guitar upright, and started playing it like a cello!" It wasn't long before Abe was given his very own real cello to play.

LISTENING CD 2:28

Sonata for Cello and Piano, Op. 40, Second Movement
by Dmitri Shostakovich

Listen to Abraham's performance and interview on the national radio program From the Top.

RECORDED INTERVIEW

Spotlight on the Saxophone

While earning a graduate degree as a bassoonist, Erika Kirsch learned the music library was separate from the university's main library. Her experience as an assistant there prepared her for a music librarian's career.

Conductors choose the music for their concerts, but music librarians work months before rehearsals start to get the music ready. Whether the performing group owns the music or needs to rent it, it has to be gathered. If it's copyrighted, permission fees must be paid. Making sure all players have special markings from the director or the same bowings for string players is also part of the job.

"You need to be a musician and know a lot about publishers, copyright law, and managing budgets," explains Ms. Kirsch. "It's never boring!"

Did You Know?

The saxophone, invented in 1846 by Adolphe Sax, is one of very few instruments named after its creator.

Although this single-reed instrument is considered a woodwind instrument, it is made of brass.

With its straight body, the soprano saxophone looks like a metal clarinet. Alto, tenor, and baritone saxophones have longer bodies that bend back up at the bottom and wider bells that curve out.

LISTENING CD 3:1–2

Boléro **(excerpt)** by Maurice Ravel

Take Five
by Paul Desmond

Listen for the saxophone in these two pieces. Since the saxophone was invented in France, it is not surprising that many French composers, like Ravel, have used it in their music. The saxophone is also a favorite with jazz musicians. In "Take Five," a classic jazz piece in $\frac{5}{4}$ meter, you can hear its composer, Paul Desmond, on saxophone.

Musical Messages, Musical Journeys

Music is a special force in people's lives. You can express joy, love, hope, and sadness with music. When you share music with others, you are sending musical messages. In Unit 2 you will sing and play musical messages that will take you on journeys beyond your imagination.

Coming Attractions

Sing and play a popular song in Spanish.

Read a listening map of movie music.

Sing a call-and-response song.

What message does this song send?
Sing the song.

PLEASE, MR. POSTMAN

CD 3:4

Words and Music by Robert Bateman, Georgia Dobbins,
William Garrett, Freddie Gorman and Brian Holland

do

Oh yes, wait a min-ute, Mis-ter Post-man. Wait____

____ Mis-ter Post-man. Please Mis-ter Post-man, look and see,____

is there a let-ter in your bag for me?__ I've been wait-ing a

long, long time,__ since I heard from that friend of mine.__

1. There must be some word to - day____
2. So man-y days__ you've passed me by,____

____ from my friend so far a-way.__ Please, Mis-ter Post-man,
____ see the tears in__ my eyes.__ You did-n't stop to

Rhythm, Rhythm, Rhythm

CONCEPT
RHYTHM
SKILLS
SING, PERFORM, LISTEN
LINKS
FINE ART, LANGUAGE ARTS

The verses of "Frog Went A-Courtin'" tell a story. Some phrases have nonsense words that are fun to sing, but they may take practice!

Sing "Frog Went A-Courtin'" and enjoy the nonsense words.

Frog Went A-Courtin'

CD 3:7

Kentucky Folk Song
Additional Words by MMH

Verse
Dm

do

1. Frog went a - court - in' and he did ride.
(2.) rode right___ to___ Miss Mous - ie's door,
(3.) took Miss___ Mous - ie on his knee,
(4.) out my___ Un - cle Rat's con - sent,
5. Un-cle Rat___ laughed_ and shook his sides,

G   F   G

Rink - tum bod - y min - chy cam - bo.

Dm

Sword and buck - ler by his side,
Found Miss Mous - ie sweep-in' the floor.
And said, "Miss Mous-ie, will you mar - ry me?"
I could not mar-ry the pres - i - dent."
To think his niece would be a bride.

G   F   G

Rink - tum bod - y min - chy cam - bo.

Perform the rhythm of verse 1 using body percussion.

- **Clap** every syllable of words that tell the story.
- **Pat** the rhythm of the nonsense words.

Refrain

Ki - man-ee - ro down to Cai - ro, Ki - man-ee - ro Cai - ro.

Shad-dle - ad - dle - ad - a - ba - ba, lad - da - ba - ba link - tum.

Rink - tum bod - y min - chy cam - bo.

2. He
3. He
4. "With -

6. Who will make the wedding gown?
Old Miss Rat from Pumpkin Town.

7. Where will the wedding supper be?
Way down yonder in a hollow tree.

8. What will the wedding supper be?
A fried mosquito and black-eyed pea.

9. First to come was a bumblebee,
He set his fiddle on his knee.

10. Next to come was a doodle bug,
Carrying a water jug.

11. Next to come was a flying moth;
She laid out the tablecloth.

12. Next to come was an itty-bitty flea
To dance a jig for the bumblebee.

13. Next to come was a big old cow;
She wanted to dance but she
didn't know how.

14. Next to come was a big black snake;
He ate up all the wedding cake.

15. Last to come was an old gray cat;
She swallowed up the mouse and
ate up the rat.

16. Mr. Frog went hopping over the
brook;
A duck came along and swallowed
him up.

17. Now is the end of him and her;
Guess there won't be no
tadpoles covered with fur!

18. Little piece of cornbread lying on
the shelf,
If you want any more you can sing
it yourself!

Rapping, Tapping Rhythms

Read the poem below. Then listen to the recording. You will learn rhythm patterns that go with the words in bold type.

The Woodpecker

 CD 3:10

The **woodpecker** pecked out a little round hole
And made him a house in the **telephone pole.**
One day when I watched, he poked out his head
And he had on a hood and a collar of red.

When the streams of rain pour out of the sky
And the sparkles of **lightning** go flashing by
And the big, big wheels of thunder roll ...
He can snuggle back in the **telephone pole.**

—Elizabeth Madox Roberts

Art Gallery

Exhausted Bird

For many artists, birds are a favorite subject. The British artist Marg Hewson (b. 1936) made this sculpture out of an automobile exhaust pipe, bedsprings, a metal tube, and metal reinforcing rods.

48

Each word or phrase below from the poem totals one beat.
Tap the beat as you say each one four times.

pole

light-　ning

wood-　peck- er

tel-　e-　phone

he　can snug- gle

(a beat of rest, or silence)

Which words or phrases have three sounds on a beat?
Are the sounds equal, or are some longer than others?

Which phrase has four sounds on a beat?
Are the sounds equal, or are some longer than others?

Use the words above to help you perform the rhythm patterns below:

Clap the rhythms printed in red. **Pat** the rhythms in blue.

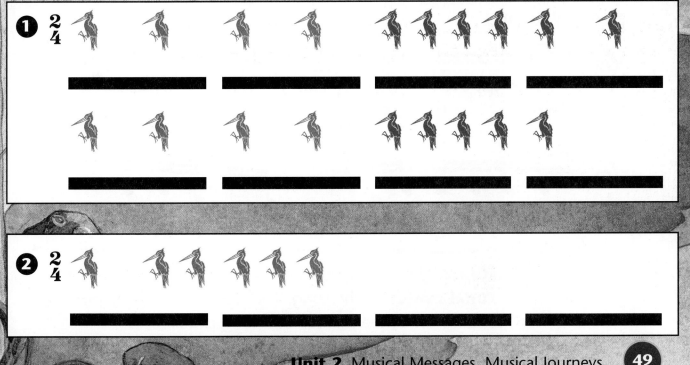

CONCEPT
MELODY
SKILLS
SING, PERFORM, ANALYZE
LINKS
SOCIAL STUDIES, DANCE

Early settlers of North America sang and danced when taking a break from their hard work. What do you do when taking a break from hard work?

"Cedar Swamp" is one song these pioneers would sing and dance to. **Sing** "Cedar Swamp."

Cedar Swamp

CD 3:13

Appalachian Folk Song

Verse

1. 'Way low down in the ce-dar swamp, Wa-ter's deep and mud-dy.
2. Built my love a— big fine house, Built it in the gar-den.

There I met a pret-ty lit-tle miss, There I met my hon-ey.
Put her in and she— jumped out, Fare you well my dar-lin'.

Refrain

Swing a la-dy up and down, Swing a la-dy home,—

Swing a la-dy up and down, Swing a la-dy home.

Identify the final pitch of "Cedar Swamp." This is the **tonal center** of the song. The tonal center is the pitch around which the melody of a song is built.

Dancing in a Longways Set

The dance formation you see below is called a longways set. The pair of dancers at one end of the set is called the "head couple." The pair at the other end is called the "foot." **Perform** these movements as you sing "Cedar Swamp."

FORMATION

longways set

VERSE

right-elbow swing

For the verse, all couples perform a right-elbow swing and a left-elbow swing.

For the refrain, the head couple gallops sideways to the bottom of the set.

REFRAIN

gallop sideways

Finding the Tonal Center

Look at the first verse of "Cotton-Eye Joe." Follow the outline below to trace the shape of the melody. The red line shows the tonal center of the melody.

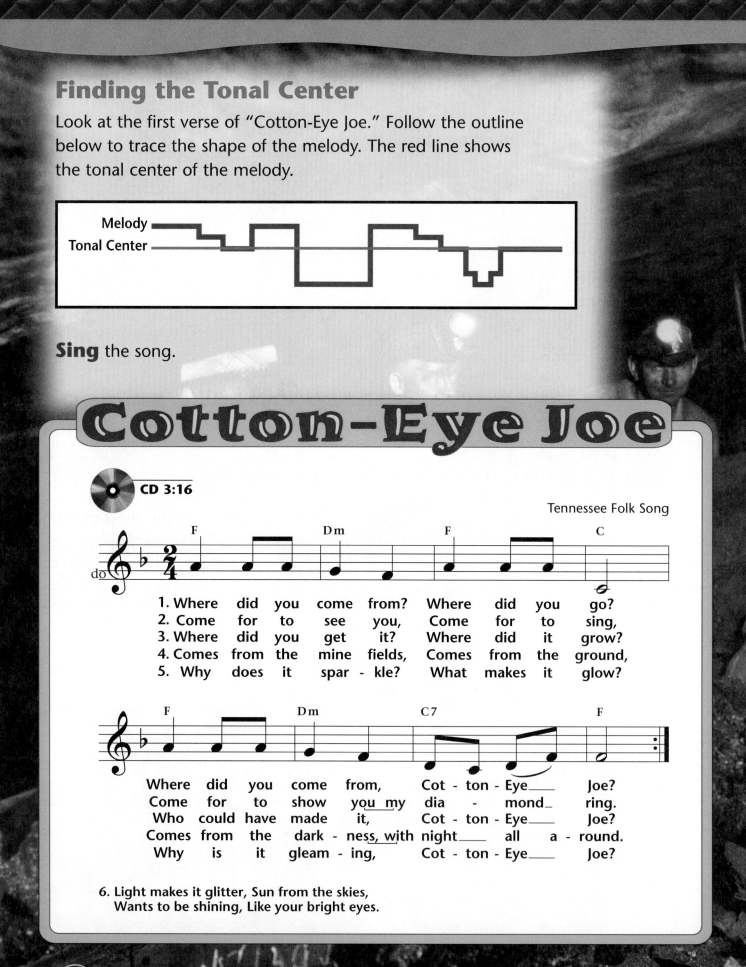

Sing the song.

Cotton-Eye Joe

CD 3:16

Tennessee Folk Song

do

	F			Dm		F			C

1. Where did you come from? Where did you go?
2. Come for to see you, Come for to sing,
3. Where did you get it? Where did it grow?
4. Comes from the mine fields, Comes from the ground,
5. Why does it spar - kle? What makes it glow?

	F			Dm		C7			F

Where did you come from, Cot - ton - Eye___ Joe?
Come for to show you my dia - mond_ ring.
Who could have made it, Cot - ton - Eye___ Joe?
Comes from the dark - ness, with night___ all a - round.
Why is it gleam - ing, Cot - ton - Eye___ Joe?

6. Light makes it glitter, Sun from the skies,
   Wants to be shining, Like your bright eyes.

Look at the melody below. Where is the tonal center? Drag your finger over the pitches to "feel" the shape of the melody.

Sing this melody. First use pitch syllables in rhythm, then use the words shown below the staff. Then sing the melody with "Cotton-Eye Joe."

Countermelody for Cotton-Eye Joe

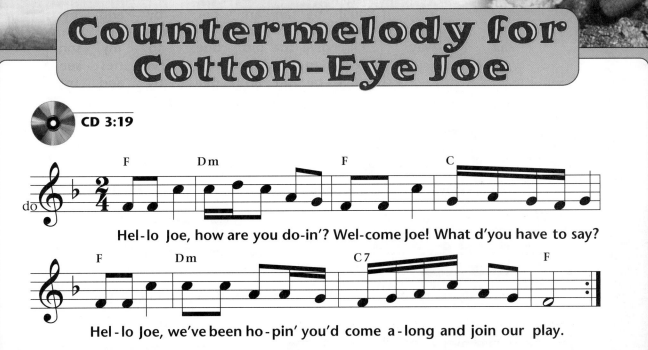

CD 3:19

Hel-lo Joe, how are you do-in'? Wel-come Joe! What d'you have to say?

Hel-lo Joe, we've been ho-pin' you'd come a-long and join our play.

CONCEPT
MELODY
SKILLS
LISTEN, SING, IDENTIFY
LINKS
SOCIAL STUDIES

"Sail Away, Ladies" is a lively mountain dance tune. **Sing** the song.

Sail Away, Ladies

CD 3:20

Mountain Dance

Verse

do

1. Ain't no___ use to sit and cry;
2. I've got a home in Ten - nes - see,
3. I ev - er get my new house done,   } Sail a-way, la - dies,
4. Come a-long,___ boys, and go with me,
5. Hush lit - tle ba - by, don't you cry,

sail a-way;   {
You'll be an an - gel by and by.
that's the___ place I wan - na be.
I'll give the old one to my son,
We'll go___ down to Ten - nes - see,
You'll be an an - gel by and by,   }

Refrain

Sail a-way, lad - ies, sail a-way. Don't you rock 'em

die - dy-o, don't___ you rock 'em die - dy-o, don't___ you rock 'em

die - dy-o, don't___ you rock 'em die - dy-o. 3. If

Pitches are written on a staff with 5 lines and 4 spaces. Both the spaces and lines are numbered from the bottom up.

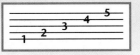

Lines of the staff

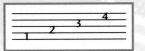

Spaces of the staff

Pitches can also be written below or above the lines.

This note is in the first space below the staff.

This note is in the first space above the staff.

When notes are higher or lower than the staff, they are written on lines above or below the staff. These lines are called **ledger lines**.

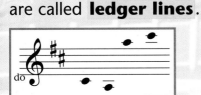

These notes are on ledger lines. What are the names of the notes on the ledger lines?

Where is *do* in this song? **Identify** the line or space where *do* is found.

When the word "ladies" is sung, notice that the pitches are lower than *do*. These pitches are called *low la* (*la₁*) and *low so* (*so₁*). What other word or words occur on *low la* or *low so* in the song?

 **LISTENING** CD 3:23

Sail Away mountain dance

This recording features Malcolm Dalglish playing the hammered dulcimer.

Listen to "Sail Away." The hammered dulcimer has a unique sound. What instruments does it remind you of?

Music from a Movie

Listen to "Augie's Great Municipal Band." How do the instruments you hear sound different from instruments on this planet?

 **LISTENING** CD 3:24

Augie's Great Municipal Band from *Star Wars Episode 1: The Phantom Menace* (excerpt)
by John Williams

"Augie's Great Municipal Band" is heard during a celebration at the end of the movie *Star Wars Episode 1: The Phantom Menace*.

Identify low *la* and low *so* in the melody below as you listen to the recording again.

Meet the Musician

John Williams (b. 1932), composer and conductor, has written film scores for more than 80 movies. He began his career as a pianist for Hollywood movie studios while in his early twenties. Soon after, he became popular as a composer and conductor of musical film and television shows. His scores can be heard in such films as *Jurassic Park*, *Home Alone*, *Hook*, the *Star Wars* films, *E.T.: The Extra-Terrestrial*, and the *Harry Potter* films.

Follow the listening map below as you listen to the recording again.
Listen for the sung A melody and the jagged rhythms of the B melody.

Listening Map for Augie's Great Municipal Band from
Star Wars Episode 1: The Phantom Menace (excerpt)

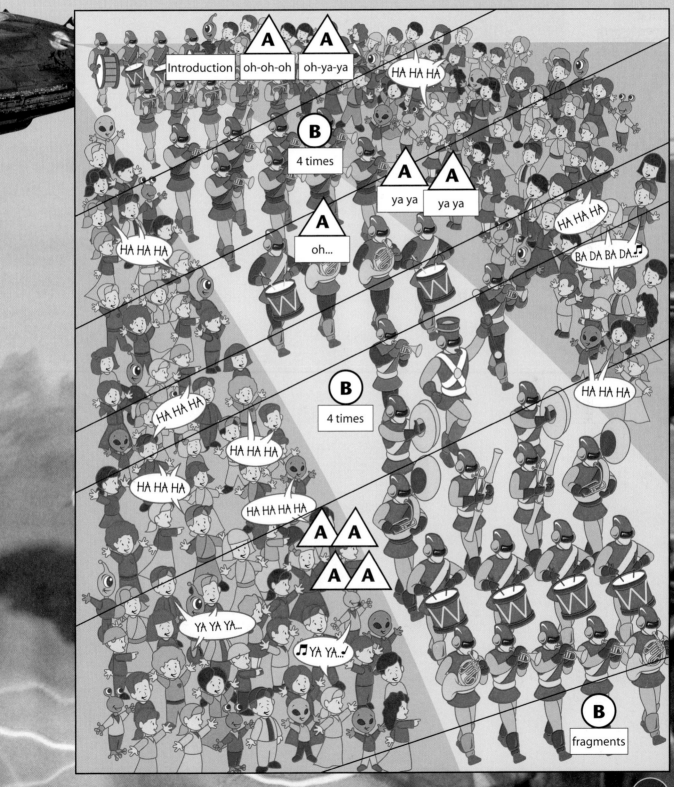

LESSON
4

CONCEPT
RHYTHM
SKILLS
CLAP, SING, LISTEN
LINKS
SOCIAL STUDIES

Mystery Musical Messages

When you see music on a page, you may not know the rhythm right away. Think of the printed music as a message. Here are four steps that will help you decode a musical message.

1 **Speak** the rhythm of the song using jazz syllables. Say

- "dit" for ♩
- "doo wah" for ♫
- "dooby dooby" for 𝅘𝅥𝅯𝅘𝅥𝅯𝅘𝅥𝅯𝅘𝅥𝅯
- "doo dooby" for ♪𝅘𝅥𝅯𝅘𝅥𝅯
- "dooby doo" for 𝅘𝅥𝅯𝅘𝅥𝅯♪

2 **Clap** and speak the rhythm of the song.

3 **Sing** the song using jazz syllables.

4 **Sing** the song with the words.

Now try these four steps with "Early in the Morning" on the next page.

Sing "Early in the Morning at Eight O'Clock."

Four equal sounds to a beat can be written like this: ♫♫
Play this accompaniment with "Early in the Morning at Eight O'Clock." **Identify** ♫♫ each time it occurs.

Flute Rhythms

One of the oldest known musical instruments is the flute. The flute is a woodwind instrument, or a wind instrument that is, or was originally, made of wood. At one time, flutes were made of wood, but today most flutes are made of metal. The sound of the flute is produced by blowing across a hole, like blowing across the mouth of a bottle.

Native American flute

Clap the first rhythm below and pat the second rhythm.

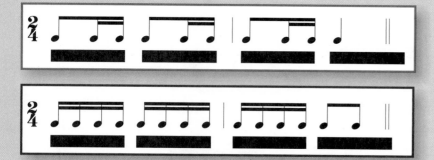

Create a musical conversation. Choose a partner. Perform these two rhythm patterns, then switch parts.

CD-ROM

Use *World Instruments* **CD-ROM** to learn more about flutes from all over the world.

Fife player in ▶ Colonial Williamsburg, Virginia

Flute player in ▶ South Africa

flute

Badinerie from Suite for Orchestra No. 2 in
B Minor by Johann Sebastian Bach

"Badinerie" is a movement from the *Suite in B-minor*
for solo flute and orchestra.

Listen for the rhythm that your group performed in this
recording.

Meet the Musician

Johann Sebastian Bach (1685–1750) spent all
of his life in Germany writing enormous amounts of
music for organ, orchestra, solo instruments, choirs,
and solo voices. As a church organist, he had to
compose a new work for church services nearly
every week. After his death, his music was almost
forgotten. Yet today his music is widely performed
and enjoyed around the world.

Mongolian flute ▶
player in New
York, New York

◀ Hmong flute
player in
traditional dress

Where's the Center?

CONCEPT
TONALITY
SKILLS
SING, LISTEN, PLAY
LINKS
HISTORY, SOCIAL STUDIES

"La otra España" is a song about hope for freedom and a better life. This song is about life in the Americas when settlers came from Spain. **Sing** the song.

La otra España

The Other Spain

CD 4:5

Juan Carlos Calderón
Arranged by Gilberto D. Soto
English Words by Linda Worsley

Verse

Spanish: Con som - bre - ro de a - la an - cha y un cla -
Pronunciation: kon som bɾe ɾo ðea la an cha iun kla
English: With a wide-brimmed hat, a red__ car - na - tion

vel en la so - la - pa, un don Juan se hi-zo a la
βel en la so la pa un don xwan si soa la
tucked in his la - pel,__ a rov - ing sai - lor went to

mar. Con la tie - rra a sus es - pal - das la a - ven -
maɾ kon la tye ɾa sus es pal ðas la βen
sea. With the land be - hind his back,__ ad - ven - ture

tu - ra en su mi - ra - da su gui - ta - rra y un can -
tu ɾen su mi ɾa ða su gi ta ɾa i un kan
in his sight, he sang_ and played gui - ta - rra, and went to

tar. ¡Ay ma - ri - ne - ro,__ Ay ma - ri - ne -
taɾ o ma ɾi ne ɾo o ma ɾi ne
sea. Oh ma - ri - ne - ro!__ Oh, ma - ri - ne -

Play and Listen

Play this accompaniment with the refrain of "La otra España."

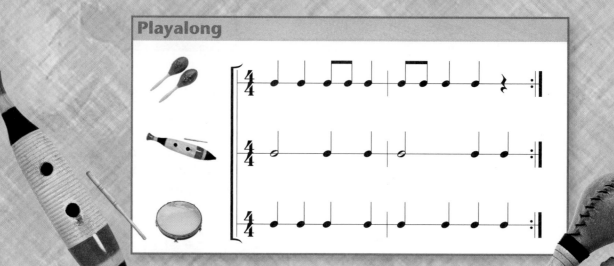

Playalong

Listen to this version of "La otra España." How is this recording similar to the recording with which you sang?

🔘 **LISTENING** CD 4:9

La otra España (The Other Spain) by Juan Carlos Calderón

Juan Carlos Calderón wrote this song for the band Mocedades.

Meet the Musician

Juan Carlos Calderón (b. 1936) was born in Spain, but has worked all over the world. Like the sailor in "La otra España," Calderón left his home to find success in other countries. As a songwriter, a record producer, and a bandleader, he has been making music for more than forty years. He has written hits for Latin stars like Ricky Martin, Luis Miguel, and the band Mocedades.

Over 300 years ago, people were taken from their homes in Africa to the United States against their will. These enslaved people sang songs that expressed their longing for freedom, their homeland, and a better life. Such songs are called **spirituals**.

Sing the spiritual "'Most Done Ling'rin' Here." How is the tonal center of "'Most Done Ling'rin' Here" different from the tonal center of "La otra España"?

'Most Done Ling'rin' Here

CD 4:10

African American Spiritual

If you get there be - fore I do, 'Most done ling - 'rin' here.

Look out for me I am com - in' too, 'Most done ling - 'rin' here.

I'm go - in' a - way, go - in' a - way, I'm 'most done ling - 'rin' here.

I'm go - in' a - way to Ga - li - lee, and I'm 'most done ling - 'rin' here.

THINK! How do you think this song would give someone hope for a better life?

Phrases of Hope, Sections of Peace

CONCEPT
FORM
SKILLS
SING, LISTEN, PLAY
LINKS
SOCIAL STUDIES, CULTURE, FINE ART

"Hine Ma Tov" is a Hebrew song from Israel that speaks of hope for people to live together peacefully. **Sing** the song.

Hine Ma Tov
How Good It Is

MAP
ISRAEL
GAZA
WEST BANK
JORDAN
EGYPT
SAUDI ARABIA

CD 4:13

Music by Allan E. Naplan
Words from Psalm 133:1

Refrain

F *mf*   Gm   C 7   F

Lai lai lai lai   lai lai lai lai lai lai lai   lai   lai lai lai   lai

B♭   Gm   Am   Dm

Last time to Coda

Lai lai lai lai   lai lai lai lai lai lai lai   lai   lai lai lai   lai

Dm   **Verse**   F

Hebrew: הִ - נֵּה מַה טּוֹב וּ - מַה - נָּ - עִים שֶׁ - בֶת אַ - חִים גַּם יַ -
Pronunciation: hi   ne ma tov u   ma na   yim she vet a xim gam ya
English: How_ good it_ is for_ all of_ us to_ join to-geth-er in

Groups of phrases make up **sections** of songs. Sections are labeled with capital letters. The first section is A, the next B, and so on.

Look at the song. **Identify** the form of "Hine Ma Tov."

? THINK! **Describe** the difference between the A and B sections of "Hine Ma Tov."

Gm   B♭   C   F   Dm

חַד   הִ - נֵה מַה טוֹב וּ - מַה נָ - עִים שֶׁ - בֶּט

xad   hi   ne   ma   tov   u   ma   na   yim   she   vet

song.   Let   our   voi-ces   raise   with   songs_ of_ praise   that   we'll

Go back to the beginning.
Last time to refrain then Coda

1. B♭   C 7   2. B♭   C 7   F

אַ - חִים גַּם יַ - חַד הִ -   אַ - חִים גַּם יַ - חַד

a   xim   gam   ya   xad   hi   a   xim   gam   ya   xad

sing   the   whole   day_ long.   How_   sing   the   whole   day_ long.

Coda   Dm   B♭   C 7   F

שֶׁ - בֶּט   אַ - חִים גַּם יַ - חַד

she   vet   a   xim   gam   ya   xad

A Dance from Israel

Listen to "Erev Shel Shoshanim."

🔘 **LISTENING** CD 4:17

Erev Shel Shoshanim by Josef Hadar and Moshe Dor

"Erev Shel Shoshanim," or "Night of Roses," also comes from Israel. The dance has four sections: AABB.

Play these rhythm patterns as you listen to the recording again.

Art Gallery

Dance

This painting by Marc Chagall (1887–1985) shows another kind of dance, called ballet. A ballet usually tells a story in dance form. It is usually performed with music played by an orchestra.

A

Face and travel counterclockwise, or the opposite of the way the hands of a clock move.

A

Face and travel clockwise. Turn yourself around in 4 steps.

B

Face your body "in" toward the center of the circle.

Calling for the Response

CONCEPT
FORM
SKILLS
SING, CREATE, LISTEN
LINKS
SOCIAL STUDIES, CULTURE

The form of many African American spirituals and work songs is **call and response**. Enslaved people brought this form of song to the United States from Africa. Usually, a leader sings a phrase (the call) and the whole group answers with another phrase (the response). Singers might also form two groups, with the first group singing the call and the second group singing the response.

Sing "Oh, Won't You Sit Down?" in two groups. One group will sing the call and the other group will sing the response.

Oh, Won't You Sit Down?

CD 4:18

African American Spiritual

Freely
Refrain

Oh, won't you sit down?_ Lord, I can't sit down._

Oh, won't you sit down?_ Lord, I can't sit down._

Oh, won't you sit down?_ Lord, I can't sit down._

'Cause I just got to Heav-en, gon-na look a-round._

Pitches or Letters?

To the right are the pitches from the refrain of "Oh, Won't You Sit Down?" The pitch syllable is given below each pitch.

Pitches can also be named using **letter names**. The pitches of most musical instruments are identified with letter names. A pitch that is named by a letter always makes the same sound.

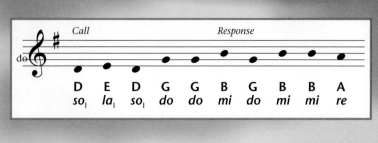

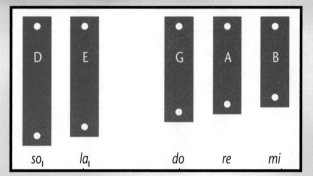

THINK!

Compare the pitches used in the call and response from the verse below. How is the response different from the call?

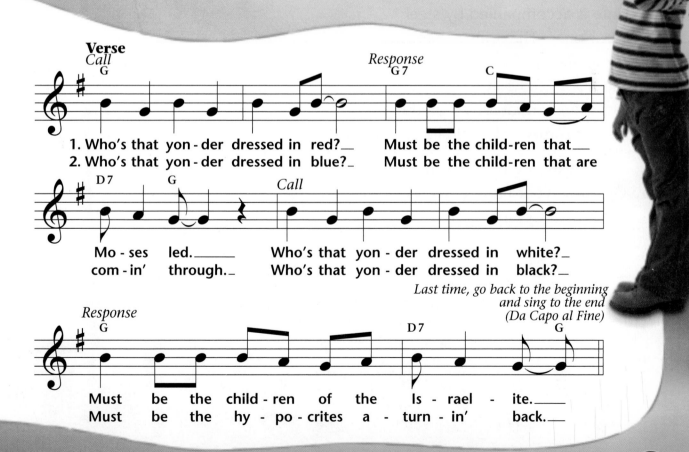

Verse

Call
G

1. Who's that yon-der dressed in red?___   *Response* G7   C
   Must be the child-ren that___
2. Who's that yon-der dressed in blue?_   Must be the child-ren that are

D7   G   *Call*

Mo-ses led._____   Who's that yon-der dressed in   white?_
com-in' through._   Who's that yon-der dressed in   black?_

Last time, go back to the beginning and sing to the end (Da Capo al Fine)

Response
G   D7   G

Must   be   the   child-ren   of   the   Is-rael-ite._____
Must   be   the   hy-po-crites   a-turn-in'   back.__

Unit 2 Musical Messages, Musical Journeys   **71**

Learn About Calypso

"Day-O," sometimes known as "The Banana Boat Song," is a **calypso** song. Calypso-style music and dance comes from the southern and eastern Caribbean. Calypso was developed on the island of Trinidad from the *gayup*, a West African work song brought to the area by enslaved people working on plantations. Calypso songs often have a call and response structure. The leader of a calypso song is called a chantwell.

Listen to the recording of "Day-O."

LISTENING CD 4:21

Day-O (excerpt) by Harry Belafonte, Irving Burgie, and William Attaway

In this recording, the singer Harry Belafonte is accompanied by steel drums, or pans. These instruments were first made in the 1940s in Trinidad from used oil drums. Steel pans are now considered to be the national instrument of Trinidad.

Look at the response below from "Day-O." Raise your hand each time you hear the response.

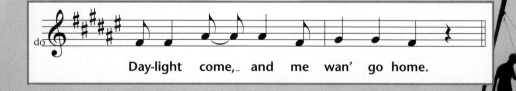

Day-light come,_ and me wan' go home.

Create a new melody to the response *Daylight come an' me wan' go home* by using the pitches below. Use these bells or the black keys on a keyboard.

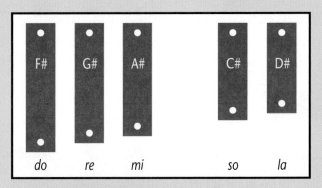

F#   G#   A#   C#   D#
do   re   mi   so   la

Your new melody should end on F♯ (*do*) because the tonal center of the song is *do*.

Listen to the recording. What instruments do you hear?

LISTENING CD 4:22

Jamaica Farewell by Irving Burgie

This recording features Harry Belafonte. "Jamaica Farewell" is one of his most popular songs.

Meet the Musician

Harry Belafonte (b. 1927) was born and raised in New York City. He developed an interest in calypso music from his parents, who came from the Caribbean. In 1955 he made a recording of the song "Jamaica Farewell" that launched a nationwide interest in calypso music. Two years later, his recording of "Day-O" was one of the most popular songs in the country.

Joes and Jugs

CONCEPT
RHYTHM

SKILLS
SING, COMPOSE, PLAY

LINKS
SCIENCE, CULTURES

"**O**ld Joe Clark" is a folk song from the Appalachian Mountains region of the United States. People have sung and danced to this popular tune for hundreds of years.

Sing the song.

OLD JOE CLARK

CD 4:23

American Folk Song

Refrain

'Round and 'round, Old Joe Clark, 'Round and 'round I say;

'Round and 'round, Old Joe Clark, I have-n't long to stay.

Verse

1. Old Joe Clark, he had a house, six-teen sto-ries high.
2. I went down to Joe Clark's house, nev-er been be-fore.
3. Joe Clark had a vi-o-lin, he fid-dled all the day.

Go back to the beginning and sing to the end (Da Capo al Fine)

Ev'-ry sto-ry in that house was full of chick-en pie.
He slept on the feath-er bed and I slept on the floor.
An-y-bod-y start to dance and Joe would start to play.

Creating Your Own Rhythm

Create your own rhythm to perform between the verses and at the end of "Old Joe Clark." Choose from these rhythms to fill in the beats shown by the blank jugs below.

Play this accompaniment while the class sings the song.

A Different Kind of Band!

The jug band is a true American musical creation! The centerpiece of the band is the jug, or ceramic bottle. The player buzzes the lips to get a tone, similar to playing a brass instrument. Different pitches are played by tightening or loosening the lips.

The washtub bass, also known as the "gut bucket," is another instrument of the jug band. Players build their own instruments using a metal washtub, a broomstick or garden-tool handle, and some cotton jùte or nylon line. Players change the pitch by moving the stick to tighten or loosen the single string.

The washboard is a grooved piece of metal, glass, or hard wood set in a wooden or metal frame. It was used for scrubbing clothes by hand before the invention of the washing machine. Players scrape their fingernails, fingers covered with metal thimbles, or spoons across the grooved section to create a rhythm part in the jug band.

What other jug band instruments do you recognize?

jug

▲
washboard

washtub bass
▼

banjo

Listen to "Brooklyn Jugs." What instruments do you hear in this recording?

LISTENING   CD 4:26

Brooklyn Jugs by Brooklyn Jugs

This recording features the New York City-based jug band, Brooklyn Jugs.

RECORDED INTERVIEW   CD 4:27

Brooklyn Jugs

bones

spoons

kazoo

77

Spotlight Your Success!

REVIEW

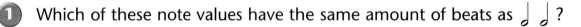

1 Which of these note values have the same amount of beats as 𝅗𝅥 𝅗𝅥 ?

a.

b.

c.

d.

2 What are the letter names of the pitches shown on the staff?

a. D E G   **b.** E A B   **c.** F A C

3 Which is usually longer in music?

a. a phrase

b. a section

c. a note

READ AND LISTEN

1 **Read** these rhythm patterns. Then listen. Which rhythm pattern do you hear?

a. 2/4

b.  2/4

c.  2/4

2 **Read** these pitch patterns. Then listen. Identify the pattern that matches the pitches you hear.

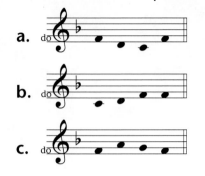

a.

b.

c.

THINK!

1 What is the relationship of the tonal center to a melody in a song?

2 If *do* in a song is on the first space of the staff, how would you determine where on the staff *la* is?

3 When you dance or perform movement, which would be the best to listen for: melody, rhythm, or steady beat? Why?

4 **Write** a short paragraph. First, think about several composers from this unit. Choose a piece you like best and explain what you like about it.

CREATE AND PERFORM

1 Use ♩, ♩, ♫ to build a four-measure phrase in 2/4 meter.

2 **Create** a melody for your four-measure phrase. Decide which pitch you want for your tonal center: C, G, or F.

3 **Sing** your melody. If you are not pleased with it, improve it or write another melody.

Meet the Musician

ON NATIONAL RADIO!

Name: Catherine Turner
Age: 17
Instrument: French Horn
Hometown: West Chester, Ohio

When she was in the fifth grade, Catherine Turner joined the school band. She was shown many different instruments and decided she liked French horn best. "I loved the way it sounded," recalls Catherine. "I couldn't wait to start playing it."

Catherine's band teachers suggested she learn trumpet before trying the French horn, but Catherine had already made up her mind. She was determined to play the horn, no matter how difficult it was.

Catherine is now seventeen. She plays horn in both the school concert and the marching bands. In marching band, Catherine plays a mellophone, which is a French horn made especially for marching. "It looks similar to a large trumpet, but it uses a horn mouthpiece," she explains.

Catherine thinks all her hard work has paid off. "You can do anything if you try!" she states.

A Tip From the Top!

"Don't give up."

Catherine Turner knew she really wanted to play the French horn, and she didn't give up trying because it was hard. Believing you can do something is the first important step to doing it.

LISTENING CD 5:1–5

What Did You Do Today at Jeffrey's House? by Peter Schickele

Listen to Catherine's performance and interview on the national radio program From the Top.

RECORDED INTERVIEW

Spotlight on the Timpani

Did You Know?

Timpani can also be referred to as "kettle drums."

The first known timpani were used about 1,400 years ago in Persia.

Timpanists use a pedal at the base of the instrument to tighten or loosen the drumhead. These pedals change the pitch of the drum.

Timpanists are usually seated in front of two or more drums, each tuned to a different pitch.

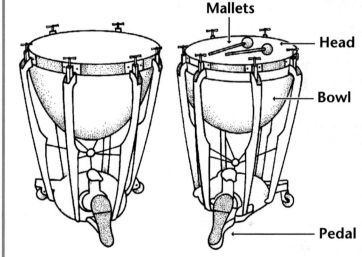

Mallets
Head
Bowl
Pedal

LISTENING CD 5:6–7

Turandot from *Symphonic Metamorphosis on Themes of Carl Maria von Weber* (excerpt)
by Paul Hindemith

Sonatina for Three Timpani and Piano, First Movement (excerpt) by Alexander Tcherepnin

Listen for the timpani solo at the beginning of Hindemith's piece and again at the end.

Some composers have even written solo pieces for timpani. In the piece by Tcherepnin, the soloist must tune all three timpani many times, often while the piano is playing.

Happy Go Lucky!

Music has the power to make you happy and helps you forget your troubles. In Unit 3 you will sing and play music from all over the world that will make you feel good inside! How does music make you happy?

Coming Attractions

Sing a song from the Philippines.

Create harmony for a cowboy song.

Play chords to accompany an Israeli folk song.

"Happy Talk" is a song from the Broadway musical *South Pacific.*

Sing "Happy Talk." What do you think the words mean?

CD 5:8

Music by Richard Rodgers
Words by Oscar Hammerstein II

Refrain

Hap - py Talk, keep talk - in' Hap - py Talk.____

Talk a - bout things you'd like to do. You

got to have a dream.__ If you don't have a dream,__

how you gon - na have a dream_ come true?

Rhythms on the Railway

CONCEPT
RHYTHM
SKILLS
LISTEN, SING,
READ, PRACTICE
LINKS
SOCIAL STUDIES,
MOVEMENT,
THEATRE

By the middle of the 1800s, railroads in the United States were being built to connect the eastern and western states. "Pat Works on the Railway" is a song about an Irishman who worked on these railroads.

Listen to the recording as you read the words of the song.

Sing "Pat Works on the Railway."

Pat Works on the Railway

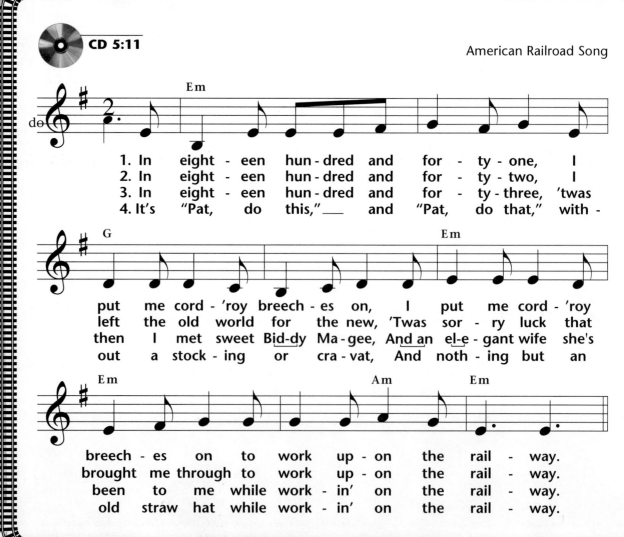

CD 5:11

American Railroad Song

1. In eight - een hun - dred and for - ty - one, I
2. In eight - een hun - dred and for - ty - two, I
3. In eight - een hun - dred and for - ty - three, 'twas
4. It's "Pat, do this," __ and "Pat, do that," with -

put me cord - 'roy breech - es on, I put me cord - 'roy
left the old world for the new, 'Twas sor - ry luck that
then I met sweet Bid-dy Ma - gee, And an el-e - gant wife she's
out a stock - ing or cra - vat, And noth - ing but an

breech - es on to work up - on the rail - way.
brought me through to work up - on the rail - way.
been to me while work - in' on the rail - way.
old straw hat while work - in' on the rail - way.

Say the phrase "Fil-li-me-oo-re-i-re-ay."

Fil-   li-   me-   oo-   re-   i-   re-   ay

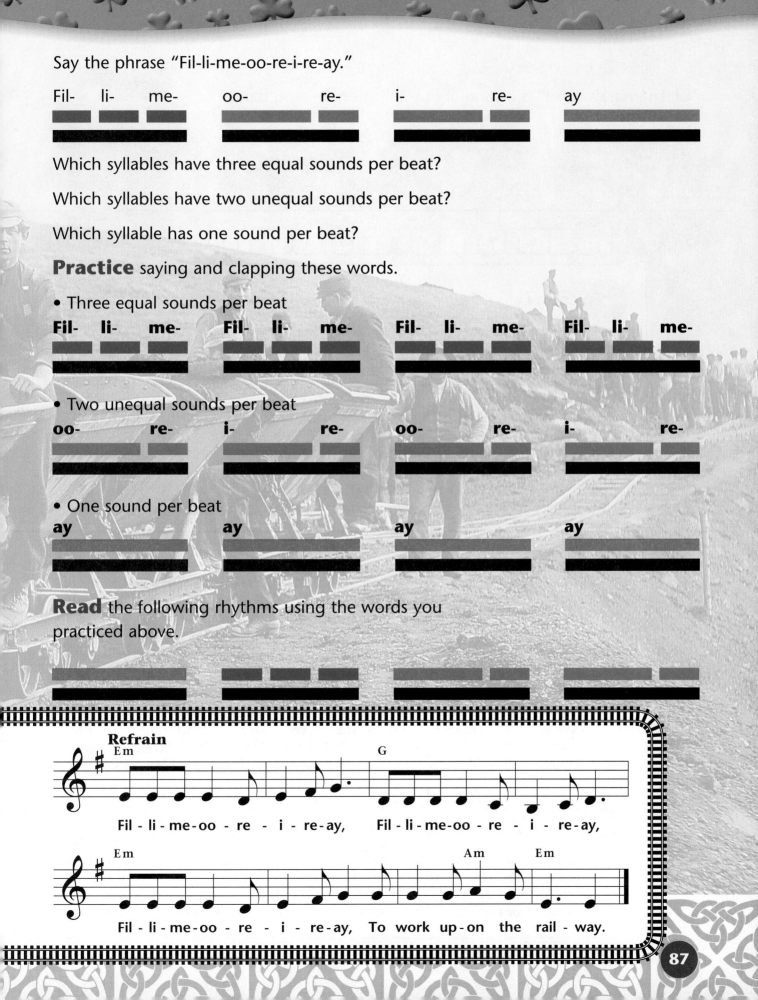

Which syllables have three equal sounds per beat?

Which syllables have two unequal sounds per beat?

Which syllable has one sound per beat?

Practice saying and clapping these words.

• Three equal sounds per beat

Fil- li- me-   Fil- li- me-   Fil- li- me-   Fil- li- me-

• Two unequal sounds per beat

oo-   re-   i-   re-   oo-   re-   i-   re-

• One sound per beat

ay   ay   ay   ay

Read the following rhythms using the words you practiced above.

Refrain

Em   G

Fil - li - me - oo - re - i - re - ay,   Fil - li - me - oo - re - i - re - ay,

Em   Am   Em

Fil - li - me - oo - re - i - re - ay, To work up - on the rail - way.

87

March to the Beat

"Macnamara's Band" is a song about an Irish marching band.

Pat with the beat as you sing the song.

Macnamara's Band

CD 5:14

Music by Shamus O'Connor
Words by John J. Stamford

Verse

1. Oh! me name is Mac-na-mar-a, I'm the lead-er of the band,_
2. Right_ now we are re-hears-in', for a ver-y swell af-fair,___
3. Oh! my name is Un-cle Yul-ius and from Swe-den I have come,_
4. Oh! I wear a bunch of sham-rocks and a un-i-form of green,_

Al-though we're few in num-bers we're the fin-est in the land.
The an-nual cel-e-bra-tion, all the gen-try will be there.
To play with Mac-na-mar-a's band and beat the big bass drum,
And I'm the fun-niest look-ing Swede that you have ev-er seen.

We play at wakes and wed-dings and at
When Gen-'ral Grant to Ire-land came, he
And when I march a-long the street, the
There's O'-Bri-ens and Ry-ans and Shee-hans and Mee-hans, they

ev-'ry fan-cy ball,_____ And when we play to
took me by the hand,_____ Says he, "I nev-er
la-dies think I'm grand,_____ They shout, "There's Un-cle
come from Ire-land,_____ But by Yim-min-y, I'm the

Rhythms o' the Irish Band

"Macnamara's Band" uses many of the same rhythms as "Pat Works on the Railway."

Identify a word from the refrain of "Macnamara's Band" that has three equal sounds per beat.

Then, find words from the refrain that have two unequal sounds per beat. How about one sound per beat?

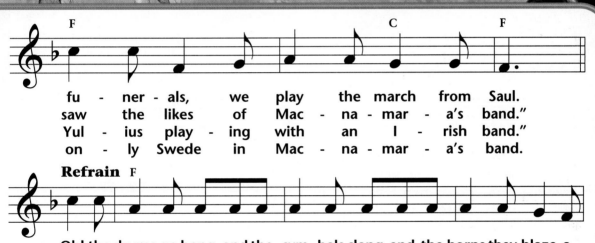

fu - ner - als, we play the march from Saul.
saw the likes of Mac - na - mar - a's band."
Yul - ius play - ing with an I - rish band."
on - ly Swede in Mac - na - mar - a's band.

Refrain

Oh! the drums go bang, and the cym - bals clang, and the horns they blaze a -

way;___ Mc - Car - thy pumps the old ba - zoon while I the pipes do play;

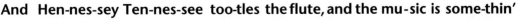

And Hen - nes - sey Ten - nes - see too - tles the flute, and the mu - sic is some - thin'

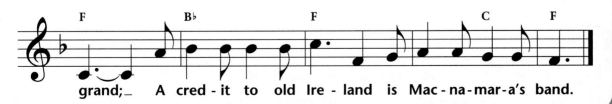

grand;___ A cred - it to old Ire - land is Mac - na - mar - a's band.

Step, Skip, Leap into Calypso

CONCEPT
MELODY
SKILLS
SING, LISTEN,
READ, PLAY
LINKS
MOVEMENT,
THEATER,
VISUAL ARTS

"**W**ater Come a Me Eye" is a calypso song from Jamaica, an island nation in the Caribbean Sea.

Sing the song. Trace the shape of the melody with your finger as you sing.

MAP
THE BAHAMAS
CUBA
JAMAICA
HAITI
PUERTO RICO
DOMINICAN REPUBLIC

Water Come a Me Eye

CD 5:17

Calypso Jamaican Song

Verse

1. Ev - 'ry time I think of Li - za,
2. Don't know why you went a - way,—
3. Time go slow when love is past,—
4. Lis - ten 'cause I'm call - in' you,—

Wa-ter come a me eye.

Ev - 'ry time I think of Li - za,
When you com - in' home to stay?—
When you come back, time go fast,—
And my heart is call - in' too,—

Wa-ter come a me eye.

Refrain

Come back Li - za, come back girl, Wa - ter come a me eye.

1., 2., 3.
4.

Come back Li - za, come back girl, Wa - ter come a me eye. eye.

Melodies can move in many ways. Look at the examples below from "Water Come a Me Eye."

Some melodies have **repeated notes**. They stay on the same pitch.

Ev-　'ry　time　I

Melodies can move by **steps**. They move by going to the next higher or lower pitch.

me
a
eye
come
ter
Wa-

When a melody moves by **skips**, it moves higher or lower by jumping over one pitch. When it moves by leaps it jumps over more than one pitch.

of

think
za
Li-

Step Over to South America

Listen to the recording. The melody in the first section of the song uses many repeated notes. How does the melody in the second section of the song move?

🎵 **LISTENING** CD 5:20

One Note Samba
by Antonio Carlos Jobim

"One Note Samba" is a song from Brazil about a melody built on one pitch. The piece has two sections.

Read the rhythms below.

Play along with "One Note Samba" on classroom instruments as you listen to the recording again.

N

BRAZIL

ARGENTINA

URUGUAY

Playalong

Listen to *Repicados sobre Madera* for each of the different drums. How can you tell the three drums apart?

🔘 **LISTENING**   CD 5:21

Repicados sobre Madera (excerpt) Uruguayan candombe

This recording features drummers from Uruguay.

◀ Candombe played in the streets of Montevideo, Uruguay

Learn About Candombe

Candombe is a type of music from Uruguay, a country in South America that borders Brazil and Argentina. Candombe is based on a rhythm brought by enslaved people from Africa to Uruguay over two hundred years ago. The rhythm is played by three types of drums: *tambor piano*, *tambor chico*, and *tambor repique*. Because each drum is a different size, each drum is also a different pitch. Candombe is played on the streets of Montevideo, the capital of Uruguay. It is also played for carnivals and festivals.

◀ Drums played in a parade in Montevideo

Unit 3 Happy Go Lucky!   93

LESSON
3

CONCEPT
MELODY
SKILLS
SING, READ,
LISTEN
LINKS
LANGUAGE ARTS,
MOVEMENT,
VISUAL ARTS

Searching for the New Pitch

"Love Somebody" is a song that features many of the pitch syllables you already know. **Name** the pitch syllables you know.

Sing the song. Find the new pitch.

Love Somebody

CD 5:22

American Folk Song

A
C   G7   C   G7

1. Love some-bod - y, yes I do. Love some-bod - y, yes I do.
2. Love some-bod - y, can't guess who. Love some-bod - y, can't guess who.

C   G7   C   G7   C

Love some-bod - y, yes I do. Love some-bod-y but I won't tell who.
Love some-bod - y, can't guess who. Love some-bod-y but I won't tell who.

B
C   G7

Love some-bod - y, yes I do. Love some-bod-y, yes I do.

C   G7   C

Love some-bod-y, yes I do. And I hope some-bod-y loves me too.

There are five pitches in the melody for the A section of "Love Somebody." These are four of the pitches:
do re mi   so

The melody has a pitch between *so* and *mi*. It is called *fa*. In this song, *so* and *mi* are on lines and *fa* is on the space between them.

do re mi fa so

On what words do you sing *fa* in "Love Somebody"?

Read the A section of the song with pitch syllables and hand signs.

Read the poem below. How is "Whispers" similar to the lyrics of "Love Somebody"?

la

so

fa

mi

re

do

Whispers

Whispers
  tickle through your ear
  telling things you like to hear.
Whispers
  are soft as skin
  letting little words curl in.
Whispers
  come so they can blow
  secrets others never know.

    —Myra Cohn Livingston

Moving to a New Key

Whatever pitch *do* is on, all of the other
pitches of the scale move with it.

Sing the first five pitches of the scale when *do* is G.

do re mi fa so

alto recorder ▶

- Where is *do*?
- Where is *mi*?
- Where is *so*?
- Where is *fa*?

Below is the melody of the A section of "Contredanse" by the
French composer Jean-Philippe Rameau.

Read the melody above using pitch syllables and
hand signs.

Meet the Musician

Jean-Philippe Rameau (1680–1764) was a
French musician and composer. While working as an
organist, he wrote one of the most important books
in Western music about harmony. When Rameau was
fifty years old, he began writing operas. They were so
popular in Paris that he continued to write more of
them until he was eighty years old.

Meet the Recorder

The recording below of "Contredanse" includes recorders. The recorder is a woodwind instrument that was popular in Europe during the 1500s and 1600s. A consort is a group of the same instruments in different sizes.

Listen to the recording. How many times do you hear the A section?

 LISTENING CD 5:26

Contredanse from *Les Indes galantes* (excerpt)
by Jean-Philippe Rameau

"Contredanse" was written in the 1700s. It is from one of Rameau's most famous operas, *Les Indes galantes* (*The Gallant Indians*).

Follow the listening map below of the B, C, and D sections for "Contredanse." The form of the piece is A B A C A D A.

▲tenor recorder

soprano recorder ▲

bass recorder ▶

Listening Map for Contredanse

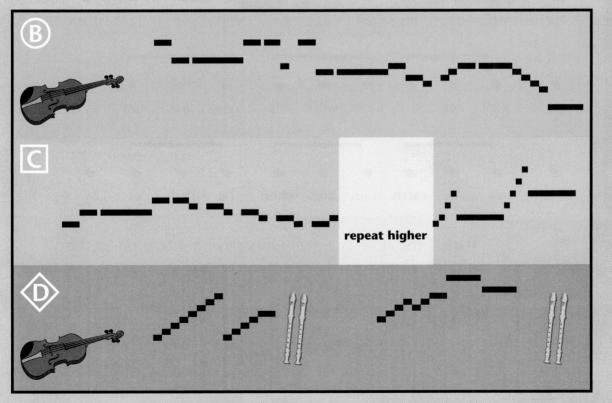

LESSON 4

On the Rail to Meter

CONCEPT
METER

SKILLS
READ, COMPARE,
IDENTIFY, SING

LINKS
VISUAL ARTS,
MOVEMENT

"**A** Modern Dragon" is a speech piece that tracks the passage of a railway train through the night.

A MODERN DRAGON

CD 5:27

Words by Rowena Bastin Bennett
Adapted by MMH

2.
A train is a dra-gon that roars through the dark.

He wrig-gles his tail as he sends up a spark.

He pier-ces the night with his one yel-low eye,

And all the earth trem-bles when he rush-es by.

Read the speech piece while paying attention to the rhythm of the words.

Compare the beat to the rhythm of the words "One yellow." Do both of these words fit into one beat?

One yel- low

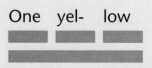

There are three equal sounds on one beat.

Finding the Meter

At the beginning of most pieces of music is a meter signature. The number on top tells how many beats there are in each measure. The number on the bottom tells what kind of note equals one beat.

Sometimes, there are two unequal sounds to a beat. It might be written like this: ♩♪ There could also be three equal sounds to a beat, written like this: ♫♪ One sound per beat would be written like this: ♩.

When you see these two types of rhythm patterns, the meter signature is usually written as $\frac{2}{?}$ or $\frac{6}{8}$. In $\frac{6}{8}$ there are six eighth notes in one measure.

Read and perform this pattern on percussion instruments.

Playalong

THINK! If a song has a meter signature of $\frac{3}{8}$, how many eighth notes are there in one measure?

San Juan Rhythms

In "La sanjuanerita," a young girl tells about living in San Juan, Guatemala. **Identify** the meter signature for the song. Then, find these two rhythm patterns in "La sanjuanerita."

Sing the song.

MAP

MEXICO

HONDURAS

GUATEMALA

NICARAGUA

La sanjuanerita
The Girl from San Juan

CD 6:1

Words and Music by Guadalupe Hernández
English Words by Linda Worsley

B♭   F7

Spanish: U - na chi - qui - lla de San Juan, quie-re ̮ a su pue-blo que ̮ es un jar-
Pronunciation: u na chi ki ya ðe san xwan kye ɾea su pwe ßlo kes un xaɾ
English: There is a   girl from old San Juan, she loves her town, a gar - den

B♭   Cm7   F7

dín, con flo - re - ci - tas de tem-po   ral   li-rios, cla - ve - les y ̮ a-lhe-
ðin kon flo ɾe si tas ðe tem po   ɾal   li ɾyos kla   ße les ia le
fair, col-or-ful i - ris bloom in the spring, lil - ies and bright car-na-tions

1.
B♭   2.
B♭   F7

lí - es. U - na chi - lí - es. Siem-bra la pa - pa, siem-bra ̮ el fri-
li es u na chi li es syem bɾa la pa pa syem bɾel fri
there. ̱ There is a   there. ̱ She sows po - ta - toes, she plants the

100

Tejedoras

This painting by Antonio Coché Mendoza (b. 1953) illustrates weavers practicing their trade in San Juan, Guatemala.

jol. Bue-na co - se-cha el cam - po le - da. Y en la
xol bwe na ko se chel kam po le ða i en la
beans, boun-ti - ful har - vest comes from the fields. Then comes fi -

fies-ta de San Juan, se po-ne a-le - gre su co-ra-zón. Con la ma-
fyes ta ðe san xwan se po nea le gɾe su ko ɾa son kon la ma
es - ta in San Juan, Her heart is light and joy-ful a - gain, to the ma-

rim - ba van a bai - lar to-dos con - ten - tos un buen son.
ɾim ba ßan a ßai laɾ to ðos ko ten tos un ßwen son
rim - ba, now she will dance, all are con - tent and hap - py then!

CONCEPT
METER
SKILLS
IDENTIFY, PAT,
PLAY, LISTEN
LINKS
CULTURES,
SOCIAL STUDIES

"Sitsiritsit" is a traditional song from the Philippines. The word "sitsiritsit" represents the sound of a rooster crowing. **Sing** the song with the Tagalog words. Find the insect names for butterfly *(alibangbang)*, firefly *(salaginto)*, and beetle *(salagubang)*.

Pat with the beat as you sing the song. Is the beat in groups of 2 or groups of 3?

The $\frac{2}{2}$ meter signature means that there are two beats per measure and the ♩ gets one beat. $\frac{2}{2}$ can also be written like this: **2/2**

Play the parts below on mallet instruments and finger cymbals as you sing the song.

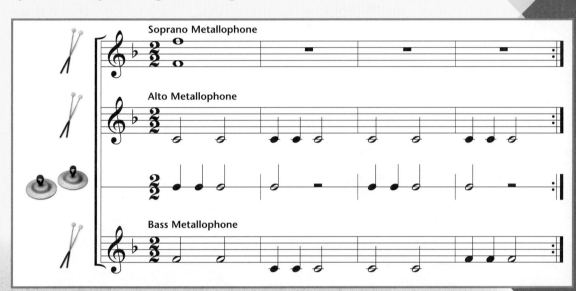

Dancing the *Tinikling*

The national dance of the Philippines is called the *Tinikling*. The dancers copy the movements of the tikling birds (similar to herons or cranes).

Tinikling originated in Leyte, one of the Visayan Islands. It is located in the middle of the country. The Spaniards took control of the Philippines in the 1500s. They forced the native Filipinos to work in the rice fields. Slower workers were rapped on the feet with bamboo poles as punishment. The workers would jump around the poles so they would miss them. This is how the dance was created.

bandurria

laud

Filipinos dancing the Tinikling

Listen to *Tinikling*. **Pat** the beat as you listen.
Is the beat in groups of 2 or groups of 3?

 **LISTENING** CD 6:9

Tinikling national dance of the Philippines

Native Filipinos do not usually sing along
when dancing *Tinikling*. It is accompanied
by a rondalla, an orchestra of plucked string
instruments. These instruments are the
bandurria, laud, octavina, guitar, and the
bajo de uñas.

▼ **These Filipino women are part of a parade in The Philippines.**

octavina

guitar

bajo de uñas

The Loud and Soft of It!

CONCEPT
DYNAMICS

SKILLS
SING, IDENTIFY, COMPARE, LISTEN

LINKS
SOCIAL STUDIES, CULTURES

Loudness and softness make music expressive. **Dynamics** refers to the loudness and softness of music. Dynamic markings in music show how loud or soft it should be performed. Read the chart below to learn about the different dynamic markings.

ff	fortissimo	very loud
f	forte	loud
mf	mezzo forte	medium loud
mp	mezzo piano	medium soft
p	piano	soft
pp	pianissimo	very soft
<	crescendo	gradually get louder
>	decrescendo	gradually get softer

Sing "El manisero," a song originally from Cuba.

Identify the dynamic markings in the song.

El manisero

Peanut Vendor

CD 6:10

Music and Spanish Words by Moises Simons
English Words by Linda Worsley

Spanish: ¡Ma-ní!___   ¡Ma-ní!___   Ca-se-ri-ta no te_a
Pronunciation: ma ni   ma ni   ka se ɾi ta no tea
English: **Ma-ní!___   Ma-ní!___   Come a-long and buy them,**

cues-tes a___ dor-mir,   sin co-mer te_un cu-cu-ru-cho de__ ma-ní.
kwes tes a   ðoɾ mir   sin ko meɾ teun ku ku ɾu cho ðe   ma ni
don't lie down_ to sleep.   You can buy   a cone of ma-ní, good_ to eat.

Dynamics on the High Seas

Listen for the expressive changes in dynamics as the orchestra plays "Guadalcanal March," from *Victory at Sea*.

 **LISTENING** CD 6:14

Guadalcanal March from *Victory at Sea*
by Richard Rodgers

Richard Rodgers was asked to create the music for *Victory at Sea*, a documentary film about World War II.

Meet the Musician

Richard Rodgers

(1902–1979) is one of the most famous composers of American musicals. He wrote many of these for Broadway, including *Oklahoma!*, *The King and I*, and *South Pacific*. Many of his musicals were turned into Hollywood movies.

THINK! Imagine a performance of "Guadalcanal March" with no changes in dynamics. **Compare** with the version you heard. Which do you like better? Why?

Read the listening map below as you listen to the recording again.

Listening Map for Guadalcanal March from *Victory at Sea*

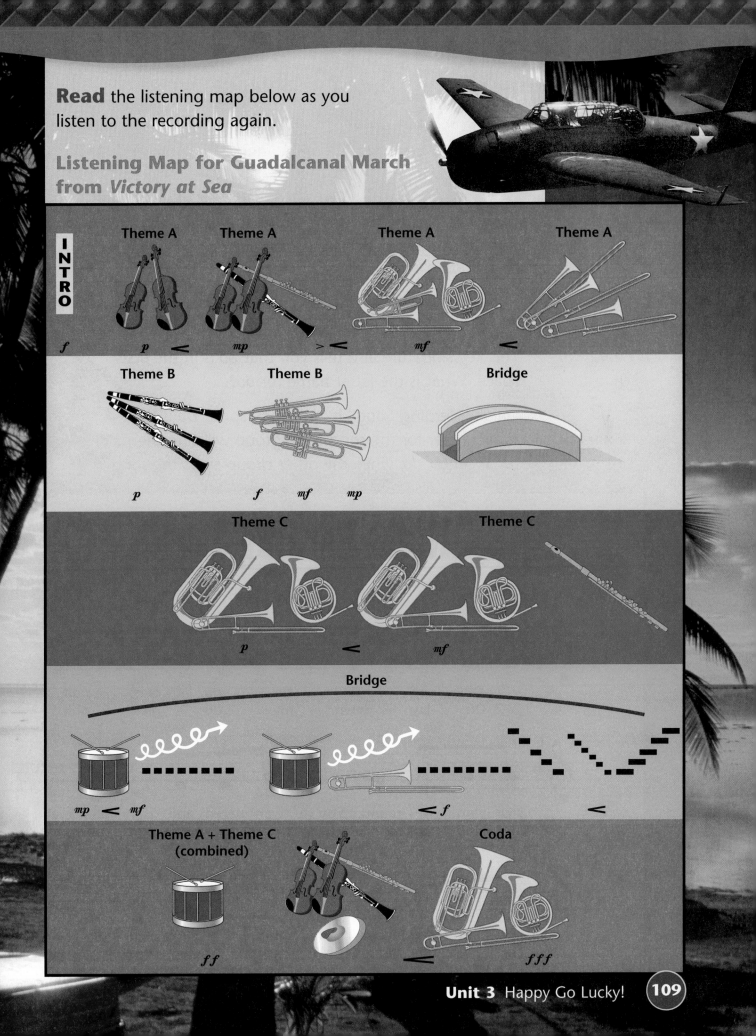

Round Up the Key

CONCEPT
HARMONY

SKILLS
SING, PLAY, LISTEN

LINKS
MOVEMENT, SOCIAL STUDIES, CULTURES

The **key signature** at the beginning of a song indicates the key of a given piece of music. In "Night Herding Song" the key signature has one **flat** (♭) on the third line. The flat comes before the meter signature. It tells you that this note is flat throughout the piece of music.

This key signature also tells you that *do* is in the first space. What is the letter name for *do*?

"Night Herding Song" is a cowboy song. *Do* is the tonal center for the song. One group will sing the tonal center *do*, while the other group sings the song.

CD 6:15

Night Herding Song

Cowboy Song

1. Oh say, lit - tle do - gies, quit
2. Oh, lay down, my do - gies, quit

rov - ing a - round. You've wan - dered and tram - pled all
shift - ing a - round. Just stretch a - way out on the

o - ver the ground. Oh, graze a - long, do - gies, and
big, o - pen ground. My horse is leg - wea - ry and

Harmony in the Corral

Singing or playing two pitches at the same time creates **harmony**. Singing the tonal center with a song is one way to harmonize the melody. Now harmonize the song another way.

Sing this pattern with two pitches: *do* (F) and *low so* (C), while the rest of the class sings the song.

THINK! Which harmony sounded better to you? Why?

move kind - a slow. And don't be for - ev - er so
I'm aw - ful tired. If you get a - way, then I'll

much on the go. Move slow, lit - tle do - gies, move
sure - ly be fired. Oh, lay down, my do - gies, lay

slow.____ Hi - o, hi - o,____ hi - o.
down.____ Hi - o, hi - o,____ hi - o.

Harmony from Israel

"Achshav" ("Now") is a folk song from Israel. **Sing** the song with both the Hebrew and the English words.

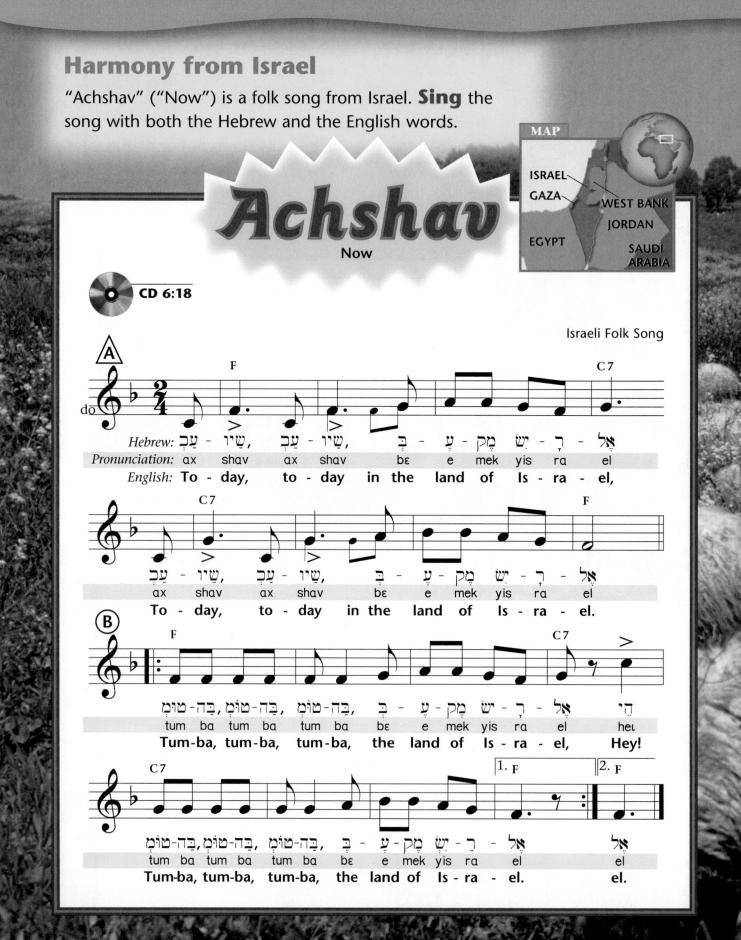

Achshav
Now

CD 6:18

MAP
ISRAEL
GAZA
WEST BANK
JORDAN
EGYPT
SAUDI
ARABIA

Israeli Folk Song

A F — C 7

Hebrew: עַכְ - שָׁיו, עַכְ - שָׁיו, בְּ - עֵ - מֶק יִשְׂ - רָ - אֵל
Pronunciation: ax shav ax shav bɛ e mek yis ra el
English: To - day, to - day in the land of Is - ra - el,

C 7 — F

עַכְ - שָׁיו, עַכְ - שָׁיו, בְּ - עֵ - מֶק יִשְׂ - רָ - אֵל
ax shav ax shav bɛ e mek yis ra el
To - day, to - day in the land of Is - ra - el.

B F — C 7

הֵי אֵל - רָ - יִשְׂ מֶק - עֵ - בְּ בַּה-טוֹם, בַּה-טוֹם, בַּה-טוֹם
tum ba tum ba tum ba bɛ e mek yis ra el hei
Tum-ba, tum-ba, tum-ba, the land of Is - ra - el, Hey!

C 7 — 1. F 2. F

אֵל אֵל - רָ - יִשְׂ מֶק - עֵ - בְּ בַּה-טוֹם, בַּה-טוֹם, בַּה-טוֹם
tum ba tum ba tum ba bɛ e mek yis ra el el
Tum-ba, tum-ba, tum-ba, the land of Is - ra - el. el.

112

Building Chords

Chords are built by sounding three or more pitches together from the scale. The tonal center for "Achshav" is *do*. This song is harmonized using two chords, one built on *do* and one built on *so*.

The first chord is built on the first step of the scale, *do*. It is called the one, or "I," chord. It sounds these pitches together:

The second chord is built on the fifth step of the scale, *so*. This chord is called the five, or "V," chord. It sounds these pitches together:

Use the I chord and the V chord to accompany "Achshav" with the following rhythm pattern:

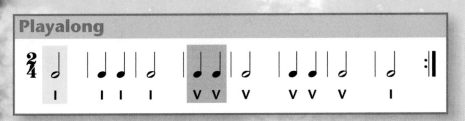

Playalong

Art Gallery

Valley of the Moon, Eilat

Judith Yellin Ginat (b. 1921) created this etching in 1968. It shows a valley in the Arava region of Israel.

CONCEPT
RHYTHM
SKILLS
SING, IDENTIFY,
READ, CREATE
LINKS
THEATER,
SOCIAL STUDIES

"**H**ey, Look Me Over" is from the Broadway musical, *Wildcat*.

Sing the song. **Identify** all of the measures in "Hey, Look Me Over" where there are three equal sounds (♩♩♩) on every beat.

From the original Broadway production of *Wildcat*

Hey, Look Me Over

CD 6:22

Music by Cy Coleman
Words by Carolyn Leigh

Hey   look   me   o - ver,   lend   me   an   ear;
Up   like   a   rose - bud,   high   on   the   vine;

Fresh   out   of   clo - ver,   mort - gaged   up   to
Don't   turn   up   your   nose,   bud,   take   a   tip   from

1.
here._____   But   don't   pass   the   plate,   folks,

don't   pass   the   cup;   I   fig - ure when-ev - er   you're

down and out, the on - ly way is up. And I'll be

mine. I'm a lit - tle bit short of the

el - bow room, but let me get me some, { And look / Hear me

out, shout, } world, here I come.

Interlude

No - bod - y in the world was ev - er with - out a pray'r;

How can you win the world, if no - bod - y knows you're there?

Kid, when you need the crowd, the tick - ets are hard to sell;

Go back to the beginning and sing to the End.
(D.C. al Fine)

Still you can lead the crowd, if you can get up and yell;

Magical Rhythms on Magical Instruments

Create your rhythm accompaniment to play with "Hey, Look Me Over." **Use** ♩., ♩ ♪, and ♫♪ to fill four measures in $\frac{6}{8}$ meter.

 **LISTENING** CD 6:25

The Sorcerer's Apprentice (excerpt)
by Paul Dukas

This piece is an example of **program music**, which is music that describes a scene or a story.

Listen for the bassoon playing three equal sounds to a beat. What other instruments pictured here play this rhythm?

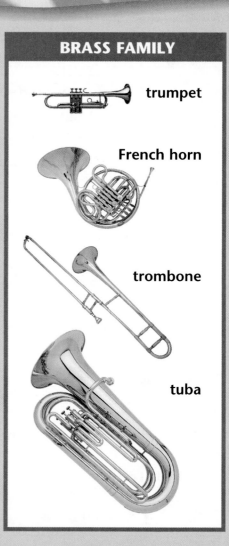

BRASS FAMILY

trumpet

French horn

trombone

tuba

STRING FAMILY

harp

double bass

cello

violin   viola

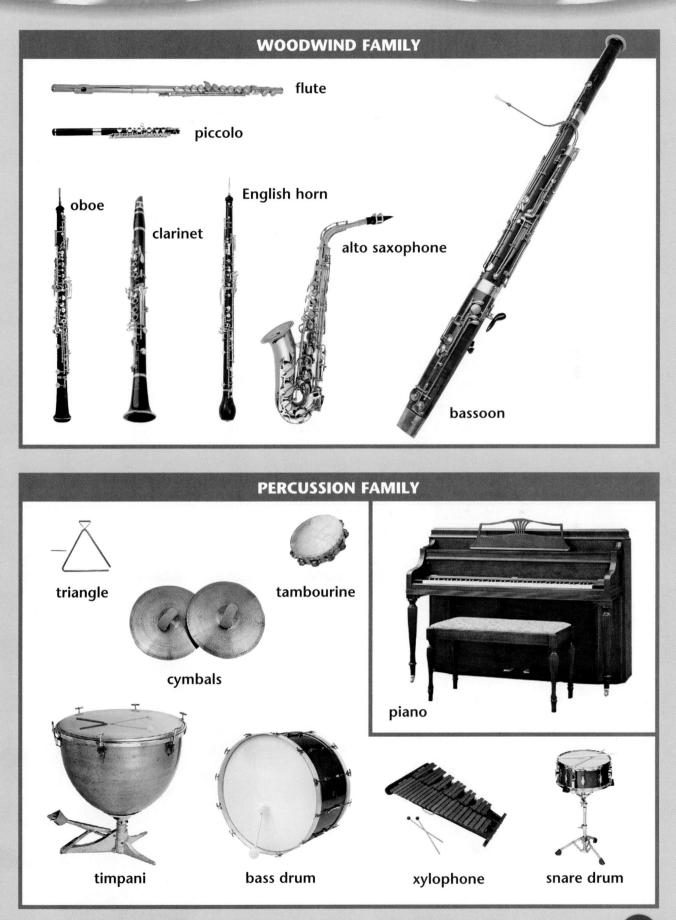

WOODWIND FAMILY

flute

piccolo

oboe

clarinet

English horn

alto saxophone

bassoon

PERCUSSION FAMILY

triangle

tambourine

cymbals

piano

timpani

bass drum

xylophone

snare drum

Spotlight Your Success!

REVIEW

1 What is a symbol that shows how many beats are in each measure and what kind of note equals one beat?

   a. meter signature   **b.** key signature   **c.** treble clef

2 Which rhythm has three equal sounds per beat in $\frac{6}{8}$ meter?

   a. ♩♪   **b.** ♫♪   **c.** ♩.

3 Which set of pitch syllables matches this melody?

   a. *do do | so   so | do do re re | do*

   b. *do do | la   la | so so mi re | do*

   c. *do do | mi   mi | fa mi re mi | do*

READ AND LISTEN

1 **Read** these rhythms. Then listen. Which rhythm do you hear?

   a. $\frac{6}{8}$ ♩ ♪♩ ♪|♩ ♪♩. ‖

   b. $\frac{6}{8}$ ♫♩. |♫♩. ‖

   c. $\frac{6}{8}$ ♩. ♩. |♩. ♩. ‖

   d. $\frac{6}{8}$ ♩. ♩. |♫♩. ‖

2 **Read** these patterns using pitch syllables. Then listen.
Which pattern do you hear?

THINK!

1 How do you know whether a phrase is just beginning or is coming to an end?

2 How can you tell the difference between repeated notes, notes that move by step, and notes that move by leap?

3 Describe the different languages that you heard in this unit. Which language do you like best? Why?

4 **Write** about something you learned from the music, instruments, and cultures in the unit. If you could choose one song or dance to perform again, which would you choose? Why?

CREATE AND PERFORM

1 **Choose** ♫ ♩ ♪, and ♩. to fill four measures in ⁶⁄₈ meter.

2 **Practice** reading your rhythm.

3 **Play** your rhythm on a classroom instrument using two or more dynamics as you play.

Meet the Musician

ON NATIONAL RADIO!

Name: Neil Vasan
Age: 17
Instrument: Marimba
Hometown: Vienna, West Virginia

Seventeen-year-old Neil Vasan plays both piano and marimba. His favorite time to practice is before he goes to bed at night. "This way, music provides a pleasant end to every day," he explains. Neil makes sure he takes a break in between practicing the two instruments, however. "If I don't, my arms cramp up from using them so much," he says.

Neil may want to be a professional musician one day. Then again, he may not.

Neil is also interested in chemistry and math, and he may decide to become a scientist. "I'm especially interested in organ transplantation," he states. "I think it's great that we are able to implant an organ into another human being and the person can live as a result."

No matter what he decides to do for a career, Neil is certain he will always love playing music. "It is very hard to imagine my life without it!"

LISTENING CD 6:27–28

Concertino for Marimba, Op. 21, First Movement ("Vigorous") by Paul Creston

Listen to Neil's performance and interview on the national radio program *From the Top*.

RECORDED INTERVIEW

Spotlight on a Wind Quintet

Did You Know?

A wind quintet is made up of five instruments: flute, oboe, clarinet, French horn, and bassoon.

The players in a wind quartet sit in a semicircle. They need to see each other to carry on their musical conversations.

The French horn is the only brass instrument in the group. Its strong sound stands out clearly from the other instruments.

The quintet's highest notes can be played by the flute and the lowest notes usually come from the bassoon.

LISTENING   CD 6:29–30

Autumn Music, First Movement (excerpt) by Jennifer Higdon

Quintet, Op. 43, Menuet (excerpt) by Carl Nielsen

Listen to these two pieces for wind quintet. The five instruments have different voices, but can make a smooth, blended sound when they play together.

UNIT 4

Musical Discoveries

Whether you are working, playing, or learning about new people and places, music is right there with you. In Unit 4 you will sing, play, and create music that makes new discoveries even more fun.

Coming Attractions

Sing a song in Mandarin.

Play chords to accompany a patriotic song.

Create your own rhythm for a Liberian song.

This song is from the musical *You're a Good Man, Charlie Brown.* It reminds you to think about the things that make you happy. How does music make you happy?

Sing the song.

The cast of the original Broadway production of *You're a Good Man, Charlie Brown*

Happiness

from the musical *You're a Good Man, Charlie Brown*

CD 6:31

Words and Music by Clark Gesner

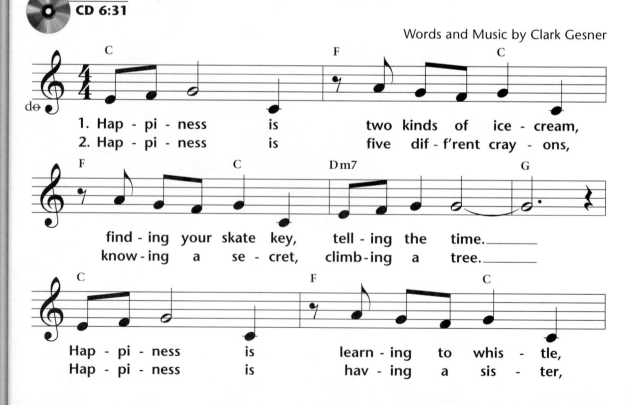

1. Hap - pi - ness is two kinds of ice - cream,
2. Hap - pi - ness is five dif - f'rent cray - ons,

find - ing your skate key, tell - ing the time.____
know - ing a se - cret, climb - ing a tree.____

Hap - pi - ness is learn - ing to whis - tle,
Hap - pi - ness is hav - ing a sis - ter,

CONCEPT
MELODY
SKILLS
SING, IDENTIFY, MOVE, PERFORM
LINKS
CULTURES, MATHEMATICS

Some songs put dreams and wishes into words.
What are the dreams and wishes in this song?
Sing "Over the Rainbow."

Over the Rainbow

CD 7:1

Music by Harold Arlen
Words by E.Y. Harburg

1. Some - where   o - ver the rain - bow   way   up   high,
2. Some - where   o - ver the rain - bow   skies   are   blue,
3. Some - where   o - ver the rain - bow   blue - birds   fly.

3rd time To Coda

there's   a   land that   I   heard   of   once   in   a   lull - a -
and   the   dreams that you dare   to   dream real - ly   do   come
Birds   fly   o - ver the rain - bow,   why then, oh   why   can't

by.   true.   Some - day   I'll wish up - on   a   star and

wake   up   where the   clouds   are   far   be - hind   me. _____

126

Think about how you move. Sometimes you take a step at a time. Sometimes it just feels great to take a flying leap! Melodies can move the same way. Sing "Over the Rainbow" again. **Identify** the melodic leaps in the song. **Move** to show the distance of the leap.

A whole note gets four beats in 4/4 and looks like this: o
An eighth rest gets one half beat in 4/4 and is written like this: ɣ Identify both of these in "Over the Rainbow."

Where trou - bles melt like lem - on drops, a-

D.C. al Coda
(Da Capo al Coda)

way, a - bove the chim-ney tops, that's where you'll find me.

Coda

I? If hap - py lit - tle blue-birds fly a-

bove the rain-bow, why, oh, why can't I?

Leap to Brazil

Oito Batutas by Pixinguinha

"Oito Batutas" is written and performed by the Brazilian composer Pixinguinha.

Listen for the wide leaps played by the clarinet in the A section of "Oito Batutas."

clarinet

Meet the Musician

Pixinguinha (1898–1973), whose given name was Alfredo da Rocha Vianna, Jr., was a composer from Brazil who played the flute and saxophone. He is known as one of the founding fathers of samba. Pixinguinha was considered a pioneer for Brazilian music, touring South America and Europe.

Playing Octaves

An **octave** leap is a wide leap. An octave is the distance between two pitches that have the same names. Find pitches that are an octave apart on the xylophone below.

Play the parts below on mallet instruments to practice playing octaves.

THINK! What do you think the number eight has to do with an octave?

LESSON 2

CONCEPT
RHYTHM
SKILLS
SING, LISTEN, WRITE, PLAY
LINKS
VISUAL ARTS, LANGUAGE ARTS, CULTURES

The Long and Short of It

The story of Noah's Ark tells about a man named Noah who prepared for a great flood by building an ark. When the rain started, Noah and his family loaded the ark with animals and watched as the floodwaters got higher and higher. After forty days and forty nights, the rain stopped and Noah and his animals were free to walk the land again.

Sing this song about Noah and his ark as you pat the beat. Then sing the song again as you clap the rhythm of the words. **Listen** to how the rhythm and beat fit together.

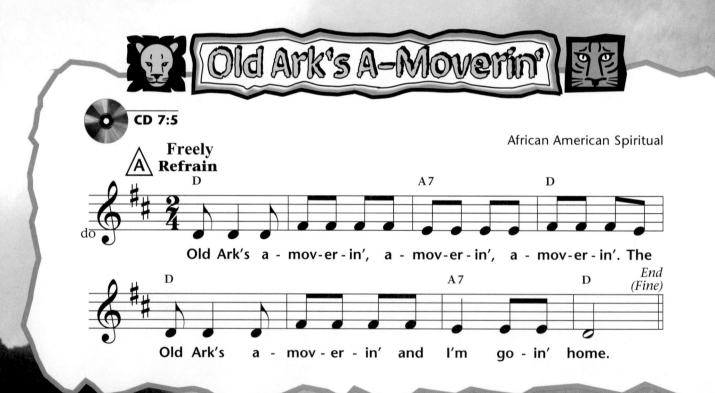

Old Ark's A-Moverin'

CD 7:5

African American Spiritual

Freely
Refrain

Old Ark's a - mov-er-in', a - mov-er-in', a - mov-er-in'. The

Old Ark's a - mov-er-in' and I'm go-in' home.

Noah's Ark

This painting was created by Edward Hicks (1780–1849) in 1846. *Noah's Ark* illustrates the story described in "Old Ark's A-Moverin'."

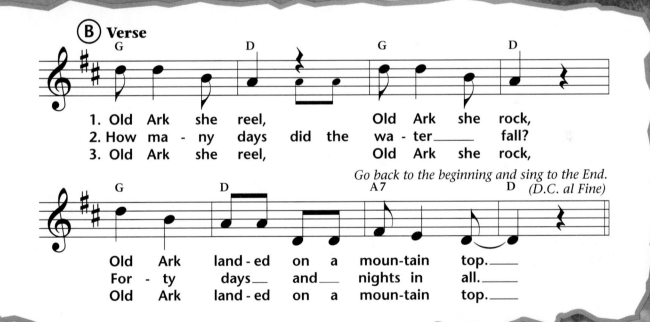

B Verse

G   D   G   D

1. Old Ark she reel,   Old Ark she rock,
2. How ma - ny days did the wa - ter_____ fall?
3. Old Ark she reel,   Old Ark she rock,

Go back to the beginning and sing to the End.
A7   D (D.C. al Fine)

G   D

Old   Ark   land - ed   on   a   moun-tain   top._____
For - ty   days_   and_   nights in   all._____
Old   Ark   land - ed   on   a   moun-tain   top._____

THINK! **Read** the lyrics "Old Ark's A-Moverin'" and look at the painting above. Sing the song again and think about the music. Do you think that the music expresses the lyrics? **Write** a short paragraph explaining why or why not.

Searching for Short-Long-Short

The short-long-short pattern in "Old Ark's A Moverin'" is two beats long. **Clap** this four-beat rhythm that starts with the short-long-short pattern.

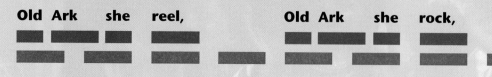

Old Ark she reel, Old Ark she rock,

Find the short-long-short pattern in the rhythm below, then clap the phrase.

Come now and join us, it's danc- ing day!

Perform this rhythm pattern as you sing "Peasant's Dancing Day," a folk song from the Balkans region of Eastern Europe.

MAP
SLOVENIA
CROATIA
BOSNIA AND
HERZEGOVINIA
SERBIA AND
MONTENEGRO
ALBANIA
ITALY   MACEDONIA

Peasant's Dancing Day

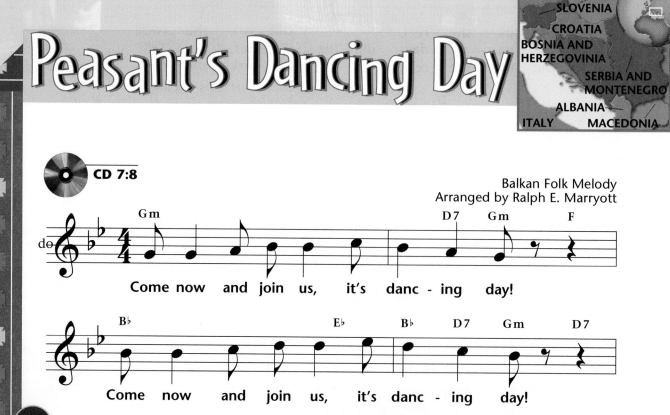

CD 7:8

Balkan Folk Melody
Arranged by Ralph E. Marryott

Come now and join us, it's danc - ing day!

Come now and join us, it's danc - ing day!

132

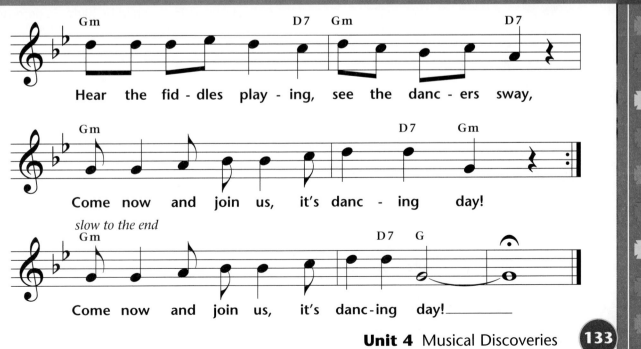

Hear the fid-dles play-ing, see the danc-ers sway,

Come now and join us, it's danc-ing day!

slow to the end

Come now and join us, it's danc-ing day!

LESSON 3

CONCEPT
MELODY
SKILLS
SING, READ, PLAY
LINKS
CULTURES, SOCIAL STUDIES

CD-ROM

Use *World Instruments* **CD-ROM** to learn more about Chinese instruments.

In Asia, bamboo has always been an important part of art, culture, and everyday life. The *dizi* is a traditional Chinese flute made from bamboo with six holes and tuned to a major scale. The *dizi* has a shrill, buzzing sound when it is played.

"Bamboo Flute" is a song from China that is sung in Mandarin. **Sing** the song. Where is the new note?

dizi

MAP
RUSSIA
MONGOLIA
KOREA
CHINA
INDIA
JAPAN

Bamboo Flute

CD 7:11

Collected and Transcribed by Kathy B. Sorensen
English Words by Linda Worsley

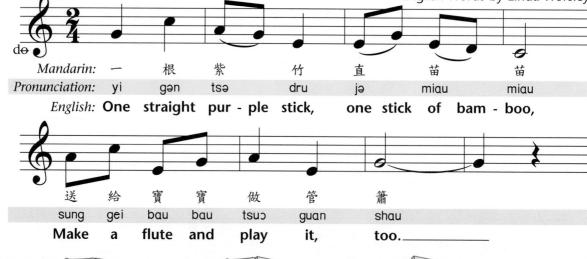

Mandarin:	一	根	紫	竹	直	苗	苗
Pronunciation:	yi	gən	tsə	dru	jə	miau	miau
English:	One	straight	pur-ple	stick,	one stick of	bam-boo,	

	送	給	寶	寶	做	管	簫
	sung	gei	bau	bau	tsuɔ	guan	shau
	Make	a	flute	and	play	it,	too._____

The pitches for the first phrase of "Bamboo Flute" are shown below, arranged from lowest to highest. The highest pitch is *high do (do¹)*. *High do (do¹)* is an octave above *do*. **Identify** *high do (do¹)* in the song. Sing the pitch syllables for this scale.

do re mi   so la   do¹

Read the first four lines of "Bamboo Flute" using pitch syllables.

More Fun with High *do*

"Buckeye Jim" is a folk song from the Appalachian region of the United States.

Sing the highlighted measures of "Buckeye Jim" using pitch syllables. What kind of scale does this song use?

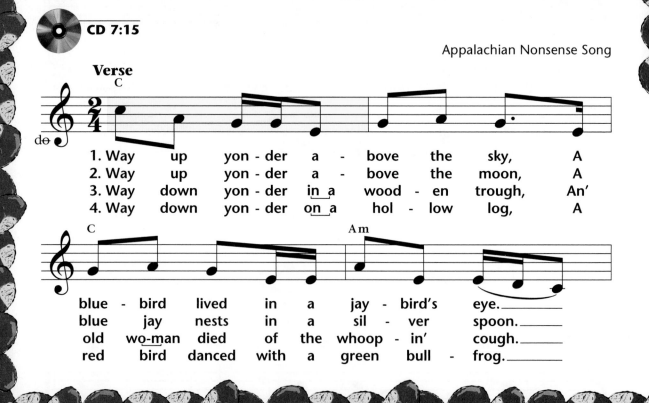

CD 7:15

Appalachian Nonsense Song

Verse

1. Way up yon - der a - bove the sky, A
2. Way up yon - der a - bove the moon, A
3. Way down yon - der in a wood - en trough, An'
4. Way down yon - der on a hol - low log, A

blue - bird lived in a jay - bird's eye. _____
blue jay nests in a sil - ver spoon. _____
old wo - man died of the whoop - in' cough. _____
red bird danced with a green bull - frog. _____

Play these parts on mallet instruments while the class sings
"Buckeye Jim."

Refrain

Buck - eye Jim, you can't go. Go
weave and spin, you can't go, Buck - eye Jim.

CONCEPT
RHYTHM
SKILLS
SING, IDENTIFY,
READ, LISTEN
LINKS
SOCIAL STUDIES,
CULTURES

Journey to the Rhythm

"Chicka Hanka" was sung by workers in
the United States as they built railroads
in the 1800s.
Sing the song. Listen for the sound of the train.

CHICKA HANKA

CD 7:18

Track Laborer's Song

Cap - 'n   go   side - track yore   train,_____

Chick-a-hank-a, chick-a -

Cap - 'n   go   side - track yore

hank-a, chick-a-hank-a, chick-a - hank-a;

train,_____

Num - ber three in

Chick-a-hank-a, chick-a-hank-a, chick-a-hank-a, chick-a-hank-a;

line,   A - com - in'   in   on

Chick - a - hank - a,   chick - a - hank - a;

time,   Cap - 'n   go   side - track yore

Chick - a - hank - a,   chick - a - hank - a;

train.

Chick - a - hank - a,   chick - a - hank - a,   chick - a - hank - a.

Short? Long? Both?

The short-long-short pattern can be written two ways:

1 A **tie** can connect the two eighth notes that sound as one quarter note.

2 A quarter note can replace the tied eighth notes.

This pattern is called **syncopation** because the long, or stressed, sound occurs between the beats, instead of on the beat.

Identify the syncopation in "Chicka Hanka."

Listening for ♪♩♪

The Inca and Quechua people are native to Bolivia and Peru. They have made flutes from wood, clay, or bone for centuries. Two of these types of flutes are called panpipes and the *quena*.

🔘 LISTENING · CD 7:21

Festival Dance Peruvian folk melody

"Festival Dance" is a traditional tune from Peru played on panpipes and *quenas*.

Clap the rhythm pattern shown below. **Listen** for this rhythm in "Festival Dance."

How many times did you hear this rhythm played?

◀ A Quechuan man from Peru playing panpipes

An Incan man from Bolivia playing the *quena* ▼

Rhythm Scramble!

Read the patterns in the boxes below. **Listen** to the recording and identify the order the patterns are played.

①

②

③

Each of these patterns comes from music you have sung or heard. One is a mystery pattern. Match the pictures below with the rhythm patterns above and provide the title of the two pieces you know.

LESSON 5

CONCEPT
HARMONY

SKILLS
SING, LISTEN, IDENTIFY

LINKS
SOCIAL STUDIES, CULTURES

In the Mood for Harmony

Often in music you hear more than one pitch sung or played at a time. Remember that this is called harmony.

Singing rounds in two or three parts is one way to create harmony. **Sing** "Sandy McNab" in unison and then as a round. **Listen** for the harmony.

CD 7:23

Anonymous, 19th Century

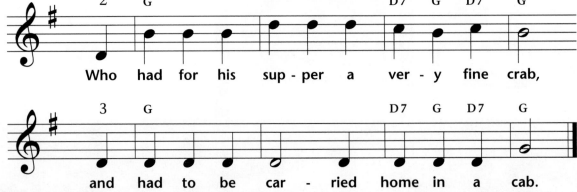

Finding the Root

The pitch on which a chord is built is called the **root**. Chords can be named by the letter of the chord root; for example, C chord or G chord.

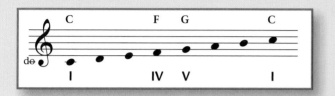

Another way to name chords is by position in the scale. The chord based on the first step of the scale is also called the "one" chord. Use the Roman numeral "I" to represent this chord.

Listen to the saxophones play "In the Mood." The harmony uses three chords: the I chord, the IV ("four") chord, and the V ("five") chord.

LISTENING CD 7:26

In the Mood by Joe Garland

"In the Mood" is a dance tune from the 1940s that is still popular today. This piece was made famous by the Glenn Miller Orchestra, featured on this recording.

Glenn Miller
Orchestra

Glass Chords

Listen for the chord changes in "Dance No. 4."

🔊 **LISTENING** CD 7:27

Dance No. 4 (excerpt) by Philip Glass

Listen to Philip Glass perform "Dance No. 4" on pipe organ.

Meet the Musician

Philip Glass (b. 1937) is an American composer and performer who first studied music in New York, and later in Paris. He has written music for ballet, musicals, opera, and movies. Glass continues to compose and explore new forms of music.

Learn About the Pipe Organ

The pipe organ is a keyboard instrument that dates back to the third century B.C. It has foot pedals and two or more sets of keys called manuals. The organ needs air to make sound. When playing the organ, air is forced through pipes of certain sizes. This creates the sound. A longer pipe will produce a lower sound. Shorter pipes produce higher sounds. Pipe organs can have hundreds and even thousands of pipes. The pipes are made of wood or metal.

Listen to "Dance No. 4" again as you follow the
listening map. **Move** to identify the chord changes
as you listen.

Listening Map for Dance No. 4

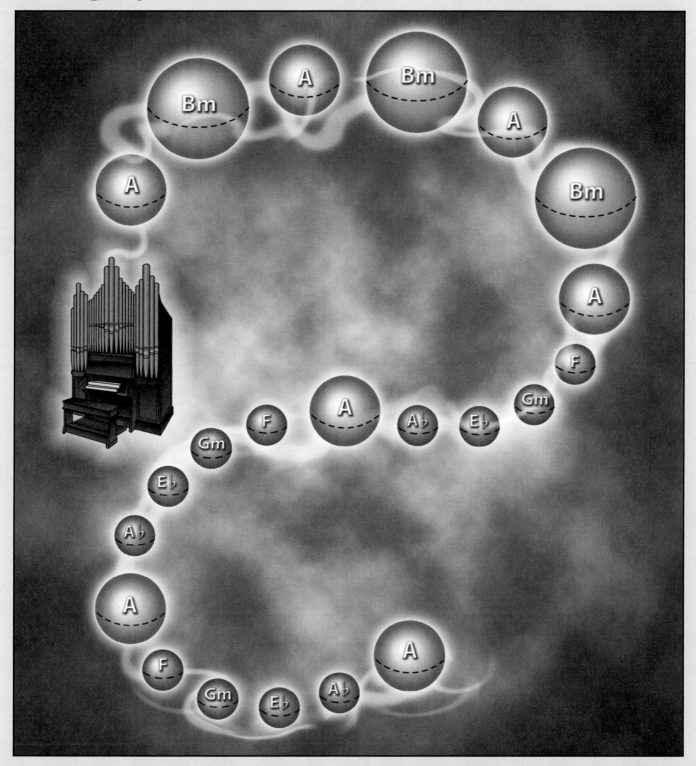

Chords in Your Land

CONCEPT
HARMONY

SKILLS
SING, PLAY, IDENTIFY

LINKS
CULTURES, SOCIAL STUDIES

"This Land Is Your Land" describes the boundaries and beauty of the United States. **Sing** "This Land Is Your Land." What do you think is beautiful about this country?

This Land Is Your Land

CD 7:28

Words and Music by Woody Guthrie

Refrain

This land is your land,___ This land is my land,___

from Cal - i - for - nia___ to the New York is - land,___

From the red-wood for - est___ to the Gulf Stream wa - ters;___

This land was made for you and me.

End (Fine)

146

One Song, America, Before I Go (excerpt)

One song, America, before I go,
I'd sing, o'er all the rest, with trumpet sound,
For thee—the Future.

—Walt Whitman

Verse

C   G

1.   As   I   was   walk - ing_____   that   rib - bon   of   high - way,_____
2.   I've   roamed and   ram - bled_____   and I   fol-lowed my   foot - steps__
3. When the sun comes shin - ing_____   and   I_____   was stroll - ing_____

D 7   G

I   saw   a - bove   me_____   that   end - less   sky - way._____
to the   spar - kling sands   of_____   her   dia - mond   des - erts,_____
and the wheat fields   wav - ing_____   and the   dust clouds   roll - ing_____

C   G

I   saw   be - low   me_____   that   gold - en   val - ley,_____
And   all   a - round   me_____   a   voice was   sound - ing,_____
As the   fog   was   lift - ing,_____   a   voice was   chant - ing,_____

Go back to the beginning and sing to the End.
G *(Da Capo al Fine)*

D 7

This   land   was   made   for   you   and   me.
"This   land   was   made   for   you   and   me."
"This   land   was   made   for   you   and   me."

Building Chords

The I, IV, and V chords are called **triads**, which means they each have three pitches. To build a triad, begin with the root of the chord, or lowest pitch. If the root is on a line, the higher pitches in the triad are on the two lines above the root. If the root is in a space, the higher pitches are in the two spaces above the root.

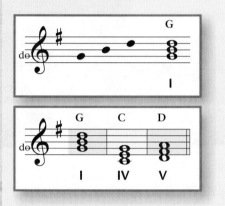

Play the harmonic pattern for the refrain of "This Land Is Your Land" with these three chords.

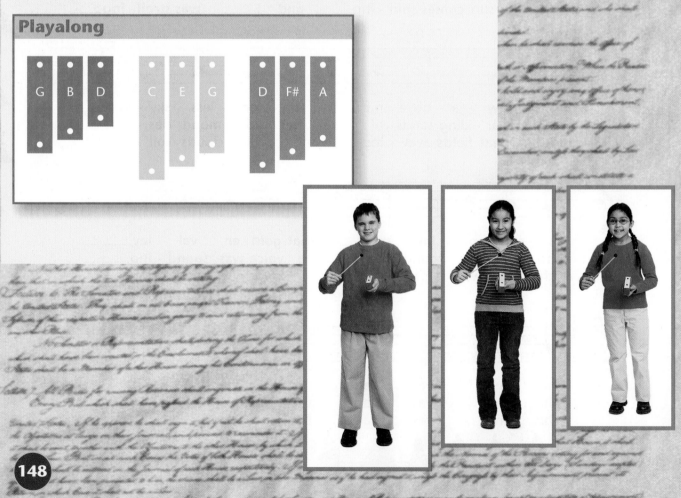

Which Chords Go Where?

Play these harmonic patterns.

A.

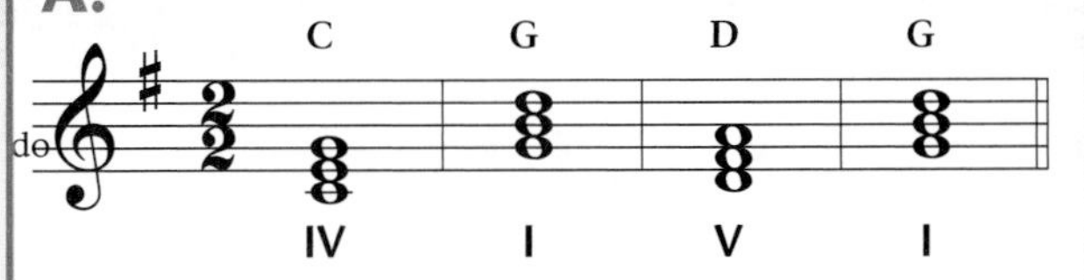

C	G	D	G
IV	I	V	I

B.

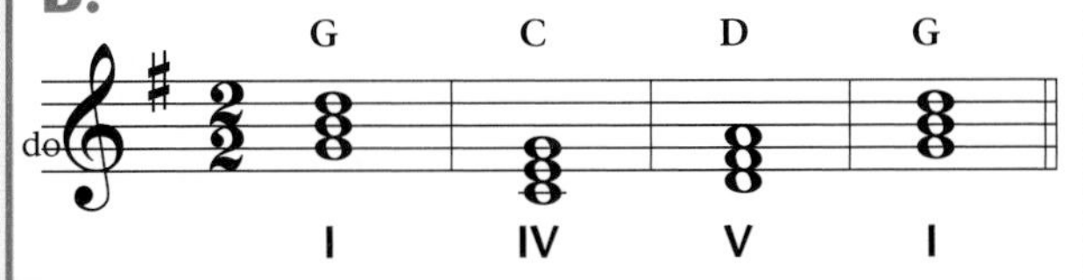 G	C	D	G
I	IV	V	I

C.

D	D	G	G
V	V	I	I

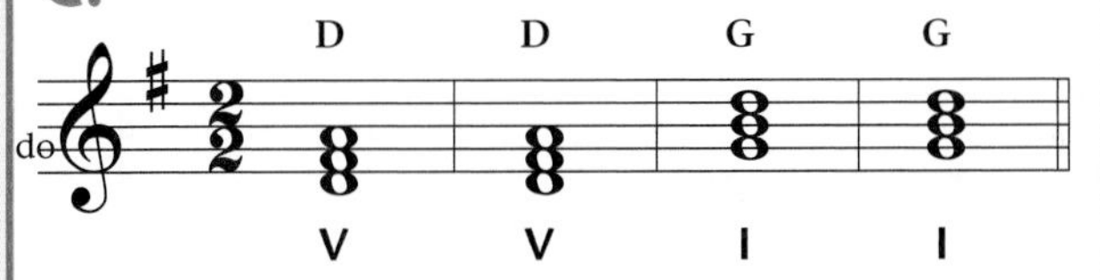

Which pattern is the correct harmonic pattern for the refrain of "This Land Is Your Land"?

THINK! What is the relationship between the harmonic pattern of the verse and the harmonic pattern of the refrain?

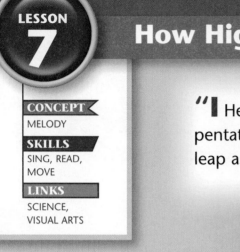

CONCEPT
MELODY

SKILLS
SING, READ, MOVE

LINKS
SCIENCE, VISUAL ARTS

"**I** Heard a Mockingbird" features only the pitches from the pentatonic scale. **Sing** the song. **Move** to show the upward leap as you sing the song.

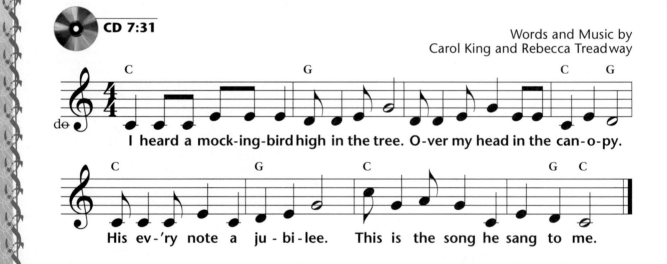

I Heard a Mockingbird

CD 7:31

Words and Music by
Carol King and Rebecca Treadway

I heard a mock-ing-bird high in the tree. O-ver my head in the can-o-py.

His ev-'ry note a ju-bi-lee. This is the song he sang to me.

Flying High for Octaves

Identify repeated notes, steps, skips, and leaps in the melody.

Practice the hand signs below. **Read** "I Heard a Mockingbird" using pitch syllables and hand signs.

do

re

mi

so

la

high *do*

Play these parts as an accompaniment to the song.

Create a Mockingbird Melody

"I Heard a Mockingbird" uses these pitches between *do* and *high do* (*do¹*). What do you call the leap between *do* and *high do* (*do¹*)?

Use the rhythm of the words in "I Heard a Mockingbird" to create your own melody. Use these pitches to sing your melody for the first and last phrases:

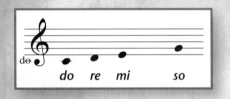

Use these pitches to sing your melody for the second and third phrases:

THINK!

Sing your melody in a different way. **Describe** how you would change your melody to make it more expressive or more interesting.

Listen to the Mockingbirds

The mockingbird is known for being a mimic. It imitates other birds' songs and sings them as part of its own song.

 LISTENING CD 7:34

Night of the Mockingbird by John Huling

This recording features John Huling playing a Native American flute.

Listen to *Night of the Mockingbird*. Move to show the way the melody moves. How does John Huling's playing sound like a bird call?

CD-ROM
Use *World Instruments* CD-ROM to learn more about the Native American flute.

Art Gallery

The Fabergé Mosaic Egg of the Royal Collection

Peter Carl Fabergé (1846–1920) created this egg in 1914. It is now part of Great Britain's Royal Collection.

Yankee Doodle Rhythm

CONCEPT
RHYTHM
SKILLS
SING, CREATE, PLAY
LINKS
SOCIAL STUDIES, CULTURES

The words of the song "Yankee Doodle" date back to the American Revolution in the late 1700s. It was a favorite with colonial soldiers.

Sing "Yankee Doodle" with a **descant**. A descant is a countermelody that is sung above the melody of a song. Singing a descant with a melody creates harmony.

CD 8:1

Traditional Melody
Words by Dr. Richard Shuckburgh
Descant by Mary Goetze

1. Fath-er and I went down to camp
2. Yan - kee Doo - dle went to town,
3. There was Cap - tain Wash - ing - ton
(4.) there I saw a swamp - ing gun,
(5.) ev - 'ry time they fired it off,

a - long with Cap - tain Good - in',
a - rid - ing on a po - ny,
up on a slap - ping stal - lion,
large as a log of ma - ple,
it took a horn of pow - der;

and there we saw the men and boys
He stuck a feath - er in his cap
a - giv - ing or - ders to his men;
up - on a might - y lit - tle cart;
it made a noise like Fath - er's gun

154

Clap the rhythm of the descant, then sing the descant with the song.

as   thick   as   hast - y   pud - din'.
and   called   it   mac - a - ron - i.
I   guess   there   were   a   mil - lion.
a   load   for   Fath - er's   cat - tle.
on - ly   a   na - tion   loud - er.

Refrain

Descant (add 6th and 7th times through)

Step with   the mu - sic and step with   the band.

Melody

Yan - kee Doo-dle keep it up,   Yan - kee Doo-dle dan - dy,

Step with   the mu - sic, it's Yan-kee Doo-dle dan - dy.

Mind the mu - sic and the step, and with the girls be han - dy.

4. And
5. And

6. And there I saw a little keg,
   Its head all made of leather,
   They knocked upon't with little sticks
   To call the folks together.
   Refrain

7. I can't tell you half I saw,
   They kept up such a smother;
   I took my hat off, made a bow,
   And scampered home to Mother.
   Refrain

Take Time for Rhythm

This song is from the West African country, Liberia. Many African songs and stories give advice to young people. What is the message in this song?

Sing "Take Time in Life."

MAP
ATLANTIC OCEAN
GUINEA
SIERRA LEONE
LIBERIA

Take Time in Life

CD 8:4

Liberian Folk Song

1. I was pass - ing by, My broth - er called me in,
2. I was pass - ing by, My un - cle called me in,
3. I was pass - ing by, Some peo - ple called me in,

And he said to me, You bet - ter take time in life.
And he said to me, My neph - ew, take time in life.
And they said to me, My young man, take time in life.

Peo - ple, take time in life, Peo - ple, take time in life,
Neph - ew, take time in life, Neph - ew, take time in life,
Young man, take time in life, Young man, take time in life,

Peo - ple,
Neph - ew, } take time in life 'cause you got far way to go.
Young man,

Use these rhythm patterns from the "Yankee Doodle" descant to create an eight-beat rhythm. Include ♪ ♩ ♪ at least once during the eight beats. Use ♩ 𝄽 for the last two beats.

Play the rhythm you created on percussion instruments as an introduction and coda for "Take Time in Life."

MIDI

For another activity with "Take Time in Life," see *Spotlight on MIDI.*

Percussion instruments from West Africa

▼ djembe

THINK!   What is the relationship between the message of "Take Time in Life" and the message of "This Land Is Your Land" earlier in the unit?

talking drum ▶

shekere ▶

Spotlight Your Success!

REVIEW

1 What is an octave?

   a. the five lines and four spaces on which musical notes are written

   b. the distance between two pitches that have the same name

   c. the stressed sounds that occur between the beats instead of on the beats of a rhythm pattern

   d. two or more pitches sung or played at the same time

2 What is a countermelody that is sung above the melody of a song?

   a. motive   **b.** round   **c.** descant

3 What is the root of this chord?

   a. A   **b.** D   **c.** G

READ AND LISTEN

1 **Read** these rhythms. Then listen. Which rhythm do you hear?

   a.

   b.

   c.

   d.

2 **Read** these patterns using pitch syllables. Then listen.
Which pattern do you hear?

a.

b.

c.

THINK!

1 How would you explain syncopation?

2 How could you determine if two notes were an octave apart?

3 What do the lyrics of "This Land Is Your Land " mean
to you? Why?

4 **Write** about a concept you learned in this unit and tell why
you think it is important.

CREATE AND PERFORM

1 Choose , and 𝄾 to fill four measures
in 4/4 meter.

2 **Create** your own rhythm composition.

3 **Play** your composition using percussion instruments.

4 For an additional challenge, use pentatonic pitches in the key
of F to create a melody for your composition.

Meet the Musician
ON NATIONAL RADIO!

Name: Lauren Criddle
Age: 17
Instrument: Voice
Hometown: Calabasas, California

When seventeen-year-old Lauren Criddle was in elementary school, the only kind of music she knew about was the pop music she heard on the radio. She wasn't exposed to classical music until she began studying voice.

When Lauren saw her first opera, she couldn't believe how magnificent it was. She said to herself, "This is me! This is what I want to do with the rest of my life!" Lauren hopes that one day she'll sing at famous opera houses all over the world. She would also like to teach because she wants to expose other kids to classical music.

Lauren recently visited an elementary school where she taught children about opera. "At first, some of them chuckled and covered their ears," recalls Lauren, "but soon they were asking me all sorts of questions." Afterward, Lauren was asked to sign many autographs!

LISTENING · CD 8:8–9

Summertime from *Porgy and Bess*
by George and Ira Gershwin

Listen to Lauren's performance and interview on the national radio program From the Top.

RECORDED INTERVIEW

Spotlight on the Violin

Did You Know?

Violinists produce sounds either by pulling a bow across the strings—*arco*—or by plucking the strings with their fingers—*pizzicato*.

Before the middle 1700s, violinists rested the instrument on their chests, not their shoulders.

The violin section is the largest group of instruments in the orchestra.

Antonio Stradivari (1644–1737) is considered the most gifted *luthier*, or violin maker, in history.

Scroll

Tuning Peg

Bow

Neck

String

Finger Board

Bridge

Chin Rest

 **LISTENING** CD 8:10–11

Scheherazade (excerpt)
by Nikolai Rimsky-Korsakov

Summer (Allegro non Molto) from *The Four Seasons* (Concerto No. 2 in G Minor) (excerpt)
by Antonio Vivaldi

Listen to the violin. In *Scheherazade* you can hear it play from a medium low register, where your own voice may reach, up to the very highest notes. In Vivaldi's *Summer*, the expressive qualities of the violin can be heard. Vivaldi was a violinist himself, and wrote many concertos for his favorite instrument.

UNIT
5

One Musical Planet

People all over the world speak different languages and have different ways of life. Music is one thing they all share. In Unit 5 you will sing and listen to music that brings to life the rich heritage of many lands. What are some songs you know that come from other lands?

Coming Attractions

Move to a Norwegian folk melody.

Perform a Korean hand-clapping game.

Sing a Russian folk song.

Music has the power to unite all people on Earth.
What are some other things that unite us?

Sing "Just One Planet."

Just One Planet

CD 8:12

Words and Music by
Sarah Stevens and Catherine Marchese

1. There are chil - dren   in   Ko - re - a,   and   Mex - i - co,
2. There are peo - ple   in   A - las - ka,   and   some in   Ne-

too, and Af - ghan - i - stan, Nor - way, and Su - dan, Aus - tra - lia,   Pe -
pal, and they sing and dance, and they want a chance to join with us

ru.   But no mat - ter where they're from, and no mat - ter where they
all. 'Cause no mat - ter where we're from, and no mat - ter where we

go,   they all live,   they all love,   and there's some - thing they should
go,   we all live,   we all love,   and there's some - thing we should

Refrain

LESSON
1

CONCEPT
METER
SKILLS
SING, IDENTIFY,
LISTEN, PERFORM
LINKS
CULTURES, VISUAL
ARTS, MOVEMENT

Running for Meter

When running, track athletes may need to run faster. Sometimes they just need to keep a steady pace. In music, this steady pace is the steady beat.

"Sansa kroma" is a game song played by children of the Akan culture in Ghana. **Sing** "Sansa kroma" and play the stone-passing game with the steady beat. **Identify** the meter of the song.

MAP

MALI BURKINA
FASO
IVORY GHANA NIGERIA
COAST
TOGO BENIN
WEST AFRICA

Sansa kroma
Little Hawk

CD 8:15

Akan Game Song
English Words by Linda Worsley

Ashanti: San - sa___ kro - ma, Ne na wu‿o ɔ - kye-kyer nko kɔ ma
Pronunciation: san sa kɾo ma ne na wuɔ ɔ che cheɾ ɳko kɔ ma
English: San - sa___ kro - ma, Lit - tle hawk, You are an or - phan now.

San - sa___ kro - ma, Ne na wu‿o ɔ - kye-kyer nko-kɔ ma
san sa kɾo ma ne na wuɔ ɔ che cheɾ ɳko kɔ ma
San - sa___ kro - ma, Lit - tle hawk, You are an or-phan now.

1. Grab
2. Pass
3. Clap
4. Clap

San - sa___ kro - ma, Ne na wu␣o nko - kɔ ma
san sa kɾo ma ne na wuo ŋko kɔ ma
San - sa___ kro - ma, steal-ing chicks for your own!

San - sa___ kro - ma, Ne na wu␣o nko - kɔ ma
san sa kɾo ma ne na wuo ŋko kɔ ma
San - sa___ kro - ma, steal-ing chicks for your own!

Dancing—Norwegian Style!

Listen to "Nokken Danser." **Pat** your legs when you feel the downbeat. **Tap** your shoulders on the other beats. Which meter signature fits best? $\frac{2}{4}$, $\frac{3}{4}$, or $\frac{4}{4}$?

 **LISTENING** CD 8:19

Nokken Danser Norwegian folk melody

"Nokken Danser" is a folk tune from Norway. The original melody has been around for hundreds of years.

Perform the dance for "Nokken Danser." Form a circle in pairs. Take one step for every downbeat.

Move counterclockwise in a circle.

Move clockwise in a circle.

Art Gallery

A Watermill in Christiania

This oil painting was created by Louis Gurlitt (1812–1897) around 1834. It shows a watermill in Norway.

Move into the circle and form a star.

Switch parts and move into the circle.

CONCEPT
TONALITY

SKILLS
SING, MOVE, LISTEN

LINKS
MOVEMENT, CULTURES, SOCIAL STUDIES

The word "Shalom" is Hebrew for "peace." "Shabat Shalom" is a joyful wish for peace. **Sing** the song.

MAP

ISRAEL
GAZA
WEST BANK
JORDAN
EGYPT
SAUDI ARABIA

shabat shalom

CD 8:20

Words and Music by N. Frankel

One reason melodies sound different from one another is that they use different sets of pitches. Some songs use a set of pitches called **major**. Others use a set of pitches called **minor**. The set of pitches used in "Shabat Shalom" is minor.

The grapevine step is often used in dances from the Middle East. **Perform** this step as you sing "Shabat Shalom."

RIGHT
Step right.

BACK
Cross your left foot behind your right and step.

RIGHT
Step right.

HOP
Hop with your right foot and kick with your left.

Major Nonsense!

"Chumbara" is a song that uses a set of pitches in major.
The words do not mean anything, but the song is fun to sing!
Sing "Chumbara."

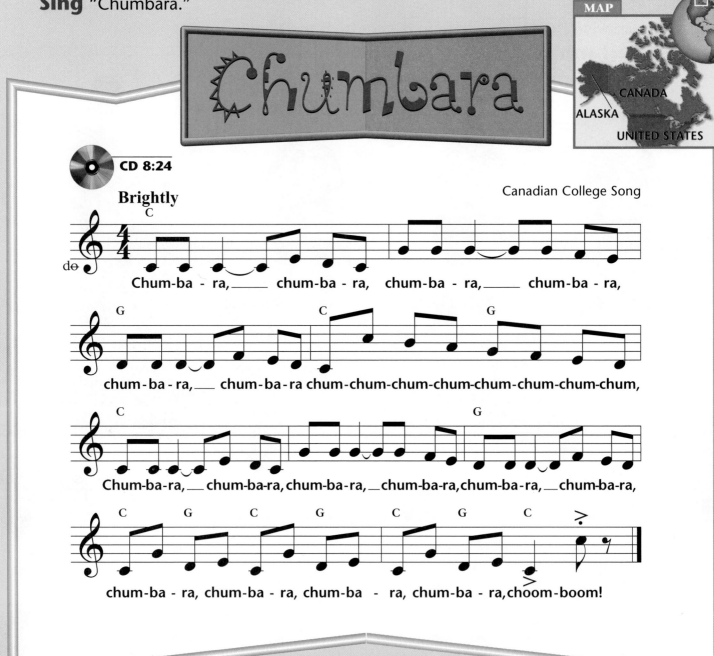

MAP

CANADA
ALASKA
UNITED STATES

CD 8:24

Brightly

Canadian College Song

Chum-ba - ra,____ chum-ba - ra, chum-ba - ra,____ chum-ba - ra,

chum-ba - ra,____ chum-ba - ra chum-chum-chum-chum-chum-chum-chum-chum,

Chum-ba-ra,____chum-ba-ra,chum-ba-ra,__chum-ba-ra,chum-ba-ra,__chum-ba-ra,

chum-ba - ra, chum-ba - ra, chum-ba - ra, chum-ba - ra,choom-boom!

THINK! How do you think "Chumbara" would sound if it were minor? How would this change the mood of the song?

172

An Ear for Major and Minor

Listen to "Dance of the Mirlitons" as you follow the listening map below.

 **LISTENING** CD 8:27

Dance of the Mirlitons from *The Nutcracker*
by Piotr Ilyich Tchaikovsky

"Dance of the Mirlitons" is from *The Nutcracker*, a ballet suite. A mirliton is a type of reed instrument. This selection has A and B sections that repeat. The A section is played by three flutes. A trumpet is featured in the B section. One section is in major, and one section is in minor.

Which section is major and which is minor?

Meet the Musician

Piotr Ilyich Tchaikovsky (1840–1893), a Russian composer, wrote ballets, operas, symphonies, concertos, and choral music. Many people said that he wrote his music from the heart, not the head.

Listening Map for Dance of the Mirlitons

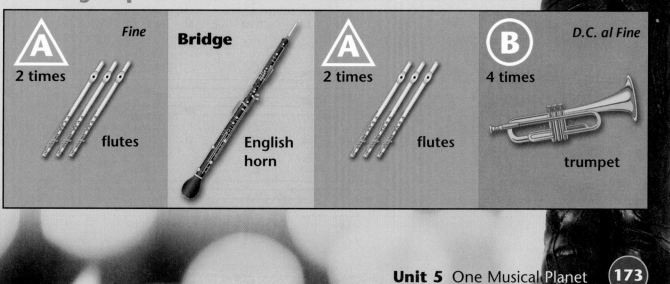

A Fine	**Bridge**	**A**	**B** D.C. al Fine
2 times — flutes	English horn	2 times — flutes	4 times — trumpet

Long Live Rhythm!

CONCEPT
RHYTHM
SKILLS
SING, IDENTIFY,
PLAY, READ
LINKS
CULTURES,
SOCIAL STUDIES

The Festival of the Rosary
(detail), 1506, by
Albrecht Dürer

The Latin words of this song declare "Long Live Music!"
Sing "Viva la musica" in unison and then as a round.

Viva la musica

CD 8:28

Music by Michael Praetorius
Words Traditional

Latin: Vi - va, vi - va la mu - si - ca.
Pronunciation: vi va vi va la mu zi ka

Vi - va, vi - va la mu - si - ca.

Vi - va la mu - si - ca.

Tying Rhythms Together

The rhythm of the first measure of
"Viva la musica" can be written like this:

or like this:

A dot following a note adds half of
the note's rhythmic value to the
note. A dot after a quarter note
makes it an eighth note longer.

Identify all of the ♩. ♪ patterns in "Viva la musica."

Play these rhythms as an accompaniment to the song.

Three Musicians
(16th century), anonymous

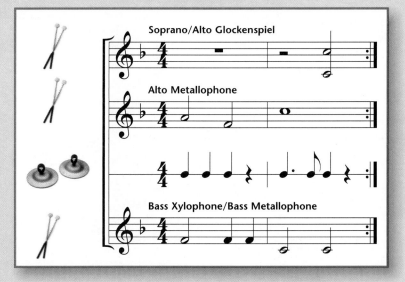

Renaissance Rhythms

Listen to "La canarie."

 LISTENING CD 9:1

La canarie from *Dances from Terpsichore*
by Michael Praetorius

"La canarie" is an instrumental piece Michael Praetorius composed for dancing. Viols, early relatives of the violin family, play the melody. Lute and tambourine accompany.

Look at the melody below from "La canarie."
Identify the ♩ ♪ rhythm each time it occurs.

▲ Lute

See **music.mmhschool.com** to research Renaissance Music.

Learn About Renaissance Music

Between 1400 and 1550, the sound of music changed very quickly. Musical forms and harmonies became more full and complex. Many of the new musical ideas were created by French and Flemish composers. With the help of the printing press, these ideas spread quickly through the churches and royal courts of Europe.

THE RAMAGE PRESS.

Michael Praetorius (1571–1621) was a German organist, composer, and scholar. Like many musicians of his time, he worked for churches and in the courts of noble families. Praetorius wrote over a thousand hymns, musical settings of psalms, and other choral pieces. He also wrote a lot about music. Much of what we know about performing and composing music 400 years ago comes from the writings of Michael Praetorius.

Art Gallery

Two Musicians

Albrecht Dürer (1471–1528) created this painting around 1504, about 70 years before Praetorius was born.

CONCEPT
MELODY

SKILLS
SING, IDENTIFY,
READ

LINKS
CULTURES,
SOCIAL STUDIES

"El coquí" ("The Frog") is a folk song from Puerto Rico. **Sing** the song with the Spanish words.

MAP
THE BAHAMAS
CUBA
JAMAICA
HAITI
PUERTO RICO
DOMINICAN REPUBLIC

El coquí

The Frog

CD 9:2

Puerto Rican Folk Song
English Version by MMH

Verse

Spanish: El co - quí, el co - quí a mi me en can - ta,
Pronunciation: el ko ki el ko kia mi men kan ta
English: The co - quí, the co - quí so en - tranc - ing,

Es tan lin - do el can - tar del co - quí;
es tan lin doel kan taɾ ðel ko ki
The co - quí sings a beau - ti - ful song.

Por las noch - es al ir a a - cost - ar - me,
poɾ las no ches al iɾ a kos taɾ me
Through the hours when I'm sleep - ing and dream-ing,

Me a - dor - me - ce can - tan - do a - sí._____
mea ðoɾ me se kan tan do a si
The co - quí sings to me all night long._____

Almost "*do*" but Just Below

Sing the last phrase of "El coquí" shown below.
Then sing just the last pitch, the tonal center, *do*.
The highlighted pitch just below *do* is called *ti*.
Identify *ti* in "El coquí."

ti

so   do¹   do¹   ti   la   ti   do¹

Read this phrase using pitch syllables and hand signs.

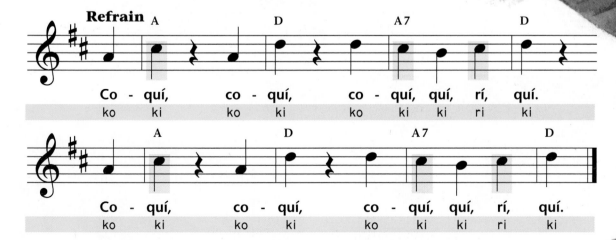

Refrain

A   D   A7   D

Co - quí,   co - quí,   co - quí, quí, rí, quí.
ko   ki   ko   ki   ko   ki   ki   ri   ki

A   D   A7   D

Co - quí,   co - quí,   co - quí, quí, rí, quí.
ko   ki   ko   ki   ko   ki   ki   ri   ki

The Major Scale

If you sing all the pitches from *do* to *do*ˈ you will be singing a
major scale. **Identify** *ti* in the scale below. Remember
that it is just below *do*.

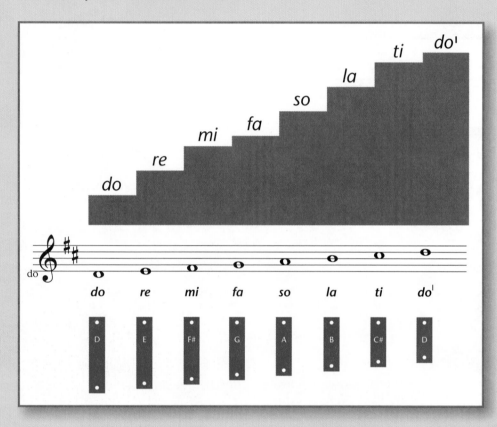

Play these chords on resonator bells to accompany
the refrain of "El coquí."

Listening for *ti*

The pitch *ti* is often referred to as the "leading tone." What do you think *ti* is leading to?

Listen for *ti* and *do* in this recording.

CD-ROM

Use *Orchestral Instruments* **CD-ROM** to learn more about the piano and how it is used in a modern day orchestra.

LISTENING CD 9:7

Vivace from *Piano Sonata No. 2 in D Minor* (excerpt) by Sergei Prokofiev

This recording is played by the pianist Barbara Nissman. The piece features *ti*, or the leading tone, throughout the movement. *Do* is not heard in this piece until the very end of the excerpt.

RECORDED INTERVIEW CD 9:6

Listen to the recorded interview with Barbara Nissman.

Meet the Musician

Barbara Nissman (b. 1944), pianist, was born in Philadelphia and has performed all over the world. She is known for playing the piano music of Prokofiev. Nissman also gives lectures and master classes on Prokofiev's music. She says his music "reveals ... a love of life that is quite wonderful."

Rolling Through Meter

CONCEPT
METER
SKILLS
SING, MOVE,
LISTEN, PAT
LINKS
LANGUAGE
ARTS, CULTURES,
MOVEMENT

"Roll On, Columbia" is about the Columbia River in the northwestern United States. Sing the song. How might you move to show the meter?

ROLL ON, COLUMBIA

CD 9:8

Music based on "Goodnight Irene"
by Huddie Ledbetter and John Lomax
Words by Woody Guthrie

1. Green Doug-las   fir where the   wa-ters   cut through,
2. Oth-er   big   riv-ers   add   pow-er   to   you,

Down her   wild   moun-tains   and   can-yons   she   flew.
Yak-i-ma,   Snake, and   the   Klick-i-tat,   too.

Ca-na-di-an   North-west   to the   o-cean so   blue,
Sand-y,   Wil-lam-ette,   and the   Hood Riv-er,   too,

Roll   on,   Co-lum-bia,   roll   on.

Corre el río
(The River Flows By)

Corre el río
decidido, sin parar
el mar sereno

The river flows by
Determined, instoppable
The ocean serene

—*Patricia Vasquez*

The meter signature of "Roll On, Columbia"
is $\frac{3}{4}$ meter. $\frac{3}{4}$ meter can also be written as $\frac{3}{4}$ meter.
How many beats are there per measure in $\frac{3}{4}$ meter?
Which note gets one beat?

Columbia River

Refrain

Roll on, Co-lum-bia, roll on. Roll on, Co-lum-bia, roll on. Your pow-er is turn-ing our dark-ness to dawn. Roll on, Co-lum-bia, roll on.

Global Voices

A Hand-Clapping Game from Korea

"Ban Dal" is a song from Korea. There is a hand-clapping game that goes with the song. **Listen** to "Ban Dal." Learn to play the game.

MAP

RUSSIA
CHINA
NORTH KOREA
JAPAN
SOUTH KOREA

 **LISTENING** CD 9:11

Ban Dal by Yoon Kyekyoung

This song was written by the Korean composer Yoon Kyekyoung in the 1920s. It is known by many Korean children. Kyekyoung is considered to be a Korean national treasure by many native Koreans.

Pat with the beat as you listen to "Ban Dal" again. The beats are in groups of three.

Look at the Korean characters. Read the translation as you listen to the song again.

반 달

Ban Dal
Half Moon

 푸른 하늘 은하수 하얀 쪽배엔
계수 나무 한 나무 토끼 한 마리
돛대도 아니 달고 삿대도 없이
가기도 잘도 간다 서쪽 나라로

 In the blue sky, the milky way and a white boat
In the boat, a laurel tree and a little rabbit
While having no mast or even a punt pole
It moves smoothly to western lands

The Key to Major and Minor

CONCEPT
TONALITY

SKILLS
PLAY, SING,
IDENTIFY

LINKS
CULTURES,
SOCIAL STUDIES

The key of a song is determined by its tonal center and scale. When a song or a scale has *do* as a tonal center, it is in a major key. **Play** and sing a major scale beginning on D.

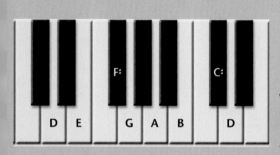

do   re   mi   fa   so   la   ti   do¹

When D is *do*, there is a sharp on both the F line and the C space. This key signature tells you to use F-sharp (F♯) and C-sharp (C♯) instead of F and C.

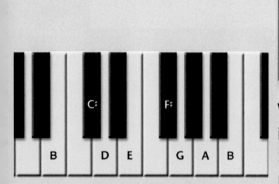

la₁   ti₁   do   re   mi   fa   so   la

When a song has *la* as its tonal center, it is in a minor key. Play and sing a **minor scale** beginning on B. This is a B-minor scale. The B-minor scale has the same key signature as the D-major scale. The D-major scale begins and ends on *do*. The B-minor scale begins and ends on *la*.

Unlock the Key

Sing "When I Was Young," a folk song from Ireland. The tonal center is D. Is this song in a major or minor key? How can you tell?

MAP
SCOTLAND
NORTHERN IRELAND
ENGLAND
IRELAND WALES

When I Was Young

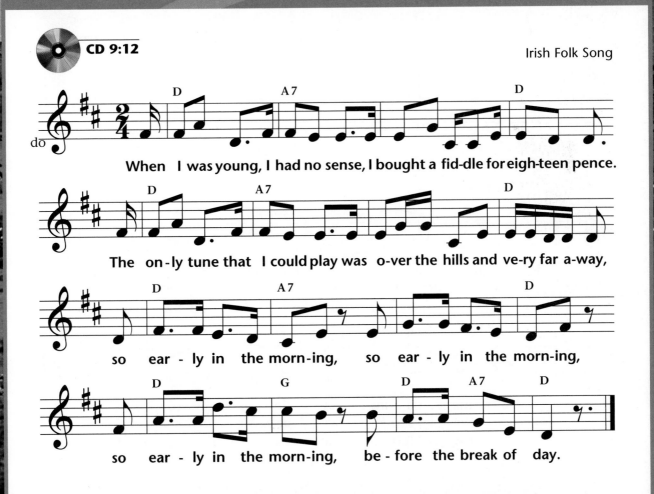

CD 9:12

Irish Folk Song

When I was young, I had no sense, I bought a fid-dle for eigh-teen pence.

The on-ly tune that I could play was o-ver the hills and ve-ry far a-way,

so ear - ly in the morn-ing, so ear - ly in the morn-ing,

so ear - ly in the morn-ing, be - fore the break of day.

Minor or Major?

"Katyusha" is a folk song from Russia. **Sing** "Katyusha" in Russian first and then in English.

CD 9:15

MAP
RUSSIA
CHINA
INDIA

Russian Folk Song
English by John F. Loud

Verse

Dm / A7

Russian: 1. Рас - цве - та - ли яб - ло - ни и гру - ши,
Pronunciation: ras tsvɛ ta li yab lɑ nyi i gɾu shim
English: 1. Bloom - ing were the ap - ple and the pear trees,

A7 / Dm

По - плы - ли ту - ма - ны над ре - кой.
pɔ pli li tu mɑ ni nɑd ɛɾ kɔɪ
Swirl - ing o'er the ri - ver was the mist.

Refrain

Dm Bb F Gm Dm

Вы - хо - ди - ла на бе - рег Ка - тю - ша,
vi hɑ di lɑ nɑ bɛ ɾɛɾ kɑ tyu sha
All at once on the bank ap - peared Ka - tyu - sha,

Gm Dm Gm A7 Dm

На вы - со - ки на бе - рег, на кру - той.
na vi sɔ ki nɑ bɛ ɾɛɾ nɑ kɾu tɔɪ
On the high, the steep ri - ver bank.

Sing the first four measures using pitch syllables.

la₁ ti₁ do la₁ do do ti₁ la₁ ti₁ mi₁

Look at the last two measures of the song.
Name the pitch syllables and then sing them.

Listen to the song. **Identify** the key signature.
Is "Katyusha" in F major or D minor?
How do you know?

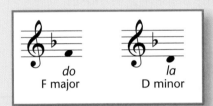

do
F major

la
D minor

Watch Your Tempo!

CONCEPT
TEMPO
SKILLS
LISTEN, SING
LINKS
SOCIAL STUDIES,
CULTURES

The speed of the beat in music is called **tempo**. The tempo can help to create a feeling or mood in a piece of music.

In "A Tragic Story," the composer used tempo to add to the drama of the words. Each verse has its own tempo.

Listen for the tempo changes in each verse of "A Tragic Story."

LISTENING CD 9:19

A Tragic Story by Benjamin Britten

"A Tragic Story" is taken from a children's song collection called *Friday Afternoons*, *Op. 7* by the British composer Benjamin Britten (1913–1976).

Here are some Italian words used to describe the tempo in music. Does "A Tragic Story" use all these tempo markings?

From the Royal Ballet production of Stravinsky's *Firebird*

andante	slow
moderato	medium
accelerando	gradually speed up
ritardando	gradually slow down
allegretto	a little fast
allegro	fast
presto	very fast

The Drama of Tempo

Tempo changes can take you by surprise and make music more interesting and expressive. The "Infernal Dance of King Kashchei" is an example of music with dramatic changes.

Listen for the tempo and dynamic changes in "Infernal Dance of King Kashchei." Follow the map below as you listen.

🎵 **LISTENING**   CD 9:20

Infernal Dance of King Kashchei from *The Firebird Suite* by Igor Stravinsky

Igor Stravinsky (1882–1971) wrote this music as part of his *Firebird* ballet. The story behind the "Infernal Dance of King Kashchei" has Prince Ivan battling the evil magician Kashchei and his monsters. When the Prince is close to defeat, the Firebird appears. The monsters are frantic when they see the Firebird. They finally collapse in exhaustion.

Adam Cooper and Fiona Chadwick in the Royal Ballet production of Igor Stravinsky's *Firebird*.

Listening Map for Infernal Dance

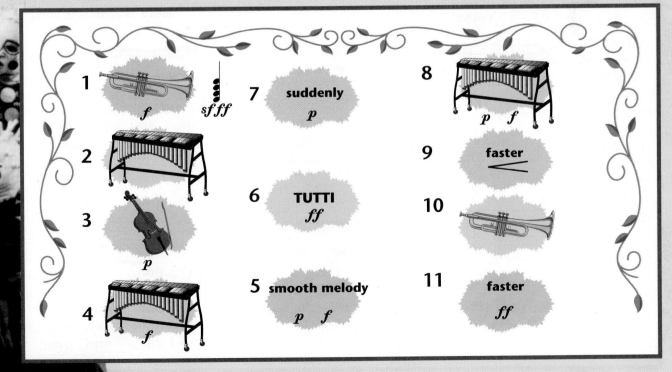

1   *f*

   s*fff*

7   **suddenly**   *p*

8   *p*   *f*

2

9   **faster**

3   *p*

6   **TUTTI**   *ff*

10

4   *f*

5   **smooth melody**   *p*   *f*

11   **faster**   *ff*

Tempo Changes for the Birds

This song tells a story about a different bird, "The Old Carrion Crow." **Listen** to the song. You will hear that the tempo of the verses is *allegro*, except for Verse 4.

Sing the song. Then choose the tempo for Verse 4 from this list.

accelerando	*ritardando*	*allegro*
presto	*moderato*	

MAP
GREENLAND
QUEBEC
NEW BRUNSWICK
NOVA SCOTIA

The Old Carrion Crow

CD 9:21

Nova Scotian Folk Song

Verse

1. Oh, the old car-rion crow was sit-ting on an oak,
2. Hur-ry now bring me my cross___ and my bow,
3. Oh, the tai - lor shot and missed___ his___ mark,
4. The___ old sow died and the bells___ did___ toll,
5. Oh,___ now the old sow's dead___ and___ gone,

Fol the rid - dle, all the rid - dle hey ding

(1.) doh,
(2.) doh,
(3.) doh, And he
(4.) doh, And the
(5.) doh, And the

THINK!

Read all the words to the song.
Why do you think the tempo is different in Verse 4?

Dm · C · Dm · Am

Watch - ing a tai - lor cut - ting out a coat.
That I may shoot yon car - ri - on___ crow.
shot the mil - ler's sow right through___ the___ heart.
lit-tle pigs___ cried and prayed___ for her soul.
lit-tle pigs___ play and wad - dle___ on,

mp *slightly held back* Dm · *a tempo*

Sing he, sing ho, the old car-rion crow, Fol the rid-dle, all the rid-dle

Refrain
Dm C Dm Am · G · F *slightly held back* C

hey ding doh. Ki - me - lea - ro kill my kea - ro, ki - me - lea - ro ki - mo,

a tempo Dm · C · Dm · Am Dm · C Dm

To me bump, bump, bump, jump Pol-ly wol-ly lee, Lin-ko kil-ly cum ki - mo.

CONCEPT
RHYTHM
SKILLS
SING, IDENTIFY, READ, CREATE
LINKS
CULTURES, SOCIAL STUDIES

Birthday Rhythms!

"Las mañanitas" (The Morning Song) is a popular birthday song from Mexico. Children in Mexico hit a *piñata* while wearing a blindfold at birthday parties. A *piñata* is a decorated object filled with candy and toys.

Sing the song. **Identify** the ♩.♪ in the song.

MAP
UNITED STATES
MEXICO   BELIZE
GUATEMALA

Las mañanitas
The Morning Song

CD 9:24

Mexican Folk Song
English Version by MMH

Spanish: És - tas son las ma - ña - ni - tas
Pronunciation: es tas son las ma nya ni tas
English: Now we sing las ma - ña - ni - tas,

que can - ta - ba el Rey Da - vid,
ke kan ta βa el ɾei ða βið
as King Da - vid long a - go

a las mu - cha - chas bo - ni - tas
a las mu cha chaz βo ni tas
sang a song to greet the morn - ing,

se las can - ta - mos a - sí:
se las kan ta mos a si
to greet the sun - light's first glow.

piñatas

THINK!

Read the song using pitch syllables.
Is this song in a major or minor key? How can you tell?

C   F

Des - pier - ta, mi bien, des - pier - ta,
des   pyeɾ   ta   mi   βyen   des   pyeɾ   ta
A - wak - en, dear one, a - wak - en

C   F

mi - ra que ya_a - ma - ne - ció,
mi   ɾa   ke   ya   ma   ne   syo
and wel - come the ros - y dawn.

B♭   F

Ya los pa - ja - ri - tos can - tan,
ya   los   pa   xa   ɾi   tos   kan   tan
Now the birds are sweet - ly sing - ing,

F   B♭   C7   F

la lu - na ya se me - tió.
la   lu   na   ya   se   me   tyo
the sil - ver moon - light has gone.

Play and Create Rhythms

Read these rhythms first using body percussion. Then play them with percussion instruments.

Perform these rhythms as an accompaniment to "Las mañanitas."

Create Rhythm!

Create your own rhythm composition to fill eight measures in ¾ meter.

Use ♩. ♪, ♩, ♫, and 𝄽 for your composition. Use ♩ 𝄾 𝄾 in the last measure of your composition. **Play** your rhythm on percussion instruments.

Listen to "Las mañanitas." How is this recording different from the song?

LISTENING CD 9:28

Las mañanitas Mexican song

This recording features "Las mañanitas" played by the mariachi group Mariachi Vargas de Tecalitlán.

guitarra del golpe

Meet the Musicians

Mariachi Vargas de Tecalitlán is named for its founder, Gaspar Vargas. Founded in 1898, it has been one of the most popular mariachi groups in Mexico. The group started with only three members playing a violin, harp, and *guitarra del golpe* (a small five-string guitar). Over the years they have added more players and instruments.

Spotlight Your Success!

REVIEW

1 What is the Italian word for tempo that means to gradually speed up?

   a. *moderato*   **b.** *allegro*   **c.** *presto*   **d.** *accelerando*

2 What is the name of the scale for the eight pitches between *la₁* and *la*?

   a. minor scale   **b.** pentatonic scale   **c.** major scale

3 What are the pitch syllables for this melody?

   a. *so fa | mi fa | so so re re | so fa so ||*

   b. *doˡ ti | doˡ ti | la la fa fa | mi re mi ||*

   c. *doˡ ti | la ti | doˡ doˡ so so | doˡ ti doˡ ||*

READ AND LISTEN

1 **Read** these rhythms. Then listen.
Which rhythm do you hear?

   a. ³⁄₄ 𝅘𝅥𝅭 𝅘𝅥𝅮𝅘𝅥𝅮 𝅘𝅥 | 𝅘𝅥𝅮𝅘𝅥𝅮 𝅘𝅥 𝄽 ||

   b. ³⁄₄ 𝅘𝅥 𝅘𝅥𝅮𝅘𝅥𝅮 𝅘𝅥𝅮𝅘𝅥𝅮 | 𝅘𝅥𝅭 𝅘𝅥𝅮𝅘𝅥 ||

   c. ³⁄₄ 𝅘𝅥𝅭 𝅘𝅥𝅮𝅘𝅥𝅮 | 𝅘𝅥𝅮𝅘𝅥𝅮 𝅘𝅥𝅮𝅘𝅥𝅮 𝅘𝅥 ||

   d. ³⁄₄ 𝅘𝅥𝅮𝅘𝅥𝅮 𝅘𝅥𝅮𝅘𝅥𝅮 𝅘𝅥𝅮𝅘𝅥𝅮 | 𝅘𝅥𝅭 𝅘𝅥𝅮𝅘𝅥 ||

Read these patterns using pitch syllables. Then listen. Which pattern do you hear?

THINK!

1. How would you change a song in duple meter to triple meter?

2. If you were to change a song in a major key to a song in a minor key, how would the sound be different?

3. If you were asked to compose a happy song, what tempo would you use? Why?

4. **Write** about two cultures you learned about in this unit. Compare language, rhythm, and instruments. Which music do you prefer? Why?

CREATE AND PERFORM

1. Choose ♩, ♩., ♪, ♩, ♫, and 𝄾 to fill eight measures in ¾ meter.

2. **Create** a melody by choosing pitches for your rhythm.

3. Use pitches from the major scale in the key of C or D. If you choose C, end your melody on C. If you choose D, end your melody on D.

4. **Sing** your melody using pitch syllables twice, once at a slower tempo, and once at a faster tempo.

Meet the Musician
ON NATIONAL RADIO!

Name: David Ross
Age: 15
Instrument: Flute
Hometown: North Mankato, Minnesota

Fifteen-year-old David Ross started playing piano at the age of seven, but it never felt quite right. He tried violin and clarinet, but they didn't seem to suit him either. Then one day he tried his sister's flute. He was surprised to find that playing it came very naturally to him. "I was immediately able to get a good sound," says David. "I figured I had a good start, so I kept on going."

Not only is David a flutist, he is also a weightlifter. "I first started lifting weights in ninth grade as part of gym class, and I really enjoyed it. I like pushing myself to the limit," he explains. These days, David can bench-press a whopping 215 pounds!

David enjoys all sorts of sports, but playing the flute is what he loves to do most of all. Next year he will attend a high school for the arts. He is looking forward to devoting more of his time to studying music.

LISTENING CD 10:1–2

Sonata for Flute and Piano, Third Movement
by Francis Poulenc

Listen to David's performance and interview on the national radio program **From the Top.**

RECORDED INTERVIEW

Spotlight on the Trombone

Christopher Cerf learned early on how joyful music should be. When he was six years old, his uncle's friend taught him a little about notes and chords and how they worked together in songs. Mr. Cerf was hooked.

He was even more excited when he heard rock and roll artists like Fats Domino. It wasn't enough just to listen to the music, though. Mr. Cerf had to play it himself. By experimenting at the piano and using what he'd learned in lessons, Mr. Cerf began recognizing chord changes and musical patterns. He could play by ear and imitate many different musical styles. Soon he began writing his own songs.

Mr. Cerf's talent for writing scripts and his knowledge of children's media led him to *Sesame Street* at its beginning. Once there, he was asked to write music for the new show. It had to be fun and teach children, too. Mr. Cerf has been writing and singing for *Sesame Street* for 35 years now and is also Executive Producer, Music Producer, and Co-Creator of *Between the Lions*.

Mr. Cerf shares some advice with teachers and students. "Music is a joyful thing. Remember that while studying the hard parts."

Did You Know?

A trombonist plays different pitches by changing the length of the instrument's tubing. To change the length, the player slides a piece of the tubing in and out.

There are seven slide positions on a trombone.

A trombone's tubing is twice as long as a trumpet's.

LISTENING   CD 10:3–4

The Big Turtle—Fanfare from *The South China Sea*
by Gyorgy Ligeti

Vivo from Pulcinella Suite
by Igor Stravinsky

Brass instruments were originally used for hunting calls and fanfares to announce important events. **Listen** to a solo trombone fanfare.

UNIT 6

A Time to Dream, A Time to Sing

Dreams are a special force in people's lives. They give people hope for a better tomorrow. Dreams give people a sense of purpose. In Unit 6 you will sing, play, dance, and create music that encourages people to dream for a better future. What are some of your dreams?

Coming Attractions

Sing exciting chords in harmony.

Create your own melody in minor.

Perform a Middle Eastern circle dance.

This song is about how one person can make a difference for a lot of people. The words talk about people who had dreams for a better future and worked to make those dreams come true.

Sing "What Can One Little Person Do?" What can you do to make a difference in other people's lives?

Rosa Parks ▲

◄ Harriet Tubman

What Can One Little Person Do?

 CD 10:5

Words and Music by Sally Rogers

Refrain

F

F7

What can one lit-tle per-son do?____ What can

B♭

F

one lit-tle me or you____ do? What can one lit-tle per-son do____

Dm

G7

C7

Repeat last time only

____ to help this world go 'round?_ One can

F

F7

B♭

help an-oth-er one____ and to-geth - er we can get the job

F

G7

C7

done. What can one lit-tle per-son do____ to help this

Martin Luther King, Jr. ▶

world?

Learn About Fusion Music

Music that blends musical traditions of more than one culture is known as **fusion music**. This includes traditional songs performed in different styles. Fusion music can also be new compositions created by blending sounds, languages, and instruments of different cultures together.

Listen to these recordings. Think about how they are alike and how they are different. Use the terms below to describe how they are alike and different.

tempo	how fast or slow the music is
dynamics	how loud or soft the dynamics are
articulation	how the notes are played, such as short and crisp—**staccato**, or smooth and connected—**legato**

LISTENING CD 10:11

Milan (Meeting of the Two Rivers) by Karsh Kale

This recording features folk and chamber music from India blended together with popular music from the United States and with unusual sounds.

LISTENING CD 10:12

Porushka-Paranya Russian folk song

This recording features a folk song from Russia blended with American bluegrass, as performed by the group Bering Strait. **Name** some of the instruments you recognize from the jug band.

Listen for the different musical styles in each piece below. Can you tell what instruments are being used? **Describe** the tone colors you hear.

LISTENING CD 10:13

Refavela by G. Gil
Performed by Angelique Kidjo

"Refavela" features rhythms and words from Benin in West Africa blended with Brazilian percussion. The message of this song is to take action and help people. What are ways you can help the other students in your school?

Meet the Musician

Angelique Kidjo (b. 1960) started performing at age 6 with her mother's theater troupe. Her music blends the styles of her West African, Brazilian, and English heritage. She toured Brazil with Ali Farka Toure. She views music as a common language shared by all people. Her songs are made up of conversations between instruments, percussion, and voices.

LISTENING CD 10:14

New Africa by Youssou N'Dour and Habib Faye

This recording features Youssou N'Dour, a singer from Senegal in West Africa. "New Africa" features traditional *mbalax* rhythms and words from Senegal blended with western-style instruments. What instruments do you recognize?

LOG
ON
Log on to **music.mmhschool.com** to learn more about fusion music.

CONCEPT
FORM
SKILLS
SING, LISTEN, DESCRIBE
LINKS
CULTURES, SOCIAL STUDIES

"**S**arasponda" came to the United States from the Netherlands. The nonsense words are used to imitate the sound of a spinning wheel. **Listen** for the two sections of the song. How are these sections different? **Sing** "Sarasponda."

MAP
UNITED KINGDOM
THE NETHERLANDS
GERMANY
BELGIUM
FRANCE

Sarasponda

CD 10:15

Dutch Spinning Song

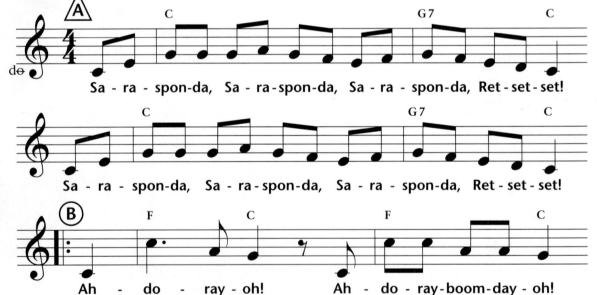

A
C   G7   C

Sa - ra - spon-da, Sa - ra-spon-da, Sa - ra - spon-da, Ret - set - set!

C   G7   C

Sa - ra - spon-da, Sa - ra - spon-da, Sa - ra - spon-da, Ret - set - set!

B
F   C   F   C

Ah - do - ray - oh!   Ah - do - ray-boom-day - oh!

G7   C   G7   C

Ah - do - ray-boom-day, Ret - set - set!   Ah - say - pa - say - oh!

Listening for Form

Listen to "Spinning Wheel" as you follow the listening map below.

 LISTENING CD 10:18

Spinning Wheel by David Clayton-Thomas

"Spinning Wheel" was a big hit in the late 1960s for the group Blood, Sweat & Tears. The group combined elements of jazz and rock and roll in their music.

Describe the ways in which Blood, Sweat & Tears made the sections different.

Listening Map for Spinning Wheel

Turn Back in Time

This song might have been sung by children in the Netherlands at a time when their mothers used spinning wheels in the early 1800s.

LISTENING CD 10:19

Twee emmertjes traditional spinning song

This singing game is about two girls carrying water. The words also speak of their traditional wooden shoes.

Listen to "Twee emmertjes."

Create different movements for each section of the song.

A pile of handmade wooden clogs in a shoemaker's shop in Vollendam, the Netherlands

A man picking tulips ▶ in the Netherlands

Wooden shoes from the Netherlands ▼

Move to show the form of "Twee emmertjes" as you listen again. Follow the translation below.

Ⓐ *Twee emmertjes water halen,*
Twee emmertjes pompen.
De meisjes op de klompen,
de jongens op de houten been,
Rij maar door mijn straatje heen!

Ⓑ *Van je ras, ras, ras,*
rijdt de koning door de plas.
Van je voort, voort, voort,
rijdt de koning door de poort.
Van je erk, erk, erk,
rijdt de koning door de kerk.
Van je één - twee - drie!

Ⓐ Getting two small buckets of water
Pumping two small buckets
Girls on the wooden shoes
Girls on the wooden leg
Feel free to drive through my path!

Ⓑ And hush, hush, hush,
the king drives through the puddle
And go on, go on, go on,
the king drives through the gate
And urch, urch, urch,
the king drives through the church
And one-two-three!

que no po - dí - a na - ve - gar.
ke no po ði a na βe ɡaɾ
a - las, it could not go to sea!

Pa - sa - ron u - na, dos, tres, cau - tro, cin - co,
pɑ sɑ ɾon u nɑ ðos tɾes kwɑ tɾo sing ko
Well it was one, two, three four, five, six, sev - en,

seis, sie - te se - ma - nas.____ Pa - sa - ron
seis sye te se mɑ nɑs pɑ sɑ ɾon
Sev - en weeks were pass - ing.____ Well it was

u - na, dos, tres, cua - tro, cin - co, seis, sie - te se - ma - nas._
u nɑ ðos tɾes kwɑ tɾo sing ko seis sye te se mɑ nɑs
one, two, three, four, five, six, sev - en, Sev - en weeks were pass - ing._

__ Pa - sa - ron u - na, dos, tres, cua - tro, cin - co,
pɑ sɑ ɾon u nɑ ðos tɾes kwɑ tɾo sing ko
__ Well it was one, two, three, four, five, six, sev - en,

seis, sie - te se - ma - nas. Y los ví - ve - res,
seis sye te se mɑ nɑs i los βi βe ɾes
Sev - en weeks were pass - ing, and our pro - vi - sions,

y los ví - ve - res, em - pe - za - ron a es - ca - se - ar.
i los βi βe ɾes em pe sɑ ɾon a es kɑ se ɑɾ
and our pro - vi - sions, soon they dwin - dled, and then were_ gone.

Stretch That Rhythm!

When you change a rhythm by making it twice as long, you augment it. This is called **augmentation**. When you augment a sound that is one beat long, it becomes a sound that is two beats long. If you were to augment a ♩ in 4/4, it would become a ♪

Compare the patterns below. **Identify** the connection between the two patterns.

Here is another example of augmentation.

How would you augment this rhythm?

THINK! Why do you think a composer would choose to use augmentation?

Art Gallery

Nevoa (Mist)
This oil painting was created by Bob Nugent (b. 1948). It shows the mist above the Amazon River in Brazil.

"Mighty River" is a fun speech piece that uses rhythms you know.
Read the speech piece.

MIGHTY RIVER

CD 11:5

Poem by Will Brecht
Adapted by MMH

Deep in the land of the jun - gle green,

Where the li - on roars and the par - rots scream,

Runs a might - y ri - ver from a ti - ny stream,

Lis - ten to it rush in - to the sea.

Now perform "Mighty River" in augmentation.
Make each rhythm, or each word, twice as long.
Keep the same beat as you perform the speech
piece in augmentation.

Perform "Mighty River" in two groups.
One group can perform the piece as written
while the other group performs the piece
in augmentation.

Unit 6 A Time to Dream, A Time to Sing   217

Voices Together in Harmony

CONCEPT
HARMONY
SKILLS
SING, PLAY, COMPARE
LINKS
SOCIAL STUDIES, CULTURES

Singing two or more melodic lines together is one way to make harmony. This is called **polyphony**. Rounds, canons, descants, and countermelodies are types of polyphony. When harmony parts have the same words and rhythm as the melody, it is called **homophony**. **Sing** homophonic voice parts in the refrain of "Bamboo."

BAMBOO

CD 11:8

Words and Music by Dave Van Ronk

1. You take a stick of bam-boo, You take a stick of bam-boo, You
(2.) trav-el on the riv - er, You trav-el on the riv - er, You
(3.) home's a-cross the riv - er, My home's a-cross the riv - er, My

take a stick of bam-boo, You throw it in the wa-ter,
trav-el on the riv - er, You trav-el on the wa-ter, Oh___
home's a-cross the riv - er, My home's a-cross the wa-ter,

Oh___ Han - nah!_____

You take a stick of bam-boo, You
You trav - el on the riv - er, You
My home's a - cross the riv - er, My

take a stick of bam-boo, You take a stick of bam-boo, You
trav - el on the riv - er, You trav - el on the riv - er, You
home's a - cross the riv - er, My home's a - cross the riv - er, My

Play these parts on mallet instruments while the class sings the song.

throw it in the wa-ter,
trav - el on the wa-ter,
home's a-cross the wa-ter,
Oh___ Oh___ Han-nah!___

Refrain

Riv - er,___ She come down.___

Riv - er,___ She come down.___ 2. You 3. My

down.___ You take a stick of bam-boo, You take a stick of bam-boo, You

take a stick of bam-boo, You throw it in the wa-ter.___

Unit 6 A Time to Dream, A Time to Sing

219

Building Chords with Voices

In "Sing Alleluia, Allelu," harmony is created by three groups singing together.

One group sings this part:

Al - le, al - le - lu - ia

A second group adds this:

Al - le, al - le - lu - ia

A third group sings:

Al - le, al - le - lu - ia

Identify all of these parts in the refrain of "Sing Alleluia, Allelu."

THINK! **Compare** the types of harmony used in "Bamboo" and "Sing Alleluia, Allelu." Give reasons why you like one type better than the other.

Sing Alleluia, Allelu

CD 11:11

Words and Music by Mary Goetze

Part I **Refrain**

do

Al - le, al - le - lu - ia, Sing al - le - lu - ia, al - le - lu.

Part II

do

Al - le, al - le - lu - a, Sing al - le - lu - ia, al - le - lu.

Part III

do

Al - le - lu - ia, al - le - lu - ia, Sing al - le - lu - ia, al - le - lu.

Decorating with Sound

CONCEPT
MELODY
SKILLS
SING, LISTEN
LINKS
VISUAL ART,
CULTURES

Many cultures take pleasure in decorating everyday items. Furniture, tools, musical instruments, and even plates are decorated. Designs are carved, sewn, etched, or painted onto objects to make them beautiful and special.

"Hala lala layya" is a folk song from Lebanon in the Middle East. **Sing** the song.

Art Gallery

Turkish table
This table is made from wood inlaid with ebony and ivory. It dates from the 1560s Ottoman Empire in Turkey.

Hala lala layya

CD 11:16

MAP
MEDITERRANEAN SEA
LEBANON
SYRIA
JORDAN
ISRAEL
EGYPT

Lebanese Folk Song
English lyrics by John Higgins

do

Pronunciation: ha la la la leι ya ha la la la leι ya

aι ni ya mu leι ya ta bιl ha wa

English: You are tru - ly_____ dear_ to__me. To me our friend - ship_

Melodies, like visual objects, can also be decorated. Extra pitches, or groups of pitches, added to melodies are called **ornaments**. In some musical styles, ornaments are added to a melody at will by the performer.

Look for the ornaments in "Hala lala layya." The ornaments add motion by filling in skips and moving by steps around pitches. **Identify** the ornaments in the song.

LOG ON

See **music.mmhschool.com** to research Middle Eastern music.

_____ ya hɪ lu   a max lɛk ɪsh wa   ya

_____ al-ways will_ be some-thing that I trea - sure.

2   *End (Fine)*   *Sing 1st time only*

læ' sʊ daī bu   ɛl wə lɪf

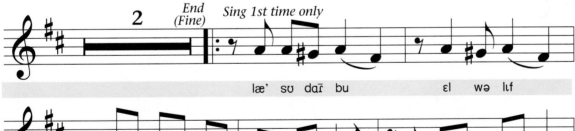

wəs æl   a   la   da   ɾu

To me our friend - ship_

Go back to the beginning and sing to the End.
(D.C. al Fine)

_____ al-ways will_ be some-thing that I trea - sure.

Ornamentation—Dutch Style!

Ornamentation has been used for hundreds of years in music from many cultures. Jacob Van Eyck composed "Al Hebben de Princen haren" in the early seventeenth century. The piece begins with a simple melody. Below is the first phrase of the melody.

The melody is repeated two times. Each time it is decorated with more ornaments, as was commonly done in those days.

The Rosenborg Castle (1615) in Copenhagen, Denmark was designed by Dutch Renaissance architects Bertel Lange and Hans van Steenwinckel the Younger.

Listen for ornamentation in "Al Hebben de Princen haren."

LISTENING CD 11:20

Al Hebben de Princen haren
by Jacob Van Eyck

This piece was written in the early 1600s. It is taken from a large collection of pieces for recorder. These pieces are playable on many instruments, such as the renaissance transverse flute played in this recording by Stefano Bet.

A woman playing a Flemish transverse flute, ▶
designed to be played from the left or right.

Meet the Musician

Jacob Van Eyck (c. 1589–1657) was born a nobleman in The Netherlands. He was blind from birth. Van Eyck was a composer, a scientist, and a designer of church bells. He was also the greatest recorder player of his time. He composed and collected hundreds of pieces for the recorder.

◀ **This detail of the Rosenborg Castle shows the ornamentation of the façade.**

A Matter of Style

CONCEPT
STYLE
SKILLS
SING, PLAY, COMPARE
LINKS
MOVEMENT, CULTURES

"**W**alk in the Parlor" is a folk song from North Carolina. **Sing** the song.

CD 11:21

North Carolina Folk Song

Walk in the Parlor

The creek's all mud-dy, the pond's all dry, 'Twas-n't for the tad-poles we'd all die.

Refrain

Walk in, walk in, walk in, I say,

Walk in the par-lor and hear the ban-jo play. Walk in the par-lor and

hear the ban-jo ring. Watch ol' Wil-lie fin-ger while he picks up-on a string.

Play this accompaniment with "Walk in the Parlor."

Introducing ... Salsa!

A music style that started in the 1970s in New York City was called **salsa**. Salsa music was originally based on accented rhythms from Cuban music, but performed by many others.

Listen for the unique rhythms of the salsa music style in "Guantanamera."

LISTENING CD 11:24

Guantanamera
by José Fernandez Dias

"Guantanamera" is a song that was sung by the Afro-Cuban singer Celia Cruz. The song is from Cuba.

What instruments accompany this song?

Pat with the beat as you listen.

Meet the Musician

Celia Cruz (1925–2003) was known as the Queen of Salsa. "Salsa means sauce," she said. "With sauce, the food tastes better. Salsa is the flavor of my music." Cruz was born in Havana, Cuba. She was already a star when she came to live in the United States in 1960. She worked with Dionne Warwick, Patti LaBelle, Gloria Estefan, and many other artists. "When people hear me sing, I want them to be happy, happy, happy," she said. "My message is always *felicidad*—happiness."

Move in Style!

Listen to "Walk in the Parlor" played in three different styles. Think about how each style is different. **Create** a movement to perform for each style you hear. **Perform** your movement as you listen to each recording.

LISTENING

Waltz in the Parlor

CD 11:27

This version is in the style of the **waltz**. The waltz is a type of dance in $\frac{3}{4}$ meter. What instruments do you hear? How is the tempo changed?

LISTENING

Parade in the Parlor

CD 11:25

This version is modeled after the kind of music you would hear in New Orleans during the festival called Mardi Gras. Compare the instruments and dynamics of this version with the original.

LISTENING

Salsa in the Parlor

CD 11:26

The rhythm of salsa style makes you want to dance! How is this different from the original "Walk in the Parlor"?

CONCEPT
TONALITY
SKILLS
SING, LISTEN, COMPOSE
LINKS
CULTURES, SOCIAL STUDIES

"A la nanita nana" is a lullaby from Spain. This song is about a mother singing to her baby.

Sing "A la nanita nana."

MAP
FRANCE
PORTUGAL
SPAIN
MOROCCO   ALGERIA

A la nanita nana

CD 11:28

A Little Lullaby

Spanish Carol
English Words by Linda Worsley

A Refrain

Spanish: A la na-ni-ta na-na, na-ni-ta na-na, na-ni-ta e-a.
Pronunciation: a la na ni ta na na na ni ta na na na ni ta e a
English: A la na-ni-ta na-na, na-ni-ta na-na, na-ni-ta e-a.

End (Fine)

Mi ni-ño tie-ne sue - ño ben-di-to, se - a ben-di-to se - a.
mi ni nyo tye ne swe nyo ßen di to se a ßen di to se a
My sleep-y lit-tle ba-by, dream in bless-ed slum-ber, in bless-ed slum-ber.

B Verse

Tor-to - li-ta que can-tas en-tre la fron-da,
tor to li ta ke kan tas en tre la fron da
Lit-tle doves in the tree-top, Joy-ful-ly sing-ing,

fuen-te ci-lla que co-rres ru - mo-ro-sa.
fwen te ði ya ke ko ɾes ɾu mo ɾo sa
Lit-tle foun-tain___ leap-ing, splash-ing and mur-mur-ing.

Identify the change from major to minor in "A la nanita nana." What is the form of the song? Which section is in minor ? Which section is in major ?

The refrain of "A la nanita nana" is made of pitches from the D minor scale.

The sound is minor . What is the tonal center of the scale?

The verse of the song is made up of pitches from the D major scale.

The sound is major . What is the tonal center of the scale?

Gm   D   A7   D

Ca - lad que es-tá dor - mi - do   el dul - ce in - fan - te
ka laδ kes ta δοɾ mi δο el dul δe in fan te
Hush, now, for he is sleep-ing, sweet lit - tle___ ba - by,

Go back to the beginning and sing to the End.

Gm   D   A7   D *(Da Capo al Fine)*

A la na - ni - ta na - na, na - ni - ta e - a.
a la na ni ta na na na ni ta e a
A la na - ni - ta na - na, na - ni - ta e - a.

Minor Changes

Listen for major and minor in "East St. Louis Toodle-Oo" as you follow the listening map below.

 **LISTENING** CD 12:1

East St. Louis Toodle-Oo
by Duke Ellington

The instruments used in this recording include trumpet, trombone, clarinet, alto saxophone, piano, banjo, bass, and drum set. Each section features a solo instrument.

Listening Map for East St. Louis Toodle-Oo

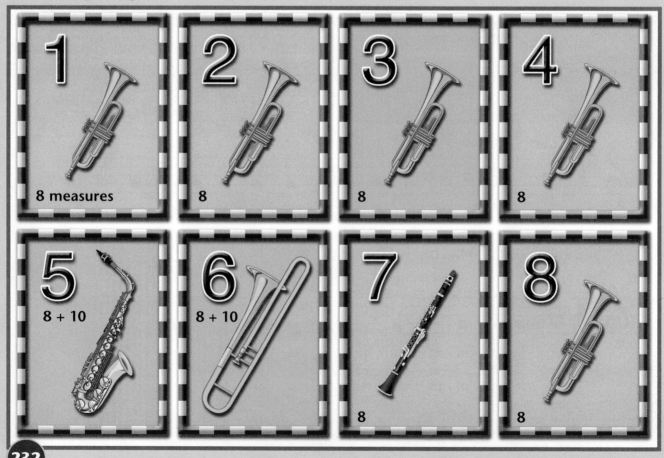

1 — 8 measures
2 — 8
3 — 8
4 — 8
5 — 8 + 10
6 — 8 + 10
7 — 8
8 — 8

Create a Verse in Minor

"Johnson Boys" is a fiddle tune from the Appalachian Mountains region of the United States. The melody is in F pentatonic, which has a major sound. **Sing** the song.

mountain dulcimer ▶

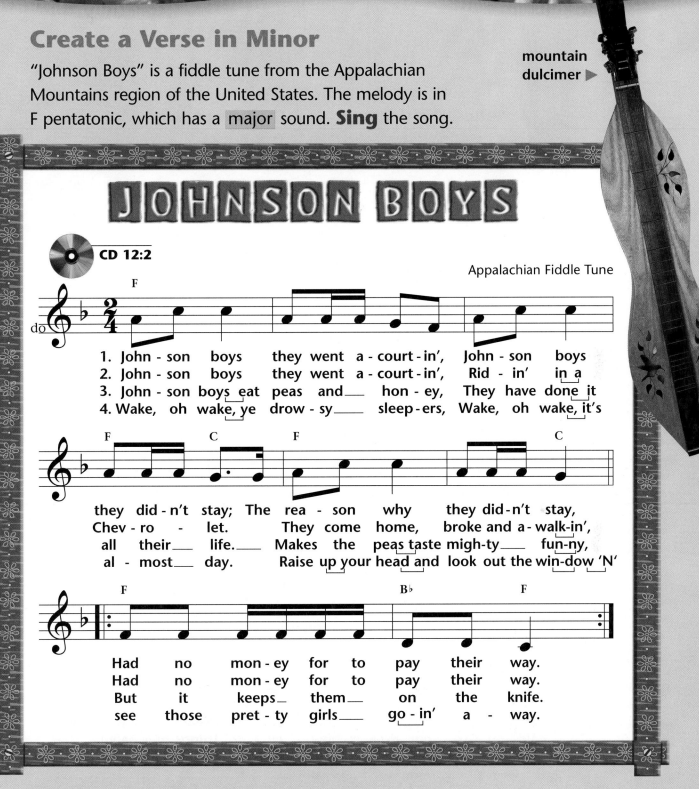

JOHNSON BOYS

CD 12:2

Appalachian Fiddle Tune

1. John-son boys they went a-court-in', John-son boys
2. John-son boys they went a-court-in', Rid-in' in a
3. John-son boys eat peas and hon-ey, They have done it
4. Wake, oh wake, ye drow-sy sleep-ers, Wake, oh wake, it's

they did-n't stay; The rea-son why they did-n't stay,
Chev-ro-let. They come home, broke and a-walk-in',
all their life. Makes the peas taste migh-ty fun-ny,
al-most day. Raise up your head and look out the win-dow 'N'

Had no mon-ey for to pay their way.
Had no mon-ey for to pay their way.
But it keeps them on the knife.
see those pret-ty girls go-in' a-way.

Create a new melody for the verse. **Use** these pitches from the pentatonic scale with *la* as the tonal center. Your new melody will have a minor sound.

la, do re mi

CONCEPT
FORM
SKILLS
SING, LISTEN, ANALYZE
LINKS
LANGUAGE ARTS, CULTURES, MOVEMENT

Dream a New Dream

This song is about following your dream no matter what happens. What are some of your dreams? **Sing** "Follow Your Dream." **Identify** the form.

Follow Your Dream

CD 12:5

Words and Music by Mary Donnelly
Arranged by George L.O. Strid

Ⓐ **Verse**

do

B♭   Dm7   Cm7

1. Ev - 'ry - bod - y needs a star to wish on__ when
2. It's the dream with - in your heart that keeps you go - ing,_ when

Cm7   B♭   F

things you want seem far, far a - way.____ But
noth - ing in the world seems_ right.____ But

B♭   F   Dm   Gm

you must al - ways strive to keep your dream a - live, 'cause
hold on to your dreams how - ev - er things may seem. That

Cm7   F7

what you long for, can be yours some - day. }
shin - ing star will guide you through the night. }

Listen to "Theme and Variations."

🔊 **LISTENING** CD 12:8

Theme and Variations (excerpt)
by Wolfgang Amadeus Mozart

This piece is from "Serenade in B♭ Major" for 13 wind instruments. It was written in the 1780s. Listen for the wind instruments you know in the recording.

Dream Dust
Gather out of star-dust
    Earth-dust,
    Cloud-dust,
    Storm-dust,
And splinters of hail,
One handful of dream-dust
    Not for sale.

—*Langston Hughes*

B **Refrain**

If you fol-low your dream,_ tho' the road seems lone-ly.
fol-low your dream,_ tho' you're tired of try-ing.

Fol-low your dream_ no mat-ter how far._____
Fol-low your dream,_ what-ev-er you do._____

Give it your best,_ you'll find suc-cess,_ if you
There'll come a time_ when you will find_ you can

1. just keep your eye_ on that star!_ If you

2. make all your dreams_ and your wish - es come true.

Making It Different

Sometimes music can be more interesting by keeping some things the same while other things change, or vary.

Vary the refrain of "Follow Your Dream." Keep the melody, or **theme**, of the refrain the same. Each time you sing it, change it in two or three of these ways to create a **variation**:

- Change the dynamics. Sing it louder, then softer. Change the dynamic level as you sing.

- Change the articulation. Sing it staccato (short and clipped), then legato (smooth and flowing).

- Change the accompaniment. Choose a percussion instrument. Add the instrument on the words *Follow your dream*.

Sing the song again. Repeat your variations as you sing. This time, add ornamentation to the melody of the refrain. Fill in skips and add steps as you sing the refrain for the last time.

THINK! How is the meaning of the words changed by the way you sing the refrain?

Very Moving!

Listen to "Debka Kurdit."

LISTENING CD 12:9

Debka Kurdit Yemeni Folk Dance

"Debka Kurdit" is a circle dance that is danced throughout the Middle East. The basic movement pattern presented in Part I is varied each time you repeat it. In the variations of the basic step, you step in and out in different ways.

Practice the steps below. **Dance** the "Debka Kurdit"!

① In

② Bend

③ Out

④ Bend

Part 1 *4 times*
in bend out bend

Part 2 *4 times*
in hop out hop

Part 3 *4 times*
bounce, bounce, bounce, step

Part 4 *4 times*
in hold out, out, out

Part 5 *4 times*
in bend out bend

Part 6 *4 times*
cross side cross side

Spotlight Your Success!

REVIEW

1 What kind of music blends musical traditions of more than one culture?

   a. salsa   **b.** calypso   **c.** fusion   **d.** folk

2 What do you do when you augment a rhythm?

   a. change a rhythm by making it twice as short

   b. change the meter signature

   c. change a rhythm by making it twice as long

3 Which set of pitch syllables matches this melody?

   a. *so fa | mi re | do re mi fa | so mi do ||*

   b. *do mi | so do' | ti la so fa | mi re do ||*

   c. *do so, | do re | mi fa so fa | mi re do ||*

READ AND LISTEN

1 **Read** these rhythms. Then listen. Which rhythm do you hear?

   a.

   b.

   c.

   d.

2 **Read** these patterns using pitch syllables. Then listen. Which pattern do you hear?

a.

b.

c.

THINK!

1 Describe what ornaments are and what they are used for.

2 What are some ways to vary a theme?

3 Tell in your own words the meaning of the lyrics of "What Can One Little Person Do?"

4 **Write** about the different styles of music you learned about in this unit. How would you describe the music using musical terms?

CREATE AND PERFORM

1 Choose ♩, ♫, ♩♫, ♫♩, and ♩ to fill four measures in ¾ meter.

2 **Create** a melody by choosing pitches for your rhythm.

3 Use pentatonic pitches in the key of F or G, where *la* is the tonal center.

4 If you choose F, end your melody on D. If you choose G, end your melody on E.

5 **Sing** your melody using pitch syllables. Use two or more dynamics as you sing.

Spotlight on
Music Reading

Spotlight on Music Reading

Spotlight on Music Reading

Unit **1** **Concepts: More Music Reading** 242
Basic Rhythms; *Do Re Mi; So;* Pentatonic Melodies

Unit **2** **Concepts: More Music Reading** 248
Low *So;* Low *La;* Sixteenth Notes; Tonal Center

Unit **3** **Concepts: More Music Reading** 256
$\frac{6}{8}$ $\frac{2}{}$ meter; Unequal Rhythms; *Fa*

Unit **4** **Concepts: More Music Reading** 264
Syncopation; High *Do;* Leap from *Do* to High *Do*

Unit **5** **Concepts: More Music Reading** 272
$\frac{3}{4}$ meter; *Ti;* The Major Scale; Chords

Unit **6** **Concepts: More Music Reading** 280
Major and Minor

Practice Basic Rhythms

Rhythms are created with combinations of notes and rests.

A quarter note ♩ = one sound to a beat.
Two eighth notes ♫ = two sounds to a beat.
A quarter rest 𝄽 = one beat of silence.
A half note ♩ = a sound lasting two beats.

Read and practice these rhythms:

Ludwig van Beethoven

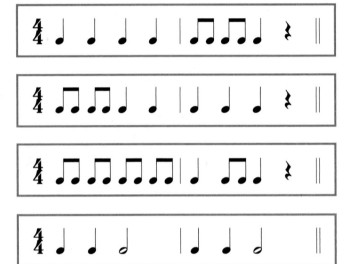

Read and play this ostinato.

LISTENING CD 12:11

Symphony No. 7 in A Major, Second Movement by Ludwig van Beethoven

This symphony uses the same rhythm pattern as the ostinato above.

Listen for the rhythm pattern in this selection.

Sing with *Do, Re, Mi*

do   re   mi

mi

re

do

Read and sing the repeated notes, steps, and skips in this song.

LONG-LEGGED SAILOR

CD 12:12

Game Chant

1.-5. Did you   ev-er, ev-er,   ev-er   in your   { long - leg-ged / short - leg-ged / knock - kneed_ / bow - leg-ged / cross - leg-ged }   life

Meet a   long-leg-ged*   sail-or   with a   long-leg-ged*   wife?

No, I   nev-er, nev-er,   nev-er   in my   { long - leg-ged / short - leg-ged / knock - kneed_ / bow - leg-ged / cross - leg-ged }   life

Met a   long-leg-ged*   sail-or   with a   long-leg-ged*   wife.

* Change word for verses 2.-5.

Music Reading   243

More *Do-Re-Mi* Melodies

Read and sing *do, re,* and *mi* in this Italian folk song.

do   re   mi

MAP
SWITZERLAND
FRANCE   ITALY
ALBANIA
GREECE

Farfallina
Butterfly

CD 12:16

Italian Folk Song
English Version by MMH

G   D7

Italian: Far-fal - li - na tut - ta bian - ca vo-la, vo-la, non si stan-ca.

Pronunciation: faɾ fal li na tut ta byang ka vo la vo la non si stang ka

English: Far-fal - li - na, with your white wings, fly a-way, do not sit still.___

G   D7   G

Vo - la li, vo - la la, po - si po - sa so-pra un fiore

vo la li vo la la po si po sa so pɾaun fyoɾe

Fly - ing here, fly - ing there, on a flow - er rest a while.

LISTENING   CD 12:15

Carillon from *L'Arlesienne, Suite No. 1*
by Georges Bizet

Bizet wrote "Carillon" for a play called *L'Arlesienne (The Girl from Arles).*

Read and play this melody as you listen to "Carillon."

mi do re mi do re mi do re mi

Improvise *do-re-mi* melodies in ¾ time as you listen again.

CONCEPT
MELODY

SKILLS
READ, SING

Sing with So

do re mi so   so

Read these songs with pitch syllables and hand signs.

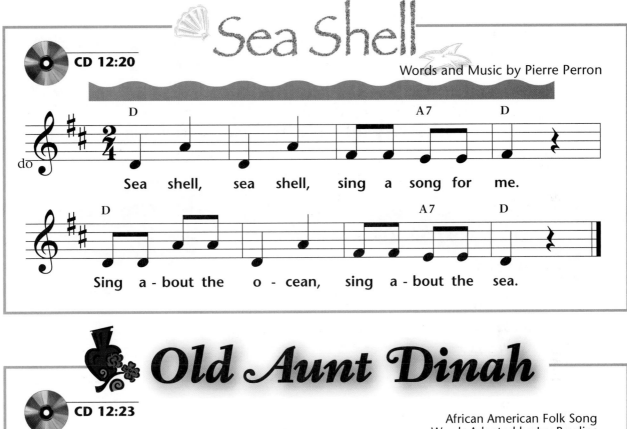

CD 12:20

Sea Shell

Words and Music by Pierre Perron

do

Sea shell, sea shell, sing a song for me.

Sing a - bout the o - cean, sing a - bout the sea.

CD 12:23

Old Aunt Dinah

African American Folk Song
Words Adapted by Ivy Rawlins

do

Old Aunt Di - nah, fare - well, fare - well, Old Aunt Di - nah,

fare thee well! Gone a - way to leave you, fare - well, fare - well,

Gone a - way to leave you, fare thee well!

Sing a Pentatonic Song

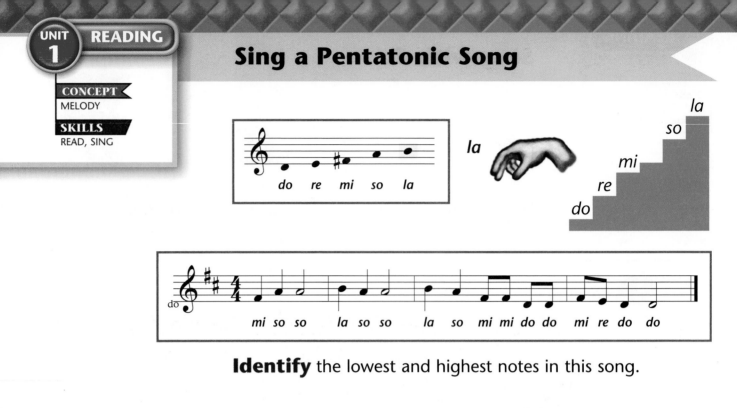

do   re   mi   so   la

la

mi so so   la so so   la so mi mi do do   mi re do do

Identify the lowest and highest notes in this song.

Page's Train

CD 12:26

North Carolina Folk Song

Pa - ge's train runs so fast,

Can't see noth-ing but the win - dow glass.

Trains at Night

I like the whistle of trains at night,
The fast trains thundering by so proud!
They rush and rumble across the world,
They ring wild bells and they toot so loud!
But I love better the slower trains.
They take their time through the world instead,
And whistle softly and stop to tuck
Each sleepy blinking town in bed! —*Frances M. Frost*

Sing and Create Pentatonic Melodies

Read this pentatonic song with hand signs.

Sing it with the words.

CD 12:29

American Folk Song

Green grav - el, green grav - el, the grass is so green.

The fair - est of maid - ens that ev - er was seen.

Create a pentatonic melody using *do, re, mi, so,* and *la.*
Play it as a B section for "Green Gravel."

CONCEPT
MELODY

SKILLS
READ, SING

Sing with Low *So* and Low *La*

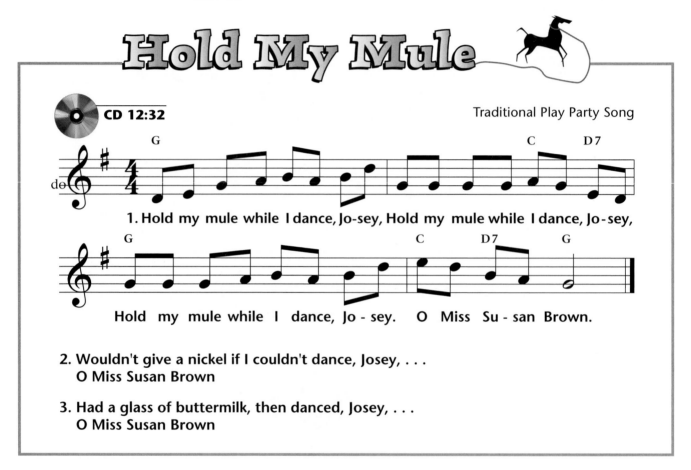

so₁ la₁ do re mi so la

Sing and play a game with this song that has low *so* and low *la*.

Hold My Mule

CD 12:32   Traditional Play Party Song

1. Hold my mule while I dance, Jo-sey, Hold my mule while I dance, Jo-sey,

Hold my mule while I dance, Jo-sey. O Miss Su-san Brown.

2. Wouldn't give a nickel if I couldn't dance, Josey, . . .
   O Miss Susan Brown

3. Had a glass of buttermilk, then danced, Josey, . . .
   O Miss Susan Brown

Sing this ostinato, first with pitch syllables then with the words.

Hold my mule, hold my mule,   hold my mule, hold my mule.

Read and clap the rhythm of the song as you sing it. What do you notice about the rhythms in the second and third verses?

Sixteenth Notes

Four equal sounds to a beat can be written as four sixteenth notes (♪♪♪♪).

♪♪♪♪ = ♫♫ = ♩

The Girl I Left Behind Me

CD 12:35

Square Dance Tune

1. First young gent a - cross the hall and
2. Oh the girl, the pret-ty lit-tle girl, and the

swing her by the right hand. Swing your part - ner by the left and
girl I left be - hind me, Ros - y cheeks, and cur - ly hair, the

prom - e - nade the girl be - hind you.
girl___ I___ left be - hind me.

Improvise a rhythm ostinato for this song.

Sing this part of the song with pitch syllables and letter names.

F F F F C D F F
do do do do so͵ la͵ do do

A *do* tonal center means the melody of a song is centered around *do*. The tonal center is often the last note of a song. What is the tonal center of this song?

Music Reading 249

Perform Sixteenth Notes

Three unequal sounds to a beat can be written with two sixteenth notes and one eighth note (♪ ♬ or ♬♪).

Remember, ♪ ♬ = ♩ and ♬♪ = ♩

Music that begins before the first beat of a complete measure begins on an upbeat. Find the upbeat.

Say and pat this game with sixteenth-note patterns.

MAP
UNITED STATES
MEXICO
BELIZE
GUATEMALA

Molinillo de café

Little Coffee Mill

CD 13:1

Latin American Children's Game
English Version by MMH

Spanish: **Mue - le el mo - li - ni - llo de ca - fé.**
Pronunciation: mwe lel mo li ni yo ðe ka fe
English: **Lit - tle cof - fee mill gives us a treat,**

Mue - le los gra - ni - tos pa - ra us - ted.
mwe le los gɾa ni tos pa ɾaus teð
Grind - ing lit - tle cof - fee beans to - day.

Gi - ra con la ma - no, gi - ra con el pie,
gi ɾa kon la ma no gi ɾa kon el pye
Turn it with your hands and turn it with your feet,

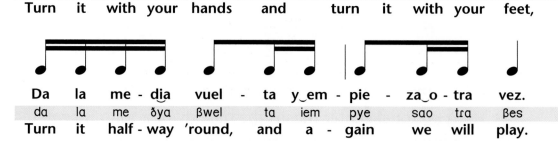

Da la me - dia vuel - ta y em - pie - za o - tra vez.
da la me ðya βwel ta iem pye sao tɾa βes
Turn it half - way 'round, and a - gain we will play.

UNIT
2 READING

CONCEPT
TONALITY
SKILLS
READ

A Different Tonal Center

Some songs have a pitch other than *do* or *la* as the tonal center. **Read** this pattern and identify the tonal center.

Ridin' of a Goat, Leadin' of a Sheep

CD 13:5

North Carolina Folk Song

Rid - in' of a goat and lead - in' of a sheep,

Rid - in' of a goat and lead - in' of a sheep,

Rid - in' of a goat and lead - in' of a sheep,

I won't be back 'til the mid - dle of the week.

Create with Sixteenth Notes

 **R**emember, an eighth rest ♪ = a silence for half a beat and ♫ = ♩

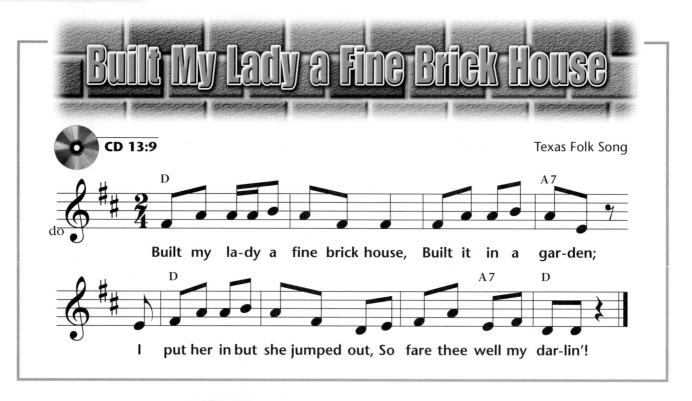

Built My Lady a Fine Brick House

CD 13:9

Texas Folk Song

Built my la-dy a fine brick house, Built it in a gar-den;

I put her in but she jumped out, So fare thee well my dar-lin'!

LISTENING CD 13:8

The Magic Flute (Overture)
by Wolfgang Amadeus Mozart

The Magic Flute is an opera that combines both serious and comical ideas and music. The overture reveals these two contrasting characteristics.

Read this rhythm pattern and listen for it in the Overture to *The Magic Flute.*

Sing Sixteenth Notes

Find the measure with ♩ ♫ and the measure with ♫♫

Swapping Song

CD 13:12 **Verse**

Appalachian Folk Song

G   C   G   D7

1. When I was a lit - tle boy I lived by my - self;___
2. Rats___ and the mice,___ they___ led me such a life, I
3. Roads___ were so long___ and the lanes were so nar-row, I
4. Wheel - bar - row broke_ and my wife got a fall;___
5. Swapped my wheel - bar-row and___ got me a horse;___

G   C   G   D7

All the bread and cheese I had, I put it on the shelf.___
had to go to Lon-don to___ get my-self a wife.___
had to bring her home_ in an old___ wheel - bar - row.
Down_ came the wheel - bar-row, wife_ and_ all.___
Then_ I___ rode_ from_ cross_ to___ cross.___

Refrain

G   C   Bm   Em

Wing wong wad-dle, to my jack straw strad-dle, To my

Am   D7   G   D7   G

John - nie fair fad - dle, to my long ways home.

6. Swapped my horse and got me a mare;
   Then I rode from fair to fair.

7. Swapped my mare and got me a mule;
   Then I rode like a doggone fool.

8. Swapped my mule and got me a goat;
   When I got on him, he wouldn't tote.

9. Swapped my goat and got me a sheep;
   Then I rode myself to sleep.

10. Swapped my sheep and got me a cow;
    And in that trade I just learned how.

Listen for Sixteenth Notes

LISTENING CD 13:15

"Galop" from *The Comedians* by Dmitri Kabalevsky

A galop is a type of fast, springy dance popular in nineteenth-century Europe. It is thought to have originated in Hungary. This music describes traveling comedians.

Look at the listening map. Find the A section rhythm, the Interlude rhythm, and the B section rhythm. Practice tapping each one at a quick tempo.

Listen to "Galop" and follow the listening map.

Listening Map for "Galop"

CONCEPT
TONALITY

SKILLS
READ, SING

Use What You Know

Clap the rhythm of the first line.
What is the tonal center?

MAP
MEDITERRANEAN SEA
LEBANON
SYRIA
JORDAN
ISRAEL
EGYPT

Zum gali gali

CD 13:16

Israeli Work Song

Ostinato

Em   Am   Em

Hebrew: זוּם גָ - לִי, גָ - לִי, גָ - לִי, זוּם גָ - לִי, גָ - לִי,
Pronunciation: zum ga li ga li ga li zum ga li ga li
English: Zum ga - li, ga - li, ga - li, Zum ga - li, ga - li.

Verse

Em   Am   Em

הֶ - חָ - לוּץ לְ - מַעַן עֲ - בוֹ - דָה,
hɛ xa lutz lɛ ma'an a vo da
Pi - o - neers work hard on the land,___

Em   Am   Em

עֲ - בוֹ - דָה לְ - מַעַן הֶ - חָ - לוּץ.
a vo da lɛ ma'an hɛ xa lutz
Men and wom - en work hand in hand.

Em   Am   Em

עֲ - בוֹ - דָה לְ - מַעַן הֶ - חָ - לוּץ,
a vo da lɛ ma'an hɛ xa lutz
As they la - bor all day___ long,___

Em   Am   Em

הֶ - חָ - לוּץ לְ - מַעַן עֲ - בוֹ - דָה.
hɛ xa lutz lɛ ma'an a vo la
They___ lift their voi - ces in song.

Music Reading 255

CONCEPT
METER

SKILLS
READ, PERFORM

A Game in 6/8 (2/•) METER

In 2/•. meter, a dotted quarter note ♩. = one beat.

At slower tempos, an eighth note ♪ = one beat. The meter is then shown as 6/8.

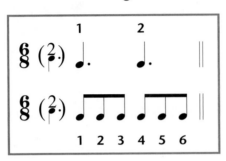

Read and pat the rhythms in the slower 6/8 meter and the faster 2/•. meter.

Perform the speech piece.

Hojas de té

CD 13:20   Tea Leaves

Mexican Children's Game
English Version by MMH

6/8

Spanish: Ho - jas   de   té,   ho - jas   de   té.
Pronunciation: o   xɑs   ðe   te   o   xɑs   ðe   te
English: Here   leaves   of   tea,   There   leaves   of   tea.

Ho - jas   y   ho - jas   y   na - da   de   té.
o   xɑs   i   o   xɑs   i   nɑ   ðɑ   ðe   te
Tea   leaves   and   tea   leaves,   but   no   cups   of   tea.

Perform the traditional Mexican hand patterns for this speech piece.

Sing Unequal Rhythms

Read and clap these rhythms.

Describe what is different about these rhythmic patterns.

Listen for unequal sounds to the beat as you learn to sing this song.

Goodbye, My Riley O

CD 13:24

African American Song
from the Georgia Sea Islands
Collected and Adapted by Lydia A. Parrish

1. Ri - ley, Ri - ley, where are you?
2. Ri - ley gone to Liv - er - pool.
3. Ri - ley gone to Lon - don Town.
4. Ri - ley gone to Mo - bile Bay.

O Ri - ley O man!

Ri - ley gone and I goin' too, Good - bye my Ri - ley O!

Music Reading 257

CONCEPT
RHYTHM

SKILLS
READ, SING

A Sea Chantey in $\frac{6}{8}$

A tie ⌣ is a curved line that connects two notes of the same pitch and means that the sound is held for the length of the two notes.

In $\frac{6}{8}$ meter,

A dotted half note 𝅗𝅥. sounds for the whole measure.

Clap these rhythm patterns in $\frac{6}{8}$ meter.

Find these patterns in the song then sing it.

Heave-Ho, Me Laddies

CD 13:27

Sea Chantey

Oh, if I were a sail - or out a sail - ing on the sea,___

I real - ly am quite cer - tain___ a cap - tain I would be.

Heave - ho, me lad - dies. Fast - en down the sails.___

This blust' - ry wind will take us___ a - sail - ing o'er the sea. sea.

Practice ⁶₈ Rhythms

Read and sing another ⁶₈ song with ties.

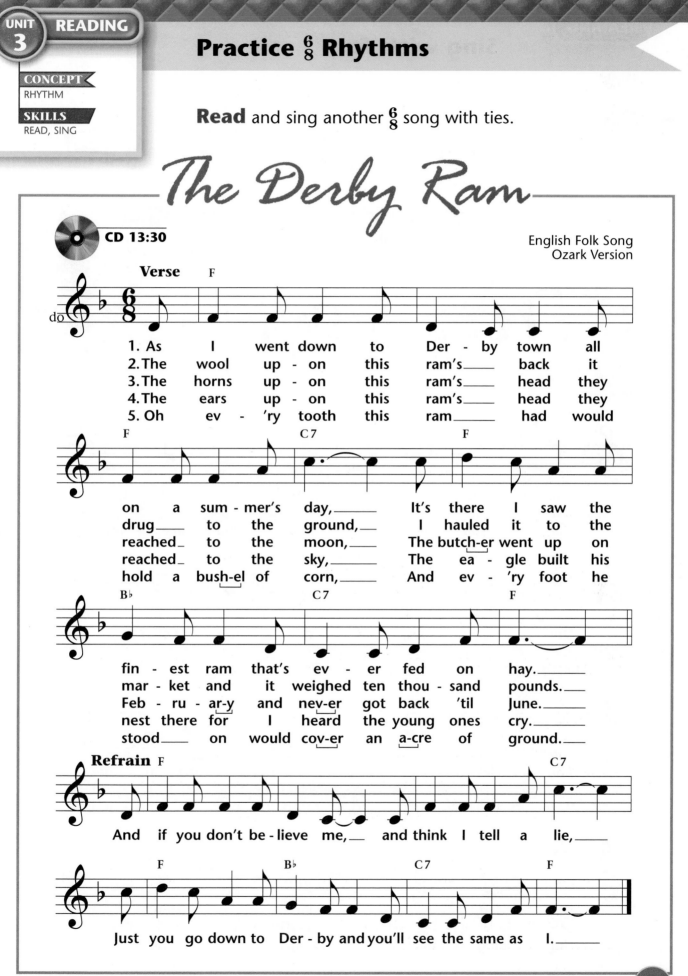

The Derby Ram

CD 13:30

English Folk Song
Ozark Version

Verse

1. As I went down to Der - by town all
2. The wool up - on this ram's____ back it
3. The horns up - on this ram's____ head they
4. The ears up - on this ram's____ head they
5. Oh ev - 'ry tooth this ram____ had would

on a sum - mer's day,____ It's there I saw the
drug____ to the ground,___ I hauled it to the
reached_ to the moon,____ The butch-er went up on
reached_ to the sky,____ The ea - gle built his
hold a bush-el of corn,____ And ev - 'ry foot he

fin - est ram that's ev - er fed on hay.____
mar - ket and it weighed ten thou - sand pounds.__
Feb - ru - ar-y and nev-er got back 'til June.____
nest there for I heard the young ones cry.____
stood____ on would cov-er an a-cre of ground.__

Refrain

And if you don't be - lieve me,__ and think I tell a lie,____

Just you go down to Der - by and you'll see the same as I.____

Sing with *Fa*

so, do re mi fa so la

fa

Sing the orange patterns in this song with pitch syllables.

MAP

SWITZERLAND
FRANCE
ITALY
SPAIN

Frère Jacques

Are You Sleeping?

CD 14:1

French Folk Song
Traditional English Words

French: **Frè** - **re** **Jac** - **ques,** **Frè** - **re** **Jac** - **ques,**
Pronunciation: frɛ rə ʒa kə frɛ rə ʒa kə
English: **Are** **you** **sleep** - **ing,** **are** **you** **sleep** - **ing,**

Dor - **mez** - **vous,** **dor** - **mez** - **vous?**
dɔr me vu dɔr me vu
Broth - **er** **John,** **Broth** - **er** **John?**

Son - **nez** **les** **ma** - **ti** - **nes,** **son** - **nez** **les** **ma** - **ti** - **nes,**
sɔ ne le ma ti nə sɔ ne le ma ti nə
Morn - **ing** **bells** **are** **ring** - **ing,** **morn** - **ing** **bells** **are** **ring** - **ing,**

Din, **dan,** **don,** **din,** **dan,** **don.**
dɛ̃ dã dɔ̃ dɛ̃ dã dɔ̃
Ding, **ding,** **dong,** **ding,** **ding,** **dong.**

More Practice with *Fa*

Find *fa* in this American song.

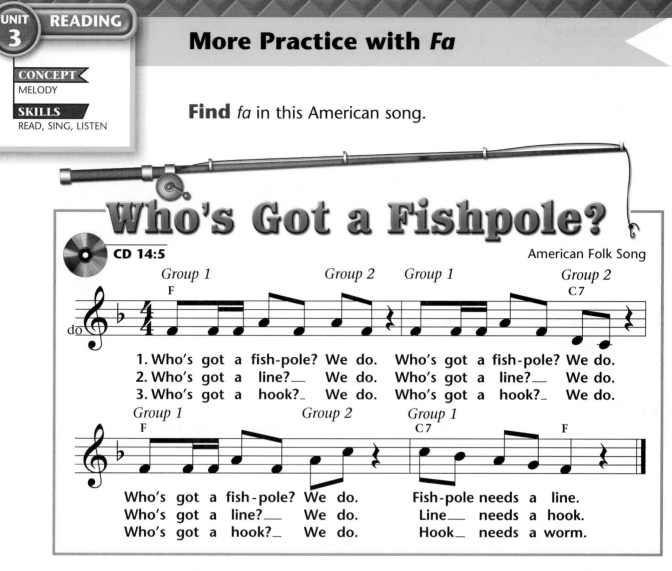

Who's Got a Fishpole?

CD 14:5

American Folk Song

Group 1   *Group 2*   *Group 1*   *Group 2*

1. Who's got a fish-pole? We do. Who's got a fish-pole? We do.
2. Who's got a line?___ We do. Who's got a line?___ We do.
3. Who's got a hook?_ We do. Who's got a hook?_ We do.

Group 1   *Group 2*   *Group 1*

Who's got a fish-pole? We do.   Fish-pole needs a line.
Who's got a line?___ We do.   Line___ needs a hook.
Who's got a hook?_ We do.   Hook_ needs a worm.

Read the rhythm of this melody by Bach then sing it with pitch syllables.

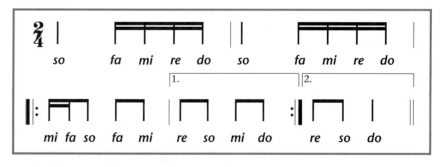

so   fa mi re do   so   fa mi re do

1.   2.

mi fa so   fa mi   re so   mi do   re so do

LISTENING   CD 14:8

Musette from *Notebook for Anna Magdalena Bach* by Johann Sebastian Bach

Listen to "Musette" and raise your hand when you hear the melody you just sang. Play the melody on a pitched instrument.

Music Reading   261

CONCEPT
MELODY
SKILLS
READ, SING, LISTEN

Use What You Know

Read and sing this pattern.

do   do   la   so   fa   mi   re   do

A slur ⌣ is a curved symbol that tells you to sing a syllable on more than one pitch.

Find the slur in this song.

What is the meter?

Identify the rhythms you know.

Sing the song with pitch syllables and hand signs then with the words.

It Rained a Mist

CD 14:9

Virginia Folk Song

It   rained   a   mist,   it   rained   a   mist.

It   rained   all   o - ver   the   town,   town,   town.

It   rained___   all   o - ver   the   town.

Sing this theme from a symphony by Haydn with pitch syllables.

 LISTENING CD 14:12

"La Chasse" ("The Hunt") *Symphony No. 73, Fourth Movement* by Franz Joseph Haydn.

Haydn wrote more symphonies than any other composer—108 in all. At the beginning of "La Chasse" ("The Hunt"), the pitches *do, mi,* and *so* suggest a hunting horn call. You will hear this theme throughout the movement.

The French horn of Haydn's time didn't have valves like horns today. That means they were not able to play all of the notes modern French horns play. Horn players had to change instruments to change keys, or insert longer or shorter "crooks" or tubing in order to play a variety of notes.

Listen for the theme played by the French horns.

Say or tap this rhythm ostinato as you listen again.

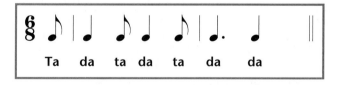

How does the music suggest galloping horses?

Modern French horn

Practice Syncopation

You know that ♩ = ♫

You can write a syncopated pattern like this: ♫♩♫ or like this: ♪♩♪

Identify the syncopated patterns in this spiritual.

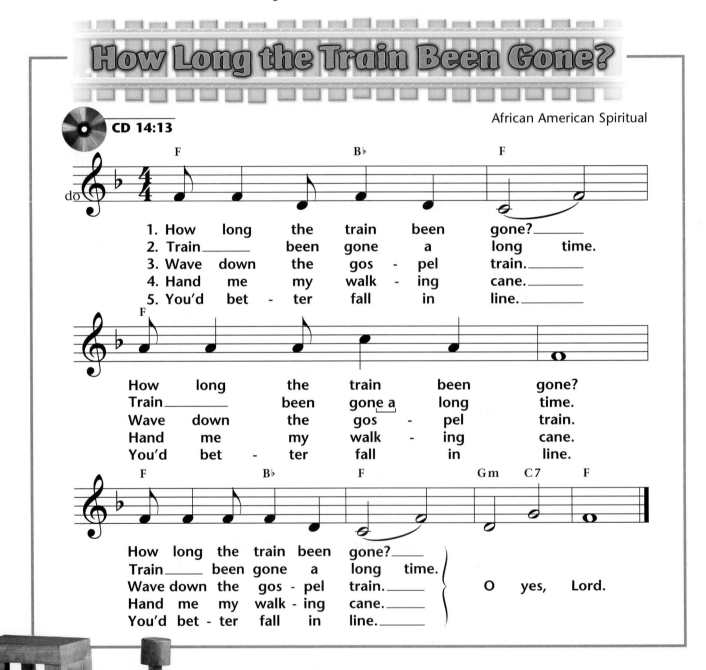

How Long the Train Been Gone?

CD 14:13

African American Spiritual

1. How long the train been gone?_____
2. Train_____ been gone a long time.
3. Wave down the gos - pel train._____
4. Hand me my walk - ing cane._____
5. You'd bet - ter fall in line._____

How long the train been gone?
Train_____ been gone a long time.
Wave down the gos - pel train.
Hand me my walk - ing cane.
You'd bet - ter fall in line.

How long the train been gone?_____
Train_____ been gone a long time.
Wave down the gos - pel train._____
Hand me my walk - ing cane._____
You'd bet - ter fall in line._____
O yes, Lord.

Syncopation in Song

This song begins on beat two.

Sing the syncopated patterns in this song.

MAP

CAMEROON

GABON CONGO

ZAIRE

Congolese Folk Song
English Version by MMH

CD 14:16

Call
F   C 7   Response F   C 7   End (Fine)

Tshiluba: **1. Ne nkan - su** *di - ma, di - ma___* **nsom-bwe - la,**
Pronunciation: ne nkan su ji ma ji ma nsom bwe la
English: **1. I'm call - ing,** *di - ma, di - ma.___* **Hear my call.**

Go back to the beginning and sing to the End.
(Da Capo al Fine)

Call
F C 7   Response F   C 7   F

Ne ku - bu - ka *di - ma, di - ma,___* **nsom bwe - la.**
ne ku bu ka ji ma ji ma nsom bwe la
I'm call - ing, now, *di - ma, di - ma.___* **Hear my call.**

2. Ne kwe-tu ...   My village, *dima, dima.*
ne kwe tu   I'm calling, now, ...

Play these patterns as you sing the song.

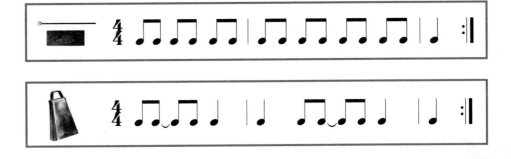

Move to Syncopated Music

A push boat pushes ships and barges, just as a tug boat pulls them.

Improvise work movements to perform with this song.

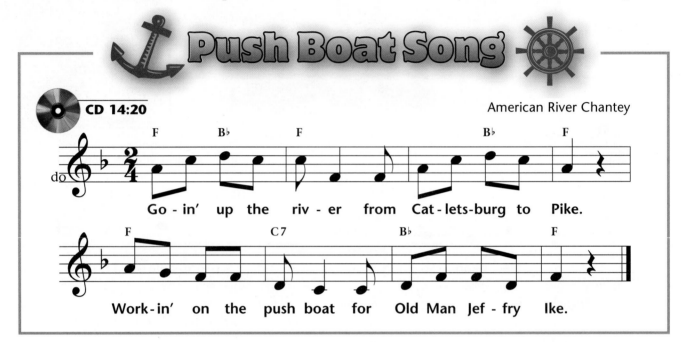

Push Boat Song

CD 14:20

American River Chantey

do

Go - in' up the riv - er from Cat - lets-burg to Pike.

Work - in' on the push boat for Old Man Jef - fry Ike.

Read and clap this rhythm from a ballet. It is the theme for a Russian sailor's dance.

la   la   mi so mi   fa re la   mi do do

re   re   la₁ do do   ti₁ la₁ ti₁ do   la₁   la₁

LISTENING CD 14:23

Russian Sailor's Dance from *The Red Poppy*
by Reinhold Glière

The Red Poppy tells the story of a Chinese dancer who gives a Russian ship captain a red poppy because she likes him.

Improvise dance movements to the theme as it changes in the music.

Use What You Know

You know the pitches and rhythms in this game song.

Find *fa* and the syncopated pattern in the song.

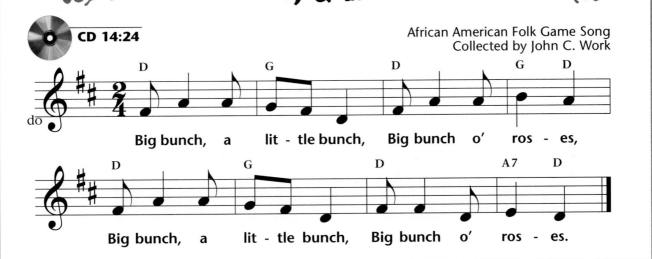

Big Bunch, a Little Bunch

CD 14:24

African American Folk Game Song
Collected by John C. Work

do

Big bunch, a lit - tle bunch, Big bunch o' ros - es,

Big bunch, a lit - tle bunch, Big bunch o' ros - es.

John Wesley Work, Jr. was a teacher and a folk song collector. A folk song collector travels to chosen areas in search of folk songs that are known only to those who live there. The collector listens as people sing their songs, records them, and writes them down.

LISTENING CD 14:27

Big Bunch of Roses by John Wesley Work III

John C. Work collected the game song you just sang and passed it on to his son, John Wesley Work III. John Wesley used the melody in this composition for piano.

Listen for the ways that John Wesley Work III varied "Big Bunch, a Little Bunch" in this piece for piano.

Music Reading 267

UNIT
4
READING

CONCEPT
MELODY

SKILLS
READ, SING, IDENTIFY

Sing with High *Do*

do   re   mi   fa   so   do¹

Sing the melody of these boats with pitch syllables.

do¹   do¹   do¹

so   so   so

mi   mi   mi

do   do   do

Row, Row, Row Your Boat

CD 14:28   Traditional Round

Row,   row,   row your boat   gent-ly down the stream,

Mer-ri-ly, mer-ri-ly, mer-ri-ly, mer-ri-ly, Life is but a dream.

Identify the meter of the song.

Leap from *Do* to High *Do*

Find the octave leaps in this English folk song.

MAP
SCOTLAND
IRELAND
WALES
ENGLAND

Oliver Cromwell

CD 14:31

English Folk Song

1. Ol - i - ver Crom-well lay   bur - ied and dead,   Hee haw,
(2.) ap - ples were ripe___ and   read - y   to   fall,   Hee haw,
(3.) sad - dle and bri - dle, they   lie on the shelf,   Hee haw,

bur - ied and dead.   There grew an   old   ap - ple tree
read - y   to   fall.   There came an   old   wom - an to
lie   on   the shelf. If   you   want an - y   more you can

o - ver his head,   Hee   haw,   o - ver his head. 2. The
gath - er them all,   Hee   haw,   gath - er them all. 3. The
sing it your - self, Hee   haw,   sing it your - self.

Sing or play this ostinato on a pitched instrument with the song.

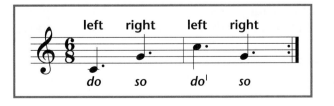

left   right   left   right

do   so   do¹   so

A Pentatonic Spiritual

Read and sing the response parts of this pentatonic song.

Read the pink part with pitch syllables then sing the song.

Train Is A-Coming

CD 15:1

African American Spiritual

1. Train is a-com-ing, Oh, yes,_____
2. Bet-ter get your tick-et, Oh, yes,_____
3. Room for man-y oth-ers, Oh, yes,_____

Train is a-com-ing,_____ Oh, yes,_____
Bet-ter get your tick-et,_____ Oh, yes,_____
Room for man-y oth-ers,_____ Oh, yes,_____

Train is a-com-ing, Train is a-com-ing,
Bet-ter get your tick-et, Bet-ter get your tick-et,
Room for man-y oth-ers, Room for man-y oth-ers,

Train is a-com-ing, Oh, yes._____
Bet-ter get your tick-et, Oh, yes._____
Room for man-y oth-ers, Oh, yes._____

Practice Pitches and Rhythms

Sing this Shaker song with high *do*.

Find the largest leap in the melody. What is this leap called?

Hop Up and Jump Up

CD 15:4

Shaker Song

Hop up and jump up and whirl 'round, whirl 'round,

Gath - er love, here it is all 'round, all 'round,

Here is love flow - ing 'round, catch it as you whirl 'round,

Reach up and reach down, here it is all 'round.

Identify high *do* each time it occurs with a hand sign.

What word would you use to describe the rhythm of the first measure below?

Say or play this ostinato with the song.

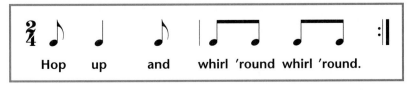

Hop up and whirl 'round whirl 'round.

Music Reading 271

Another Dotted Rhythm Pattern

A dotted quarter note is equal in length to one quarter note plus an eighth note.

$$\text{♩.} = \text{♩} + \text{♪}$$

Clap these rhythm patterns.

Read the ♩. ♪ pattern in this song as you pat with the beat.

Chairs to Mend

CD15:7

Old English Round

Chairs to mend, Old chairs to mend!

Mack - er - el, Fresh mack - er - el! An - y

old rags, An - y old rags?

Sing the song in canon.

Practice with Rhythm Patterns

This song has another kind of rhythm pattern that uses a dotted quarter note: ♪ ♩.

Read the song and find the syncopated rhythms.

Clap these rhythm patterns, and identify those that appear in the song.

Create a body percussion ostinato using the patterns above.

American Cowboy Songs in ¾

Sing and conduct these cowboy songs in ¾ meter with ♩. ♪ rhythm patterns.

1 3   2

My Home's in Montana

CD 15:14

Cowboy Song

1. My home's in Mon-tan-a, I wear a ban-dan-na,
2. When val-leys are dust-y, My po-ny is trust-y,
3. When far from the ranch-es, I chop the pine branch-es,

My spurs are of sil-ver, My po-ny is gray.
He lopes through the bliz-zard, The snow in his ears.
To heap on my camp-fire As day-light grows pale.

When rid-ing the rang-es, My luck nev-er chang-es,
The cat-tle may scat-ter, But what does it mat-ter?
When I have par-tak-en Of beans and of ba-con,

With foot in the stir-rup I'll gal-lop a-way.
My rope is a hal-ter for pig-head-ed steers.
I whis-tle a mer-ry old song of the trail.

 **LISTENING** CD 15:17

Cattle from *The Plow That Broke the Plains*
by Virgil Thomson

Listen for "My Home's in Montana" in this selection.

Read this song and identify the dotted half notes.

CD 15:18

American Folk Song
Arranged by Mary Goetze

F   C 7   F

do   Good - bye,   Old   Paint,   I'm   a - leav - in'   Chey - enne.

do   Ride!   Ride!   Gid-dy up!   Gid-dy up!

F   C 7   F

Good - bye,   Old   Paint,   I'm   a - leav - in'   Chey - enne.

Ride!   Ride!   Gid-dy up!   Gid-dy up!

F   C 7   F

I'm a - leav - in' Chey-enne,   And I'm off   to Mon - tan'._

Leav - in'   Chey - enne.   Off   to   Mon - tan'.

F   C 7   F

Good - bye,   Old   Paint,   I'm   a - leav - in'   Chey - enne!

Ride!   Ride!   Gid-dy up!   Gid-dy up!

Sing with *Ti*

so₁ ti₁ do re mi fa so la

ti

This song has an added pitch, low *ti*.

Find low *ti* in the song.

Sing the song in unison then as a canon.

The Bell Doth Toll

CD 15:22

Traditional Round

The bell doth toll, its ech - oes roll, I know the sound full well,

I love its ring - ing, for it calls to sing - ing

With its bim, bim, bim, bom, bell. Bim, bom, bim, bom, bell.

The Major Scale

When you add *fa* and *ti* to the pentatonic scale, you can read all the notes of the major scale from *do* to *do*¹.

F G A B♭ C D E F¹
*do re mi fa so la ti do*¹

la
so
fa
mi
re
do
ti₁
la₁
so₁

Read the third line of the song with pitch syllables. Notice the stepwise melodic motion that makes up the major scale.

MAP
SCOTLAND
NORTHERN IRELAND
ENGLAND
IRELAND
ATLANTIC OCEAN
WALES

All Through the Night

Welsh Folk Song

CD 15:26

1. Sleep, my child, and peace at-tend thee, } All through the night.
2. While the moon her watch is keep-ing,

Guard-ian an-gels God will send thee, } All through the night.
While the wea-ry world is sleep-ing,

Soft the drow-sy hours are creep-ing, Hill and vale in slum-ber steep-ing,
O'er thy spir-it gen-tly steal-ing, Vi-sion of de-light re-veal-ing,

I, my lov-ing vig-il keep-ing, } All through the night.
Breathes a pure and ho-ly feel-ing,

Music Reading 277

Accompany a Song with Chords

Identify the pitch from the major scale that is missing in the song.

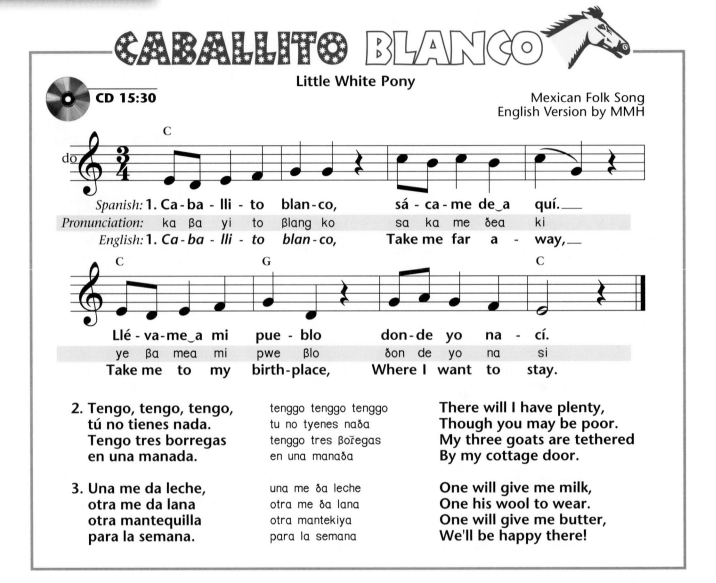

CABALLITO BLANCO

Little White Pony

Mexican Folk Song
English Version by MMH

CD 15:30

Spanish: 1. Ca - ba - lli - to blan - co, sá - ca - me de a quí.___
Pronunciation: ka βa yi to βlang ko sa ka me ðea ki
English: 1. Ca - ba - lli - to blan - co, Take me far a - way,___

Llé - va - me a mi pue - blo don - de yo na - cí.
ye βa mea mi pwe βlo ðon de yo na si
Take me to my birth-place, Where I want to stay.

2. Tengo, tengo, tengo,
tú no tienes nada.
Tengo tres borregas
en una manada.

tenggo tenggo tenggo
tu no tyenes naða
tenggo tres βoɾegas
en una manaða

There will I have plenty,
Though you may be poor.
My three goats are tethered
By my cottage door.

3. Una me da leche,
otra me da lana
otra mantequilla
para la semana.

una me ða leche
otra me ða lana
otra mantekiya
para la semana

One will give me milk,
One his wool to wear.
One will give me butter,
We'll be happy there!

Play these chords to accompany the song.

G so   D¹ re¹
E mi   B ti
C do   G so

Find the letter-name markings for these chords in the song.
In which measures do the chords change?

278

Create with the Major Scale

The *bodeen* and the *carakeen* are types of traditional Irish boats.

Read this song to practice all the pitches in a major scale.

MAP

SCOTLAND

NORTHERN
IRELAND
ENGLAND

IRELAND WALES

Oro, My Bodeen

CD 15:34

Irish Folk Song

1. O - ro, my lit-tle boat that left in the bay, } O - ro, my bo-deen.
2. Sail-ing the waves_ o - ver foam's white_ crest,
3. Rid-ing the waves_on the o - cean's_ rim,

Take up the oars and_ let__ us a - way,__ } O - ro, my bo-deen.
Hap-py and free, a - way_ to the west,__
Sail - ing_ home as the light_ grows_ dim,__

Refrain

O - ro, my__ car - a-keen low, O - ro, my bo - deen,

O - ro, my__ car-a-keen_ low,__ O - ro, my bo - deen.

Create a melody with words about sailing. Use the rhythm pattern from the first line of "Oro, My Bodeen." Use the pitches in a major scale, including *ti*.

CONCEPT
TONALITY
SKILLS
ANALYZE, READ, LISTEN

A Traditional Canon from Germany

Identify the tonal center in this song.

Analyze the pitches to find why the song is major.

MAP
DENMARK
BELGIUM
NETHERLANDS POLAND
GERMANY
AUSTRIA
CZECH
FRANCE REPUBLIC
SWITZERLAND

Himmel und Erde

Music Alone Shall Live

CD16:1

German Round
Words Adapted by MMH

German: Him - mel und Er - de müss - en ver - geh'n,
Pronunciation: hɪ məl ʊnt ɛɹ də mü sən fɛɹ gen
English: All things will per - ish be - neath the sky;

A - ber die Mu - si - ca, a - ber die Mu - si - ca,
α bəɹ di mu zi kα α bəɹ di mu zi kα
Mu - sic a - lone shall live, Mu - sic a - lone shall live,

A - ber die Mu - si - ca blei - bet be - steh'n.
α bəɹ di mu zi kα blaɪ bət bə shten
Mu - sic a - lone shall live, nev - er to die.

LISTENING CD 16:5

Children's Chorus from *Hansel and Gretel*
by Engelbert Humperdinck

In this opera, children trapped as gingerbread cookies are freed and come alive again.

Listen to this chorus that is written in the diatonic scale.

UNIT
6
READING

CONCEPT
MELODY

SKILLS
READ, SING

A Sea Chantey in F Major

Find *fa* and *ti* in this song in a major key.

Eight Bells

CD 16:6

Sea Chantey

Verse

1. My hus-band's a sau-cy fore-top-man,
2. My hus-band once shipped in a whal-er,
3. And now he's no long-er a sail-or,

A chum of the cook's, don't you know?
And sailed to the far north-ern seas,
He of-ten wakes up in the night,

He bel-lowed in-to the cook's fun-nel,
But be-ing a good heart-ed sail-or,
And think-ing he's still on the whal-er,

And shout-ed, "Come up from be-low!"
He cared not for ice, sea, nor breeze.
Calls out with the great-est de-light.

Refrain

Eight bells! Eight bells! Rouse out there the watch from be-low!

Eight bells! Eight bells! Rouse out there the watch from be-low!

A Song with a Different Tonal Center

Sing this song with pitch syllables and identify the tonal center.

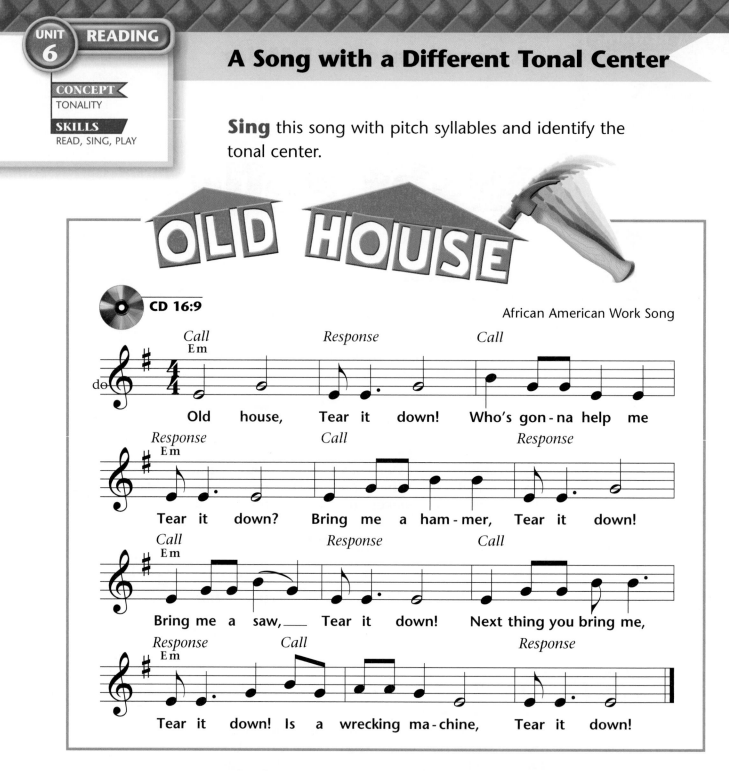

CD 16:9

African American Work Song

OLD HOUSE

Call — Old house, Tear it down! Who's gon-na help me

Response — Tear it down? Bring me a ham-mer, Tear it down!

Call — Bring me a saw,___ Tear it down! Next thing you bring me,

Response — Tear it down! Is a wrecking ma-chine, Tear it down!

Find the syncopated rhythms in the song.

An accent (>) in music puts more emphasis on a note.

Read this ostinato. Play it with the song on unpitched instruments of your choice.

Wreck it! Down it comes!

Many songs are composed using pitches from a major or minor scale.

Listen to the major scale that begins on F and the minor scale that begins on D. **Sing** them with pitch syllables.

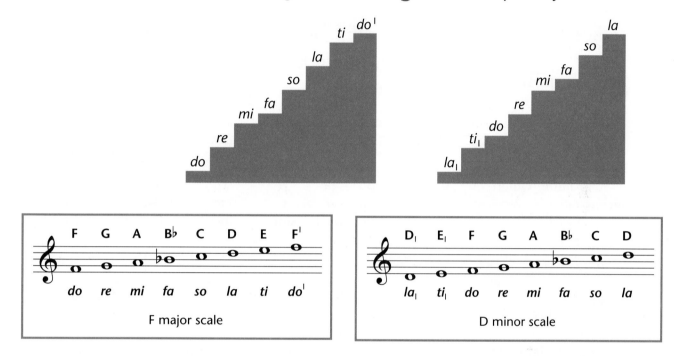

F major scale

D minor scale

Analyze the pitches of this song to identify the scale.

Rise Up, O Flame

CD 16:12

Words and Music by Michael Praetorius

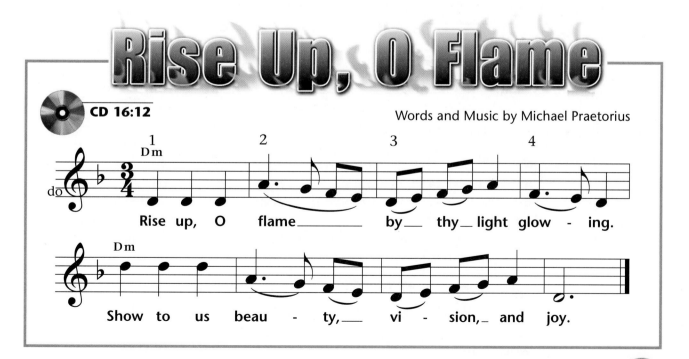

Rise up, O flame_____ by __ thy __ light glow - ing.

Show to us beau - ty, ___ vi - sion, _ and joy.

Music Reading 283

A Song in Minor

Name the minor scale used in this song.

MAP

BRAZIL
PARAGUAY
BOLIVA
CHILE   URUGUAY
ARGENTINA

¿Quién es ese pajarito?

Who Is That Little Bird?

CD 16:17

Argentine Folk Song
English Words by Linda Worsley

Spanish: ¿Quién es	e - se	pa - ja - ri - to	que	can - ta
Pronunciation: kyen es	e se	pa xa ɾi to	ke	kan ta
English: **Who is that**	**lit - tle**	**bird sing - ing,**	**Out**	**there in**

so - bre el li - món?	An - da y di - le____	que	no
so βɾel li mon	an dai di le	ke	no
my lem - on tree?	Go and tell him____	stop	his

can - te	que me ro - ba el	co - ra - zón.	
kan te	ke me ɾo βael	ko ɾa son	
sing - ing.	It____ takes my	heart from me.	

A - llí es - tá	mi____	nom - bre es - cri - to	
a ʒies ta	mi	nom bɾes kɾi to	
And my name	**is____**	**writ - ten there, oh,**	

en la ho - ja	de un	jaz - mín.	
en la o xa	ðeun	xas min	
writ - ten on the	jas -	mine tree.	

284

Create a Melody in a Minor Key

Read and sing this Russian song in a minor key.

MAP

KAZAKHSTAN

RUSSIA MONGOLIA

CHINA

INDIA

CD 16:21

Russian Folk Song
Russian Words by Nikolay Kekrasov
English Version by MMH

Create your own minor melody using rhythms from the first two lines of this song.

A Russian Melody in Minor

Read and sing this folk song in E minor.

Beryoza

The Birch Tree

CD 16:25

Russian Folk Song

Russian: Во по-ле бе-рё-за сто-я-ла,
Pronunciation: vo po le be ɾyo za sto ya la
English: In the field there stands a leaf-y birch tree.

Во по-ле куд-ря-ва-я сто-я-ла.
vo po le kud ɾya va ya sto ya la
I will make three flutes from its branch-es.

Лю-ли, лю-ли, сто-я-ла!
lyu li lyu li sto ya la
Lyu-li, Lyu-li, I'll make them.

Лю-ли, лю-ли, сто-я-ла!
lyu li lyu li sto ya la
Lyu-li, Lyu-li, from its branch-es.

Piotr Ilyich Tchaikovsky used an arrangement of this folk song in his fourth symphony. Compare Tchaikovsky's version of the melody with the song.

Symphony No. 4, Fourth Movement
by Piotr Ilyich Tchaikovsky

This movement starts off in a victorious mood. "The Birch Tree" melody is heard in a variety of ways, sometimes just as a fast fragment. Before the end, the "Fate" theme from the first movement interrupts the victorious mood.

Listen and follow the listening map to hear "The Birch Tree" melody and how it changes.

Listening Map for Symphony No. 4

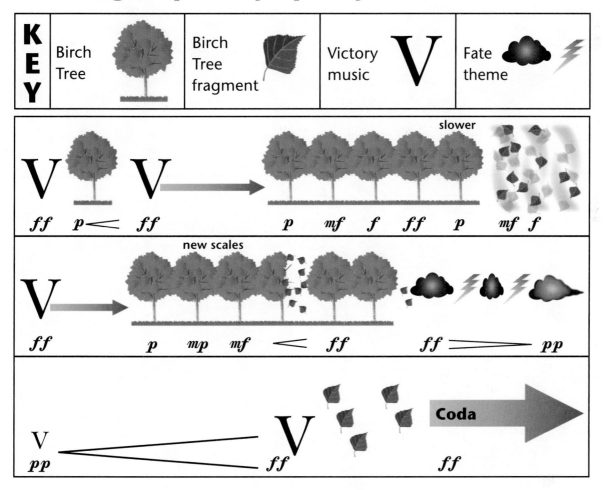

Spotlight on Performance

Spotlight on Performance

Annie Junior. 290

Choral Songs to Perform

THEME 1   Dance, Dance, Dance! 306

THEME 2   It's a Kid's World 316

THEME 3   Our Musical Lives 326

THEME 4   Nature's Songs 336

THEME 5   Over the Hills and Far Away 342

Broadway For Kids

MTI's BROADWAY junior

Annie jr.

R © Tribune Media Services, Inc.

*Mini musicals specifically designed for classroom study and presentation, featuring scenes and songs from the musical **Annie Junior**.*

Musical Numbers

It's the Hard-Knock Life

Tomorrow

I Think I'm Gonna Like It Here

N.Y.C.

You're Never Fully Dressed Without a Smile

Book by Thomas Meehan • Music by Charles Strouse
Lyrics by Martin Charnin
Based on "Little Orphan Annie®"
By permission of the *Tribune Media Service, Inc.*

ADMIT ONE
0596033
0596033
0596033

Annie Junior, Brown University School Adoption

About Rehearsals

You are about to begin rehearsals for a mini production of *Annie Junior*, one of the most popular Broadway musicals ever created. **Rehearsing** is learning and practicing something. Below are some words actors use during rehearsals.

Upstage
The area onstage farthest away from the audience.

Stage right
The area of the stage to the actor's RIGHT as she or he faces the audience.

Stage left
The area of the stage to the actor's LEFT as she or he faces the audience.

Downstage
The area onstage closest to the audience.

About the Script

CHARACTER NAMES are colored **RED**

DIALOGUE is colored **BLUE**

STAGE DIRECTIONS are colored *GREEN*

Scene 1: The New York City Orphanage

NARRATOR 1: The time is 1933.

NARRATOR 2: We're smack dab in the middle of the Great Depression in the city of New York.

NARRATOR 3: It is 4 A.M. at the New York City Orphanage.

(ANNIE has a flashlight and is trying to run away from the orphanage.)

KATE: Annie, what are you doing?

ANNIE: Runnin' away.

JULY: Annie, you're crazy. Miss Hannigan'll catch you.

ANNIE: I don't care. I'm getting outta here.

(MISS HANNIGAN enters and catches her.)

MISS HANNIGAN: Aha! Caught you! Get up and do your chores! Make this dump shine like the top of the Chrysler Building.

IT'S THE HARD-KNOCK LIFE

CD 17:1

Music by Charles Strouse
Words by Martin Charnin

All Orphans

It's the hard-knock life for us!
Got no folks to speak of, so,

It's the hard-knock life for us! 'Stead-a treat-ed,
It's the hard-knock row we hoe! Cot-ton blan-kets

Annie

All Orphans   *Annie*   *All Orphans*

we get tricked! 'Stead-a kiss-es, we get kicked!
'stead-a wool! Emp-ty bel-lies 'stead-a full!

Annie

It's the hard-knock life! Don't it

Kate & Tessie

feel like the wind is al-ways howl-in'? Don't it

Duffy & July

seem like there's nev-er an-y light? Once a

Molly & Pepper

day, don't you wan-na throw the towel in? It's

All Orphans

eas-i-er than put-tin' up a fight. No one's

More

293

there when your dreams at night get creep-y!_____ No one

cares if you grow or if you shrink! No one

dries when your eyes get wet an' weep-y!_____ From the

cry-in', you would think this place-'d sink! Ohhhh!!!!

Emp-ty-bel-ly life! Rot-ten, smel-ly life!

Molly

Full-of-sor-row life! No to-mor-row life! San-ta Claus, we

Pepper

nev-er see. "San-ta Claus," what's that? Who's he?

All Orphans

No one cares for you a smidge when you're in an

or-phan-age! It's the hard-knock life, it's the hard-knock

life, it's the hard-knock life!_____

NARRATOR 1: While everyone at the orphanage was busy cleaning, Annie escaped into the streets of New York.

Scene 2: A Downtrodden Neighborhood Street

DOGCATCHER: You seen any stray dogs around here?

ANNIE: No, sir.

DOGCATCHER: Good. Then they must all be runnin' wild a few streets over.

(The DOGCATCHER EXITS STAGE LEFT; ANNIE notices a DOG OFFSTAGE RIGHT.)

ANNIE: Hey, there's one they didn't get.

(ANNIE gets down on her hands and knees and signals for the DOG to come to her; SANDY, crawling, ENTERS from STAGE RIGHT and CROSSES to ANNIE.)

ANNIE: They're after you, ain't they? Well, they're after me, too. But don't worry, I ain't gonna let them get you or me. Everything's gonna be fine. For the both of us. If not today, well …

Tomorrow

CD 17:2

Music by Charles Strouse
Words by Martin Charnin

The sun-'ll come out to-mor-row.

Bet your bot-tom dol-lar that to-mor-row, there'll be

sun! Just think-in' a-bout to-mor-row

More

clears a - way the cob - webs and the sor - row,___ 'til there's

none! When I'm stuck_ with a day that's gray and

lone - ly, I just stick_ out my chin and grin and

Annie, Citizen

say, "Oh, the sun - 'll come out___ to - mor - row,

With more Citizens

so ya got - ta hang on 'til to - mor - row, come what

All

may." To - mor - row! To - mor - row! I

love ya, To - mor - row! You're al - ways a day a -

way! To - mor - row! To - mor - row! I

love ya, To - mor - row! You're al - ways a

rall.

day a - way!___

LIEUTENANT WARD: Hey you! Little girl. Come here.

ANNIE: Yes, Officer?

LIEUTENANT WARD: You're that runaway orphan Miss Hannigan reported. Come with me, I'm taking you back!

(WARD takes ANNIE by the arm and leads her OFFSTAGE. As they EXIT, ANNIE motions for SANDY to follow along.)

NARRATOR 2: Lieutenant Ward took Annie back to the orphanage.

Scene 3: Back at the Orphanage

NARRATOR 3: That afternoon the orphanage received an unusual visitor …

(GRACE FARRELL ENTERS, carrying a briefcase.)

GRACE: Good afternoon. Miss Hannigan?

MISS HANNIGAN: Yes?

GRACE: I'm Grace Farrell, private secretary to Oliver Warbucks.

(GRACE sits in the office chair, STAGE LEFT of the desk.)

MISS HANNIGAN: Oliver Warbucks the millionaire?

GRACE: No, Oliver Warbucks the billionaire. Mr. Warbucks has decided to invite an orphan to spend the Christmas holidays at his home.

MISS HANNIGAN: What sort of orphan did he have in mind?

GRACE: Well, she should be friendly.

(ANNIE waves to GRACE.)

GRACE: And cheerful.

(ANNIE laughs.)

GRACE: And oh, I almost forgot: Mr. Warbucks prefers redheaded children.

MISS HANNIGAN: A cheerful redhead? Sorry, we don't have any orphans like that.

NARRATOR 1: But Grace insisted that Annie be the chosen orphan.

NARRATOR 2: And Annie was off to the Warbucks mansion!

Scene 4: The Warbucks Mansion

NARRATOR 3: Welcome to the Warbucks mansion.

(GRACE and ANNIE ENTER through the door. ANNIE is wearing a new hat and a new coat.)

DRAKE: Good afternoon, Miss Farrell.

GRACE: Good afternoon, Drake. *(To EVERYONE.)* Everyone. This is Annie and her dog, Sandy. *(To ANNIE.)* Annie, this is everyone.

ANNIE: Hi, everyone.

GRACE: Now, what do you want to do first?

ANNIE: The floors. I'll scrub them first; then I'll get to the windows.

DRAKE: Annie, you won't have to do any cleaning. You're our guest.

***Annie Junior**, Enrico Fermi Elementary School, Yonkers, NY*

GRACE: And, for the next two weeks, you're going to have a swell time. Now …

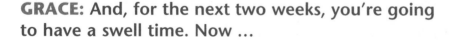

I Think I'm Gonna Like It Here

CD 17:3

Music by Charles Strouse
Words by Martin Charnin

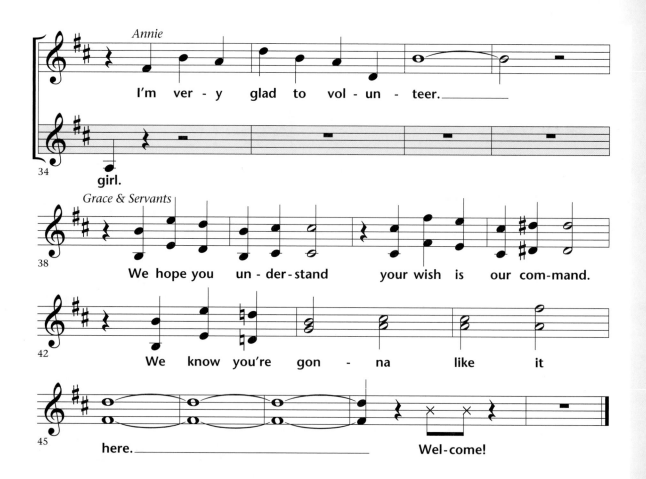

Annie
I'm ver-y glad to vol-un-teer.____

34
girl.

Grace & Servants
38
We hope you un-der-stand   your wish is   our com-mand.

42
We know you're gon - na   like   it

45
here._____   Wel-come!

Scene 4: The Warbucks Mansion (continued)

WARBUCKS: *(From OFFSTAGE RIGHT.)*
Where is everybody?
*(OLIVER WARBUCKS ENTERS with his CHAUFFEUR.
WARBUCKS is carrying a briefcase and
the CHAUFFEUR is carrying two suitcases.)*
Hello, everybody. Drake, dismiss the staff.

DRAKE: Yes, sir.

(The SERVANTS, not including GRACE, EXIT; WARBUCKS turns to speak to GRACE. NOTE: At this point the SERVANTS could change to become an array of New Yorkers.)

WARBUCKS: Well, Annie, I guess we ought to do something special on your first night. *(Has an idea.)* Would you like to go to a movie?

ANNIE: Gosh, Mr. Warbucks, I've never been to one.

WARBUCKS: *(Calls OFFSTAGE LEFT.)* Drake!

DRAKE: *(From OFFSTAGE LEFT.)* Yes, sir?

WARBUCKS: Get our coats. We're going to the movies!

ANNIE: Leapin' lizards!

(DRAKE ENTERS with three coats.)

DRAKE: Which car will you be wanting, sir?

WARBUCKS: This child's been cooped up in an orphanage. We'll walk.

(DRAKE helps WARBUCKS into his coat.)

NARRATOR 2: Oliver Warbucks and Grace showed Annie a part of New York she'd never known before.

Scene 5: The Streets of New York City

N.Y.C.

CD 17:4

Music by Charles Strouse
Words by Martin Charnin

Warbucks & Grace
N. Y. C. The shim-mer of

Warbucks *Grace* *Warbucks & Grace*
Times Square, the pulse, the beat, the drive!

Warbucks
N. Y. C. You might say that

I'm square, but wow! I come a - live.

All
The cit - y's bright as a pen - ny ar - cade. It

Annie
blinks, it tilts, it rings. To think that

I've lived here all of my life____ and

All
nev - er seen these things! N. Y.

C. The whole world keeps com - ing,

by bus, by train; you can't ex - plain

their yen for N. Y.

(ALL FREEZE as one by one, three NARRATORS step forward.)

NARRATOR 1: This was the beginning of many adventures for Little Orphan Annie.

NARRATOR 2: The nation may have been depressed that Christmas of 1933 ...

NARRATOR 3: ... but Annie gave everyone she met, rich or poor, the gift of hope and goodwill.

(EVERYONE unfreezes.)

Annie Junior, Enrico Fermi Elementary School, Yonkers, NY

You're Never Fully Dressed Without a Smile

CD 17:5

Music by Charles Strouse
Words by Martin Charnin

Hey, ho - bo man, hey, Dap - per Dan, you've both got your style, but, bro - ther, you're nev - er ful - ly dressed with - out a smile! Your clothes may be Beau Brum - mel - ly, they stand out a mile, but, bro - ther, you're nev - er ful - ly dressed with - out a smile! Who cares what they're wear - ing on Main Street or Sa - ville Row? It's what you wear from ear to ear, and not from head to toe, that mat - ters. So Sen - a - tor, so jan - i - tor, so long for a

33 while. Re-mem - ber, you're nev - er ful - ly dressed, though

36 you may wear your best. You're nev - er ful - ly

39 dressed with - out a smile!

42 Smile! Smile!! Smile, darn ya, smile!

CURTAIN CALL

Meet the Musicians

Annie Junior, Brown University School Adoption Program

Book by:
Thomas Meehan

Thomas Meehan began his career by writing comic stories for magazines such as *The New Yorker*. In addition to *Annie*, Mr. Meehan has written scripts for the musicals *The Producers* and *Hairspray*. He has also written screenplays for movies.

Lyrics by:
Martin Charnin

Martin Charnin started his career with a role in *West Side Story*. Mr. Charnin is also a director, composer, and lyricist. He has worked on more than seventy-five shows.

Music by:
Charles Strouse

Charles Strouse's first Broadway musical was *Bye, Bye Birdie*. His other musicals include *It's a Bird, It's a Plane, It's Superman; Golden Boy;* and *Annie's* sequel, *Annie Warbucks*.

Dance, Dance, Dance!

Music and dance go together like peanut butter and jelly. It's hard to have one without the other. All over the world, music gets people on their feet and moving to the beat. As you sing the five super dance hits in this theme, it won't take long before the rhythm grabs you. You will feel the need to dance, dance, dance!

At the HOP

CD 17:16

Words and Music by Arthur Singer, John Madara, and David White

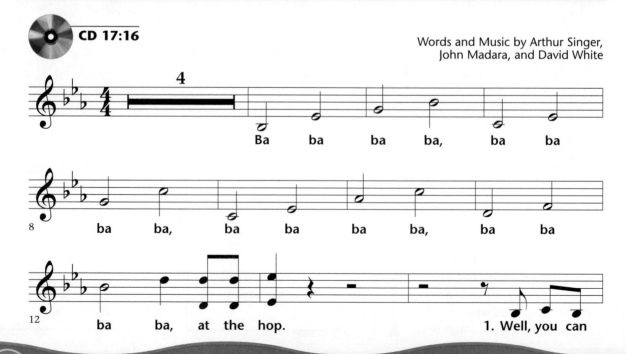

Ba ba ba ba, ba ba

ba ba, ba ba ba ba, ba ba

ba ba, at the hop. 1. Well, you can

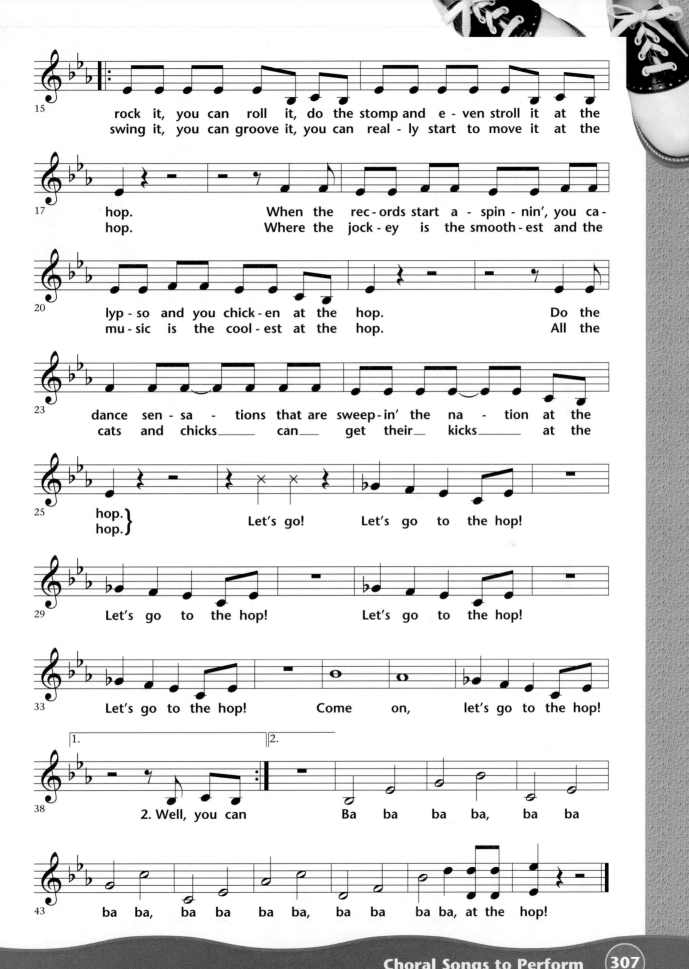

CONCEPT
MELODY
SKILLS
SING

Have you ever heard a tune that you couldn't get out of your head? Mary Chapin Carpenter wrote "Down at the Twist and Shout" after hearing Cajun music from Louisiana for the first time. She was afraid that if she went to Louisiana to hear some live Cajun music, she'd never come back!

Down at the Twist and Shout

CD 17:19

Words and Music by
Mary Chapin Carpenter

And I never have wandered down to

New Orleans,— never have drifted down a bayou stream. But I

heard that music on the radio and I said someday I was

gonna go: down a highway 10, past a La-fay-ette; there's a-

D.S. al Coda

Baton Rouge.— And I won't forget to send you a card with

my regrets 'cause I'm never gonna come back home.—

Coda

2

CONCEPT
RHYTHM
SKILLS
SING

In 1978, four women from California formed a rock band called the Go-Gos. Three years later, they had a number one album and a huge radio hit called "We Got the Beat." Even today this upbeat song still has the power to get you "off your feet"!

SKILL BUILDER: Rhythm

Clap the pattern and then sing the words.

Ev - 'ry bod - y   get off your feet.

We know you can   dance to   the beat.

CD 17:22 **We Got the BEAT**

Words and Music by
Charlotte Caffey

1. See the peo - ple   walk-ing down the street;
2. See the kids just   get-ting out   of school.

fall   in   line   just   watch - ing   all   their   feet.____
They can't wait   to   hang____ out   and   be   cool.____

They don't know   where___ they want   to   go,   but they're
Hang a - round   'til quart - ter   af - ter   12.   That's___

CONCEPT
RHYTHM

SKILLS
SING

If you love to dance, "The Loco-Motion" is the perfect song for you. The song has great dance moves that go with the song. All you need to do is read the words to learn the moves.

SKILL BUILDER: Beat in Your Feet

Speak the syncopated rhythm in the example below. Then tap your feet to the beat.

Come on ba-by, do___ the lo-co-mo-tion

The Loco-Motion

CD 17:25

Words and Music by
Gerry Goffin and Carole King

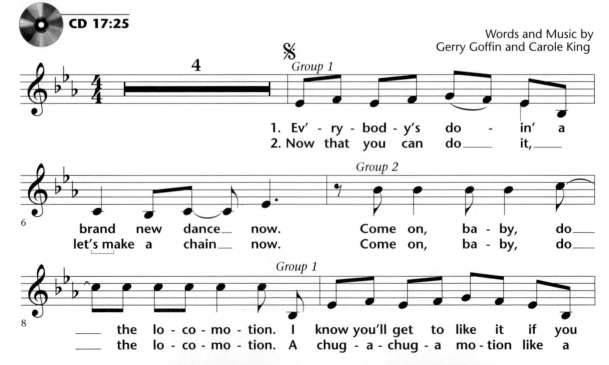

1. Ev' - ry - bod - y's do - in' a
2. Now that you can do___ it,___

brand new dance___ now. Come on, ba - by, do___
let's make a chain___ now. Come on, ba - by, do___

___ the lo - co - mo - tion. I know you'll get to like it if you
___ the lo - co - mo - tion. A chug - a - chug - a mo - tion like a

CONCEPT
HARMONY
SKILLS
SING

"Twist and Shout" is one of the most popular rock and roll songs of all time. Famous bands such as the Isley Brothers, the Beatles, and the Who have played this classic song. When it comes on the radio, people all over the world know exactly what to do: start twisting!

SKILL BUILDER: Harmony Building

Singing in harmony is one of the greatest things about being in a choir.

Practice building three-part vocal harmony by singing the exercise below.

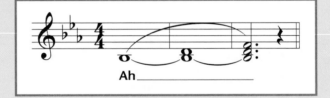

Ah _____

The Beatles

🔘 CD 18:1

Words and Music by
Bert Russell and Phil Medley

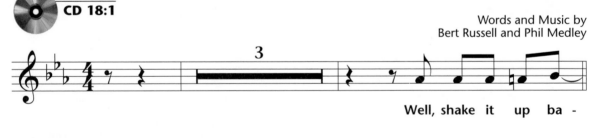

Well, shake it up ba-

-by, now.
(Shake it up ba - by.)
Twist and

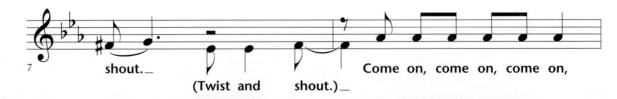

shout.___
(Twist and shout.)___
Come on, come on, come on,

It's a Kid's World

What is it like being a kid? You have times when you need to be serious, like when you do your homework. There are also times when you can relax. Being a kid isn't always easy, but it definitely can be a lot of fun!

Have you ever waited and waited for a special day to come? When that day finally comes, you can't wait to jump out of bed and get the day started. "The New Day" is the perfect song to start one of these great, new days.

"The New Day" is a three-part round. This means there are three groups of singers. When performing a round, each group sings the same melody, but starts at different times.

The New Day

CD 18:4

Anonymous

1
The new day is dawn-ing, let's greet it with danc-ing. The

2
hills and_ the_ moun-tains with shep-herd_ tunes_ ring-ing. Hey

3
tu-li tu-li tu-li tu-la, hey tu-li tu-li tu-li ho!

CONCEPT
MELODY
SKILLS
SING: VOCAL QUALITY

Have you ever imagined that you could fly? In a book called *The Snowman*, one boy's dream of flying comes true. He builds a snowman who takes him on a flight high over his town. "Walking in the Air" is a song about their magical trip.

VOICE BUILDER: Clear Vocal Tone

How would you feel flying through the air on a cold, winter night? Put this feeling in your voice as you sing the exercise below. Use a light and clear voice. Then **sing** "Walking in the Air" with this same vocal tone.

Oo_____ We're walk-ing in the air.

CD 18:7

Music and Lyrics by Howard Blake
Arranged by Audrey Snyder

Dreamily, legato

Solo or Unison
mp

We're walk-ing in the air,_____ We're

5 float - ing in the moon - lit sky._____ The

More

LISTENING CD 18:10

Walking in the Air by Howard Blake

The King's Singers are a group of six men from England who sing classical and popular songs.

Listen to their performance of "Walking in the Air." How is their version similar to the one you sing?

CONCEPT
MELODY
SKILLS
SING

The words to "The Swing" are from a book of poems written by Robert Louis Stevenson called *A Child's Garden of Verses*. These poems are about things children liked to do in the 1800s. More than 100 years later, you probably enjoy doing some of the same things.

VOICE BUILDER: High to Low

When you play on a swing you go up and down.
Your voice does the same thing when you sing.

Practice the melody in the exercise.
What direction does it move?

Ah
Up   in the   air   so   blue
Up   in the   air   and   down

The Swing

CD 18:11

Music by John Chorbajian
Words by Robert Louis Stevenson
from *A Child's Garden of Verses*

Moderately, with motion

How do you like to go up in a swing,

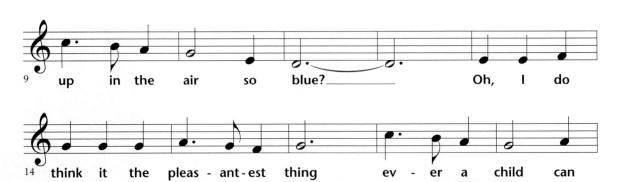

9   up in the air so blue?_____   Oh, I do

14   think it the pleas - ant - est thing   ev - er a child can

19 do!_____ Up in the air and o - ver the

24 wall, till I can see so wide,_____

29 riv - ers and trees and cat - tle and all o - ver the

34 coun - try - side_____ till I look down on the

39 gar - den green, down on the roof___ so brown,_____

44 ___ Up in the air I go fly - ing a - gain,

49 up in the air and down,_____ up in the air I go

55 fly - ing a - gain, up in the air, up in the air,

61 up in the air and down!_____

CONCEPT
MELODY

SKILLS
SING: DICTION

"Little David Play on Your Harp" is an African American **spiritual**. African American musicians created spirituals. They mixed church hymns with music their ancestors brought from different parts of Africa. This song is about a brave boy named David whose courage helps him with a great challenge.

VOICE BUILDER: Good Diction

When you sing all the sounds of all the words clearly, including consonants, you have good **diction**. To make consonant sounds, you use the lips, the teeth, and the tongue.

Sing this exercise to improve your diction.

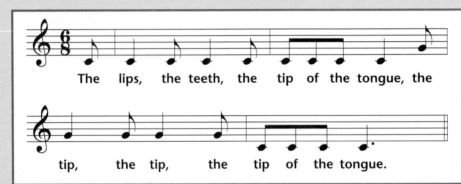

The   lips,   the teeth,   the   tip   of   the tongue, the

tip,   the   tip,   the   tip   of   the tongue.

Little David Play on Your Harp

CD 18:14

African American Spiritual
Arranged by Emily Crocker

More →

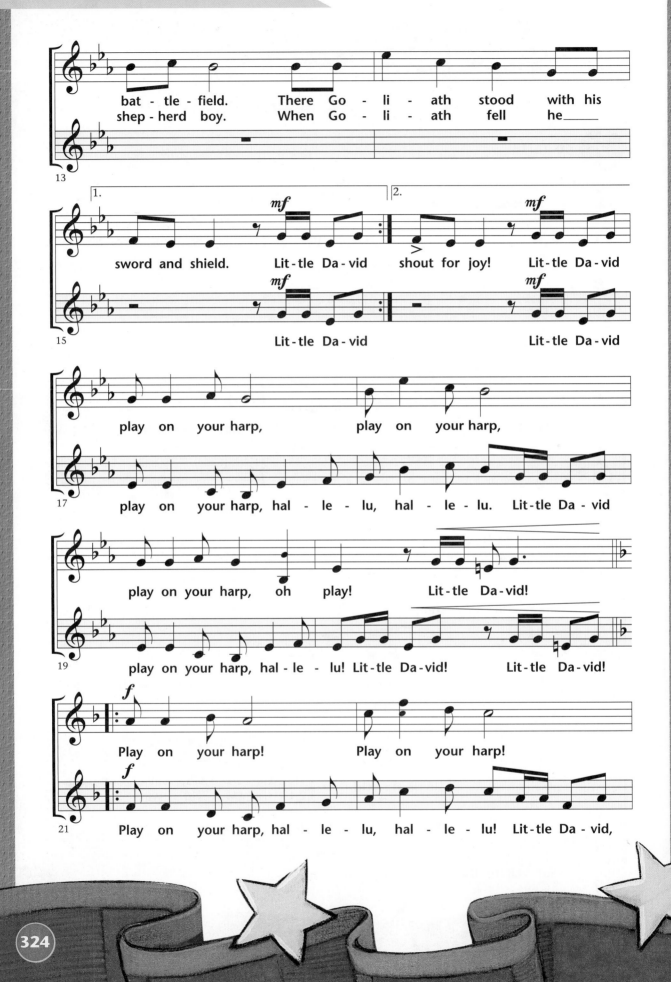

Our Musical Lives

The sounds of music fill our lives. Music from a clock radio might wake you up in the morning. You might put headphones on to listen to music on the way to school. You probably listen to or play music at parties with your friends and family. If you watch television, you hear music in nearly every program. When it's time for bed, music might even help you fall to sleep. We really do have musical lives!

VOICE BUILDER: Project Your Voice

Have you ever called to a friend across a playground or field? You may notice your voice carries farther when you project your voice at a high pitch.

Sing this melody and project your voice as if you were calling someone far away. Repeat it at higher and lower pitch levels.

Hey you!   Hey you!   Hey you!
Wake up!   Wake up!   Wake up!

Wake Up Canon

CD 18:18

American Folk Song

Now all the woods are wak - ing, the sun is ris - ing high. Wake up now, get up now, be - fore the dew is dry.

CONCEPT
EXPRESSION
SKILLS
SING

"Ogguere" is a beautiful lullaby from Cuba that celebrates the birth of a prince named Ogguere. He lived in the country of Nigeria in West Africa, a place where the ancestors of many Cubans came from. The words are in an Afro-Cuban dialect of Spanish. They describe Ogguere's mother telling him to go to sleep because she has many things to do.

VOICE BUILDER: Expression

In a lullaby, the singer gradually sings softer as the baby is going to sleep. Singing softly is a type of **expression**. Expression is the way a musician puts feeling into a song.

Sing this exercise three times. Sing more softly each time through. Hum the tune on the last time.

Repeat 3 times

mp - p 1.-2. O - ggue - re, o - ggue - re, o - ggue - re.

pp 3. hmm

MAP
FLORIDA
CUBA
HAITI
DOMINICAN REPUBLIC

CD 18:21

Ogguere

An Afro-Cuban Cradle Song
by Gilberto Valdés
Arranged by Carlos R. Abril

Afro-Cuban Spanish: O - ggue - re, o - ggue - re, o - ggue -
(Dialect)
Pronunciation: o ge ɾe o ge ɾe o ge

p

12 re o - ggue - re, o - ggue - re, o - ggue -
ɾe o ge ɾe o ge ɾe o ge

More

16
re La cam - pa - na la sei____ ta re - so - na ba -
ɾe la kam pa na la sei ta ɾe so na βa

19
tey____ y la gen - te do - ta - sion Va re -
tei i lo xen te ðo ta syon ba ɾe

24
sá la o - ra - sion____ O -
sa lo ɾa syon o

2

30
ggue - re, o - ggue - re, o - ggue - re o - ggue - re, o -
ge ɾe o ge ɾe o ge ɾe o ge ɾe o

35
ggue - re, o - ggue - re O - ggue - re dru - me -
ge ɾe o ge ɾe o ge ɾe ðɾu me

38
ri____ que yo tien que su - sí
ɾi ke yo tyen ke su si

The waterfront in Havana, Cuba

328

LISTENING CD 18:25

Ogguere An Afro-Cuban Lullaby

Listen to "Ogguere." Describe the tempo changes as sung by Bola de Nieve.

CONCEPT
MELODY

SKILLS
SING: DICTION

Circles are everywhere around us. Circles are on your bike and on the buttons on your shirt. The sun and moon are circles in the sky. Our own planet is a circle! You also have your very own family circle and a circle of friends. As you sing "Circle of Song," you will find even more examples of circles in our lives.

VOICE BUILDER: Tongue-Tied

Tongue twisters are always fun to say and sing. They also help you improve your diction. Challenge yourself to **say** and **sing** these musical phrases. Sing at a faster tempo each time.

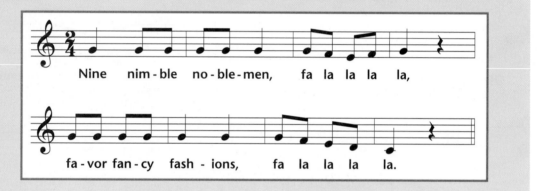

Nine nim-ble no-ble-men, fa la la la la,

fa-vor fan-cy fash-ions, fa la la la la.

CD 18:26

Words and Music by
Emily Crocker

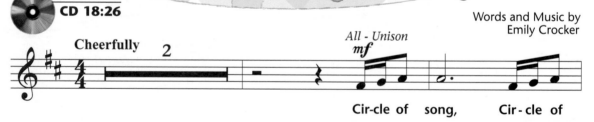

Cheerfully   2

All - Unison
mf

Cir-cle of song, Cir-cle of

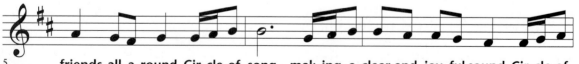

5   friends all a-round. Cir-cle of song, mak-ing a clear and joy-ful sound. Cir-cle of

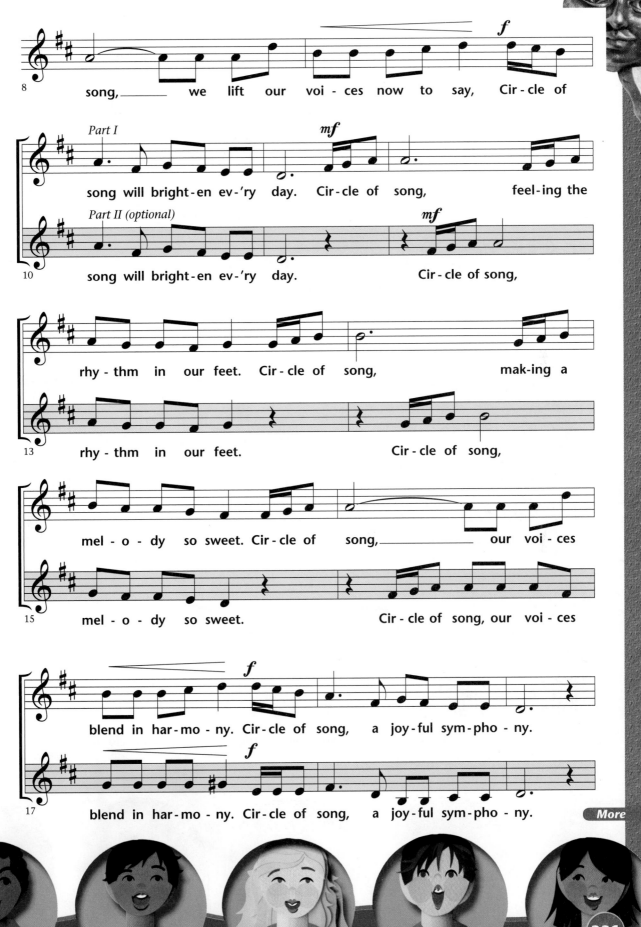

More

clear and joy - ful sound. Cir-cle of song,_____ we lift our

clear and joy - ful sound. Cir-cle of song, we lift our

voi - ces now to say, Cir-cle of song will bright - en ev - 'ry

voi - ces now to say, Cir-cle of song will bright - en ev - 'ry

(All) *mf*

day. Our song will bright-en ev - 'ry day.

CONCEPT
MELODY
SKILLS
SING

"**D**on't Let the Music Stop" gives your choir the chance to sing in two parts. You will learn to sing each part separately. When you hear them sung together, you won't want the music to stop!

VOICE BUILDER: High and Low

Sing both high and low pitches in this exercise that comes from "Don't Let the Music Stop."

Repeat at higher pitches

Ah_____ Oh_____
I hear sing - ing.

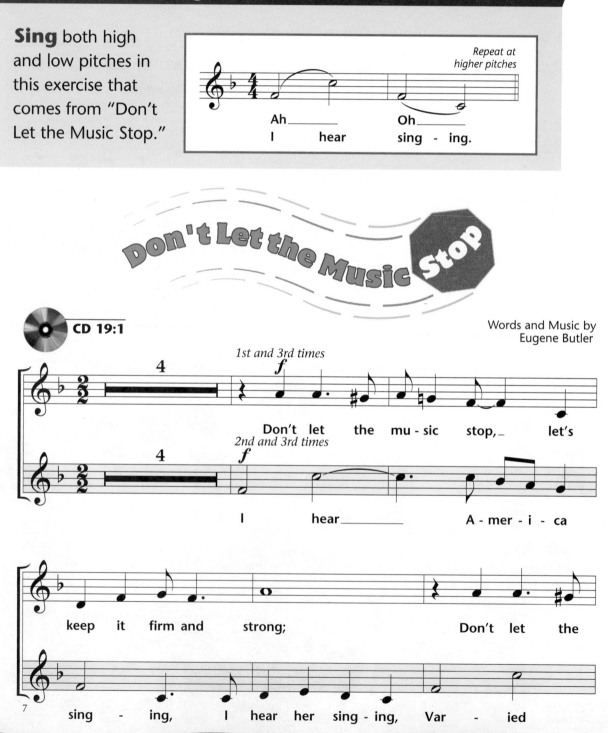

Don't Let the Music Stop

CD 19:1

Words and Music by
Eugene Butler

1st and 3rd times
Don't let the mu - sic stop,__ let's

2nd and 3rd times
I hear_____ A - mer - i - ca

keep it firm and strong; Don't let the

sing - ing, I hear her sing - ing, Var - ied

334

mu - sic stop, ___ let's sing the whole day long.

car - ols I hear. _____

Don't let the mu - sic stop, ___ don't let it ev - er

I hear _____ A - mer - i - ca sing - ing, I

cease, 'Cause the mu - sic that I sing makes the

hear her sing - ing, Var - ied

(4-measure interlude after 1st time only)

world go round, ___ It brings love and joy ___ and peace.

car - ols I hear. _____

Nature's Songs

If you take a walk through the woods, the music of the natural world fills your ears. You might hear a gurgling stream, the cry of an eagle in the sky, or the whoosh of the wind through the trees. In this theme, you will sing songs that all express the beauty of the natural world.

VOICE BUILDER: Singing Long Phrases

Practice this breathing exercise to expand your breathing capacity. This will improve your ability to sing longer phrases.

- Imagine you have a milkshake as large as the room. "Drink" the air through a giant straw.
- Imagine there is an elevator at the bottom of your lungs. Take the elevator from the basement to the first floor over 4 counts.

Now can you sing this full musical phrase in one breath?

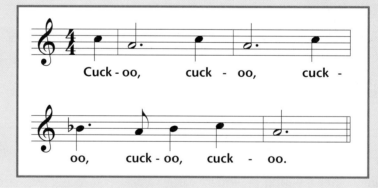

Cuck - oo, cuck - oo, cuck -

oo, cuck - oo, cuck - oo.

The flight of a bird moves up and down like the melody of a song. As you sing the two rounds below, imagine your voice is a bird flying through the air. When the melody goes up, your voice soars toward the clouds. When the melody goes down, your voice floats to the ground.

EAGLE

CD 19:5

Music by Moritz Hauptmann (adapted)
Words by MMH

Andantino, legato

Wheel - ing and turn - ing, an ea - gle in flight Will

fly a - way, will fly a - way, will soar out of sight.

The Owl and the Cuckoo

CD 19:8

Anonymous

We hear the night owl call - ing from for - est still and

dark, While from the tall - est oak tree the cuck - oo an - swers

back: Cuck - oo, cuck - oo, cuck - oo, cuck-oo, cuck -

oo. Cuck - oo, cuck - oo, cuck - oo, cuck-oo, cuck - oo.

After a visit to the mountains of the Hawaiian island of Moloka'i, Herb Mahelona wrote a song to ask people to help take special care of nature.

VOICE BUILDER: Blend Your Voice

Blend your voice with others by matching your vowel sounds. The five basic vowels are *ee, eh, ah, oh, oo*. **Sing** vowels with a relaxed jaw, vertical mouth shape, and space inside the mouth.

loo loo loo loo loo   loo,   loo loo loo loo loo _____ loo
la la la la la   la,   la la la la la _____ la
le - le wa - le la - kou,   le - le wa - le la - kou

E nānā kākou i nā manu

Let's Watch the Birds

CD 19:11

(The sound of birds and the wind through the ironwood trees.)

Text and Music by Herb Mahelona

Hawaiian:	**1. E nā-nā kā-kou i nā__ ma-nu i nā__ ma-nu**
Pronunciation:	ɛ na na ka kou i na mʌ nu i na mʌ nu
	2. E nā-nā kā-kou i kō__ lā-kou, i kō__ lā-kou
	ɛ na na ka kou i ko la kou i ko la kou

ma ka___ la - ni.
mʌ kʌ lʌ ni
kī - ka-ha 'a - na.
ki kʌ hʌ 'ʌ nʌ

Ma - lu - na lo - a   o ka ho - nu - a,
mʌ lu nʌ lo ʌ   o kʌ ho nu ʌ

1.
le - le wa - le lā - kou,   le - le wa - le lā - kou.
lɛ lɛ vʌ lɛ lɑ kou   lɛ lɛ vʌ lɛ lɑ kou

2.
le - le wa - le lā -
lɛ lɛ vʌ lɛ lʌ

CONCEPT
RHYTHM

SKILLS
SING

The Spanish words to the song "Arroyito serrano" describe a little mountain stream. The stream's beautiful song calls a person to come and hear its sweet music.

Arroyito serrano

CD 19:15

Little Mountain Stream

Words and Music by
Carlos Guastavino

Allegretto

Spanish: **A - rro - yi - to   se - rra - no___   Que**
Pronunciation: a   ɾo   yi   to   se   ɾa   no   ke

Spanish: **To - das las   ma - ña - ni - tas___   Me**
Pronunciation: to   ðas las   ma   nya   ni   tas   me

vie - nes   ba - jan - do_ha - cia_el   lla - no,___   A - gua cla - ri - ta
βye   nes   βa xan   doa   syel   ʒa   no   a   gwa kla   ɾi   ta

lla - ma   tu   can - to   le - ja - no,___   Ven - go   co - rrien - do_a
ya   ma   tu   kan   to   le   xa   no   beng   go   ko ɾyen   ðoa

tra - es.___   Per - fu - me   de   miel   y   de_a - zaha - res.___
tɾa   es   peɾ   fu   me   ðe   myel   i   ðea   sa   ɾes

ver - te___   Que - ri - do_a - rro - yi - to   se - rra - no.___
βeɾ   te   ke   ɾi   ðoa   ɾo   yi   to   se   ɾa   no

Co-rre a-rro - yi - to can - ta que can - ta Co - mo un pa - ja -
ko ɾea ɾo yi to kan ta ke kan ta ko mun pa xa

ri - to,___ Si-gue a-de - lan - te Lim-pio y fres - qui - to
ɾi to si gea ðe lan te lim pyoi fres ki to

Can - ta y co - rre más. La la la la la
kan tai ko ɾe mas la

la la la la la la la la la la la la___ la

la la la la la la la la la la la la la la la

la la la la la la la la la la la la la la la.

LISTENING CD 19:19

Arroyito serrano by Carlos Guastavino

Listen to "Arroyito serrano" performed by the Indiana University Children's Choir. Performing in a children's choir requires dedication and a commitment to practice. The excitement of singing and performing makes the hard work worth it.

Over the Hills and Far Away

Taking a journey to new places far away from home can be an exciting experience. Jump in the car, hop on a train, or get on a plane, and you are like an explorer discovering new lands. Some of the songs you will learn in this theme are about traveling. Others describe the place where the journey ends. Whether you like the trip or the place you end up, songs always help brighten your journey.

VOICE BUILDER: Energy Boost!

The song "This Train" sounds best when you sing it with energy.

Practice speaking the words three different ways:

1. Slowly and clearly as a group.
2. Quickly and clearly as a group.
3. In a fast whisper. Speak all the consonants clearly.

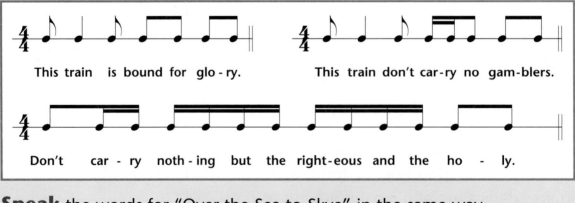

Speak the words for "Over the Sea to Skye" in the same way.

"This Train" is a great way to begin a journey over the hills to far away places. Get on board the train and sing this African American spiritual with energy.

CD 19:20

This Train

African American Spiritual

1. This train is bound for glo - ry,
2. This train don't car-ry no gam - blers,
3. This train is bound for glo - ry,

this train,_____ This train is bound for glo - ry,
this train,_____ This train don't car-ry no gam - blers,
this train,_____ This train is bound for glo - ry,

this train,_____ This train is bound for glo - ry,
this train,_____ This train don't car-ry no gam - blers,
this train,_____ This train is bound for glo - ry,

if you ride it, you must be ho - ly,
No hy-po - crites,__ no mid - night ram - blers,
Don't car-ry noth - ing but the right-eous and the ho - ly,

This train is bound for glo - ry, this train.____
This train is bound for glo - ry, this train.____
This train is bound for glo - ry, this train.____

LISTENING CD 19:23

This Train African American Spiritual

Listen to Big Bill Broonzy's version of "This Train."

CONCEPT
MELODY
SKILLS
SING

"**O**ver the Sea to Skye" describes a narrow escape to sea after a battle on land. Though the waves are rough, the sea is a safe place for the people in the song.

Over the Sea to Skye

CD 19:24

Music by Annie MacLeod
Words by Sir Harold Boulton

Refrain

"Speed, bon-nie boat, like a bird on the wing:
"Car-ry the lad that's born to be king

1.   2. (last time) Fine

On-ward! the sail-ors cry!
O-ver the sea to Skye!"

Verse

1. Loud   the   winds   howl,   loud   the   waves   roar,
2. Tho   the   waves   leap,   soft   shall   ye   sleep,
3. Man-y's   the   lad   fought   on   that   day,
4. Burned   are   our   homes,   ex-ile   and   death

Thun-der clouds rend   the   air;_____   Baf-fled   our   foes,
O-cean's   a   roy-al   bed;_____   Rocked   in   the   deep,
Well the   clay   more   could   wield,_____   When the   night came,
Scat-ter   the   loy-al   men;_____   Yet   ere   the   sword

*Last time to Refrain
and end at Fine*

stand   on   the   shore,   Fol-low   they   will   not   dare._____
flo-ra   will   keep   Watch   by   your   wea-ry   head._____
si-lent-ly   lay   Dead   on   Cul-lo-den's   field._____
cool   in   the   sheath,   Char-lie   will   come   a-gain._____

CONCEPT
MELODY

SKILLS
SING, READ

Trips are often filled with exciting experiences. However, they can make you feel homesick, too. In the Japanese words to "Hitori," a young girl sadly sings as she thinks about the beautiful cherry trees at her home in Japan.

VOICE BUILDER: Legato

Sing the exercise below in a smooth, **legato** style. Legato is marked in music notation with a long, curving arc. Look for legato marks in "Hitori," and then sing the song using legato style.

do re mi so la do¹ la so mi re do

Hitori

Japanese Folk Song
Additional Lyrics and Arrangement by
Mary Donnelly and George L.O. Strid

CD 19:27

Gentle rocking
10

All - Unison
mp

Japanese: ひ と____ り で せ び し い ふ た り で
Pronunciation: hi to ɾi de sa bi shi fu ta ɾi de
English: (optional) **Here am__ I, so all a-lone dreaming of the**

14

ま い り ま しょ ひ と 、 り で せ び し い
ma i ɾi ma sho hi to ɾi de sa bi shi
cher-ry trees of home. Here am__ I, so all a-lone

More

(3rd time) Fine

2

17

ふ　た　り　で　ま　い　り　ま　しょ
fu　ta　ɾi　de　ma　i　ɾi　ma　sho
dream-ing　of　the　cher-ry　trees　of　home.

Part I

1. There by the riv-er sits a pret-ty maid-en watch-ing the wa-ter
2. Now, as the moon-light dan-ces on the riv-er, sad-ly the maid-en

Part II (1st time only)
div.

21 Slow-ly mov-ing. Mov-ing

24 move a-long. She sees a love-ly blos-som-ing cher-ry tree
must de-part. Each gen-tle breeze that sighs_ through the cher-ry tree

slow. Slow-ly mov-ing.

1.

27 and her_ heart is filled with song. "Some day I will_ go
ech-oes the song that fills her heart.

Mov-ing slow. "Some day I will go

31 to my home that I love_ so. Once more I will_ be
to my home that I love so. Once more I will be

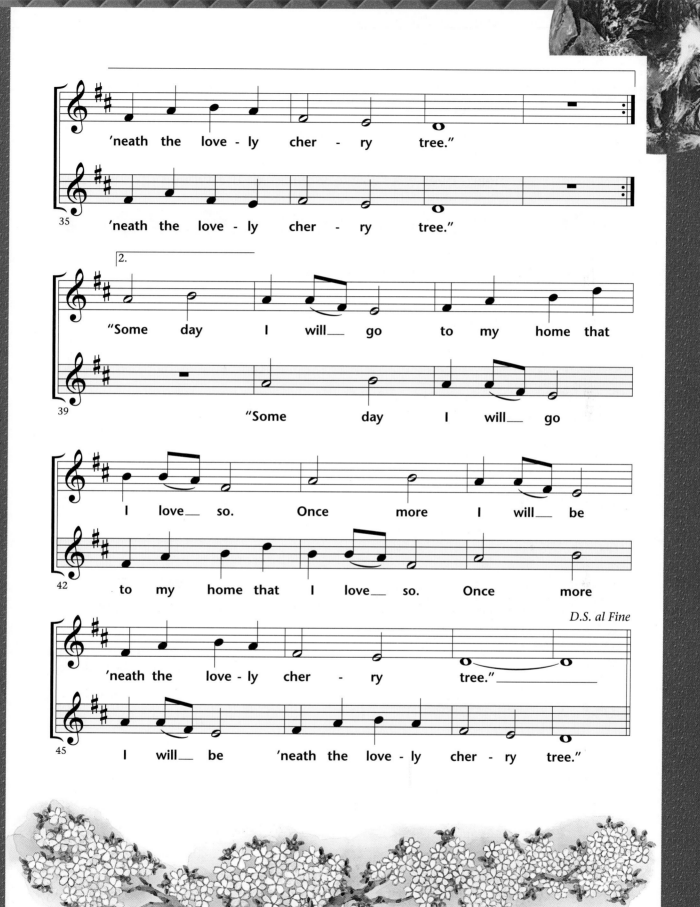

'neath the love - ly cher - ry tree."

'neath the love - ly cher - ry tree."

2.

"Some day I will__ go to my home that

"Some day I will__ go

I love__ so. Once more I will__ be

to my home that I love__ so. Once more

D.S. al Fine

'neath the love - ly cher - ry tree."_____

I will__ be 'neath the love - ly cher - ry tree."

CONCEPT
RHYTHM

SKILLS
SING

"The Kettle Valley Line" is about an old railway that connected parts of British Columbia, Canada with the Pacific Ocean. Imagine you are riding a train on the Kettle Valley Line. You must sing loud, crisp, and clear to be heard over the "clackety-clack" of the wheels on the tracks.

VOICE BUILDER: Keeping the Beat

Practice these speech patterns to keep a steady rhythm. Form three groups with your class. Groups 1 and 2 chant the patterns below while Group 3 sings "The Kettle Valley Line." Then, play the patterns on instruments with the song.

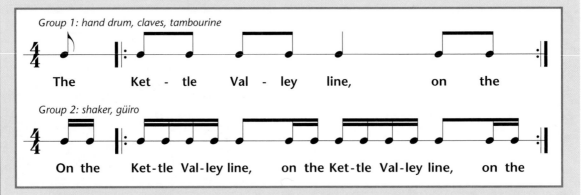

Group 1: hand drum, claves, tambourine

The   Ket - tle   Val - ley   line,   on   the

Group 2: shaker, güiro

On the   Ket-tle Val-ley line,   on the Ket-tle Val-ley line,   on the

The KETTLE VALLEY Line

CD 20:1

Words and Music by Ean Hay
Arranged by Robert J. de Frece

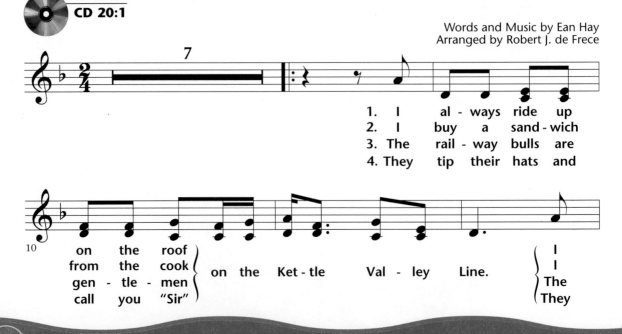

1. I al - ways ride up
2. I buy a sand - wich
3. The rail - way bulls are
4. They tip their hats and

on   the   roof
from   the   cook
gen - tle - men
call   you   "Sir"

on   the   Ket - tle   Val - ley   Line.

I
I
The
They

13

al - ways ride up on the roof
buy a sand - wich from the cook } on the Ket - tle Val - ley Line. } I
rail - way bulls are gen - tle - men I The
tip their hats and call you "Sir" They

Part I

al - ways ride up on the roof. I could
buy a sand - wich from the cook, And he
rail - way bulls are gen - tle - men, We'll__
tip their hats and call you "Sir," Then__

Part II

17

ride_____ I

ride in - side but what's the use. So I al - ways ride up
pock-ets my mon-ey, the dir - ty crook, When I buy a sand - wich
nev - er see their like a - gain. Yes the rail - way bulls are
dunk you in the lo - cal stir But they tip their hats and

19

ride_____

So I al - ways ride up
When I buy a sand - wich
Yes the rail - way bulls are
But they tip their hats and

7

on the roof
from the cook } on the Ket - tle Val - ley Line.
gen - tle - men
call you "Sir"

7

22

on the roof
from the cook } on the Ket - tle Val - ley Line.
gen - tle - men
call you "Sir"

CONCEPT
EXPRESSION
SKILLS
SING

In certain parts of the mountains of Peru, people celebrate the Yunza Festival, or Festival of Joy, in February or March. At this festival, people fill a hollow tree trunk with gifts. People take turns chopping the trunk until it falls and the gifts spill out onto the ground. "La Yunsita" is a song people sing at the festival.

VOICE BUILDER: Expressive Singing

Expressive singing can make your performance more beautiful.

Sing this vocal exercise, which is based on the refrain of "La Yunsita." Then use your voice in a light and dance-like way to sing the song.

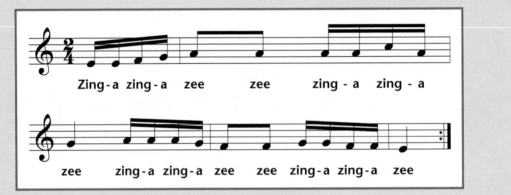

Zing-a zing-a zee   zee   zing-a zing-a

zee   zing-a zing-a zee   zee   zing-a zing-a zee

CD 20:5

Arranged by
Rosa Mercedes Ayarza de Morales

MAP

PERU   BRAZIL

BOLIVA

CHILE

ARGENTINA

Allegro   8   **Verse**

Spanish:	1. Yun - si - ta, yun - si - ta,	yun - si - ta, yun - si - ta,
Pronunciation:	yun si ta yun si ta	yun si ta yun si ta
Spanish:	2. Sau - ce - si - to ver - de,	sau - ce - si - to ver - de,
Pronunciation:	sau se si to βeɾ ðe	sau se si to βeɾ ðe

13 ¿Quién te tum - ba - rá? ¡Ja jay! ¿Quién te tum - ba - rá? ¡Ja jay!
kyen te tum ba ɾa xa xai kyen te tum ba ɾa xa xai

¿Qué ha-ces en la playa? ¡Ja jay! ¿Qué ha-ces en la playa? ¡Ja jay!
kea ses en la playa xa xai kea ses en la playa xa xai

17 Y⌣el que te tum - ba – re, y⌣el que te tum - ba – re,
yel ke te tum ba ɾe yel ke te tum ba ɾe

Prés - ta-me tu som - bra, prés - ta-me tu som - bra,
pɾes ta me tu som bɾa pɾes ta me tu som bɾa

Refrain

21 Te re-no - va - rá, ¡Ja jay! Te re-no - va - rá.
te ɾe no βa ɾa xa xai te ɾe no βa ɾa

⎰ Hua - chi - gua-
wa chi gwa

Has - ta que me vaya ¡Ja jay! Has - ta que me vaya.
as ta ke me βaya xa xai as ta ke me βaya

25 li - to, hua-chi-gua - ló, pa - ra⌣a-mar - te ¡Só - lo yo! Hua - chi-gua-
li to wa chi gwa lo pa ɾa mar te so lo yo wa chi gwa

4

29 li - to, hua - chi - gua - ló, pa - ra⌣a - mar - te ¡Só - lo yo!
li to wa chi gwa lo pa ɾa mar te so lo yo

The ruins of Machu
Picchu at sunset, ca.
1995 Peru.

Spotlight on
Celebrations

Spotlight on Celebrations

PATRIOTIC 354

AUTUMN 362

WINTER 372

SPRING 390

SUMMER 396

Songs of Our Country

The Reverend Samuel Smith wrote the words to "America" in 1831. Later he chose music from a collection of German melodies and set the words to music. The music comes from "God Save the Queen," the British national anthem.

CD 20:10

Music by Henry Carey
Words by Samuel F. Smith

1. My coun-try, 'tis of thee, Sweet land of
2. My na-tive coun-try thee, Land of the
3. Let mu-sic swell the breeze, And ring from
4. Our fa-thers' God, to Thee, Au-thor of

lib-er-ty, Of thee I sing.
no-ble free, Thy name I love.
all the trees Sweet Free-dom's song;
lib-er-ty, To Thee we sing.

Land where my fa-thers died, Land of the Pil-grim's pride,
I love thy rocks and rills, Thy woods and tem-pled hills;
Let mor-tal tongues a-wake, Let all that breathe par-take,
Long may our land be bright With Free-dom's ho-ly light;

From ev-'ry___ moun-tain-side Let___ free-dom ring.
My heart_ with_ rap-ture thrills Like_ that a-bove.
Let rocks_ their_ si-lence break, The_ sound pro-long.
Pro-tect_ us___ by Thy might, Great_ God, our King!

The Stars and Stripes Forever by John Philip Sousa

"The Stars and Stripes Forever" is a piece written for band. John Philip Sousa composed this piece on Christmas in 1896. It is the official march of the United States of America.

Listen to the different instruments playing in this band.

Listening Map for
The Stars and Stripes Forever

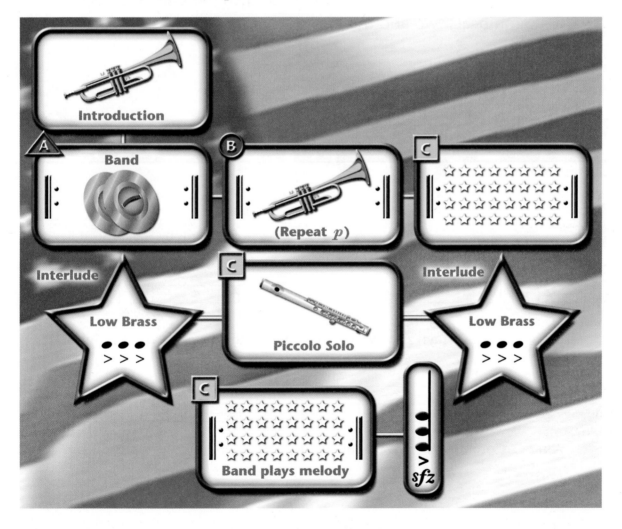

CONCEPT
BEAT/METER

SKILLS
LISTEN, PLAY

During the War of 1812, Francis Scott Key watched as the British attacked Fort McHenry in Baltimore. After the smoke had cleared, he saw the flag still waving in the breeze. He was inspired to write the words to "The Star-Spangled Banner." The words were later set to music and "The Star-Spangled Banner" was declared the national anthem of the United States.

As you listen to "The Star-Spangled Banner" tap your foot on the first beat of each measure and clap on beats two and three.

The Star-Spangled Banner

CD 20:14

Music Attributed to J.S. Smith
Words by Francis Scott Key

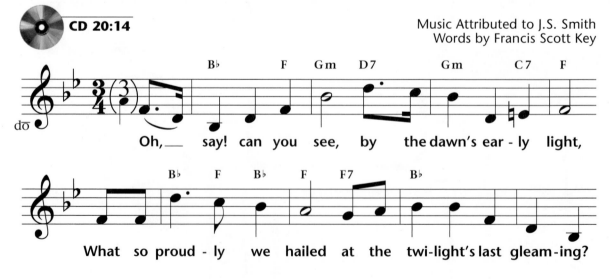

Oh, — say! can you see, by the dawn's ear-ly light,

What so proud-ly we hailed at the twi-light's last gleam-ing?

Whose broad stripes and bright stars, through the per - il - ous fight,

O'er the ram - parts we watched were so gal - lant - ly stream-ing?

And the rock - ets' red glare, the bombs burst - ing in air,

Gave proof through the night that our flag was still there.

Oh, say, does that_ Star-Span-gled Ban - ner_ yet_ wave_

O'er the land___ of the free and the home of the brave?

CONCEPT
FORM/STRUCTURE

SKILLS
MOVE, READ

People express love for their country by singing songs. Songs bring people together and help them express pride for the country in which they live. "America, My Homeland" describes the beauty of the United States.

America, My Homeland

CD 20:17

Music by Robert de Frece
Words by Robert de Frece and Shirley Funk

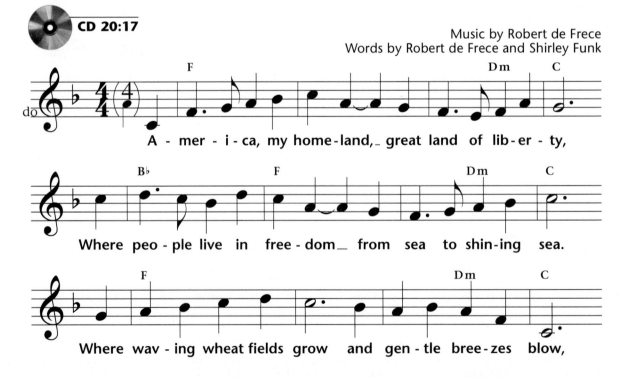

A - mer - i - ca, my home-land, _ great land of lib-er - ty,

Where peo - ple live in free-dom _ from sea to shin-ing sea.

Where wav - ing wheat fields grow and gen - tle bree-zes blow,

Where for-ests tall reach up-ward_ to moun-tains capped with snow.

A - mer - i - ca, A - mer - i - ca, we sing our praise to thee,

And proud-ly we sa-lute the flag that flies for you and me!

Sing of America

Words by H. Wilburr

Sing A - mer - i - cans, glad - ly sing

While the bells of free - dom ring!

Hail our flag on land and sea.

Sing that here we all are free!

CONCEPT
DYNAMICS
SKILLS
SING, DESCRIBE

People and events can be honored and remembered in many ways. "We Remember" honors our fallen heroes and reminds us of how we felt as a nation after September 11, 2001.

CD 20:20

Words and Music by
John Jacobson and Mac Huff
Arranged by Mac Huff

There was a day when free-dom's light seemed
day when A - mer - i - cans

ve - ry far a - way.___ There was a day that looked like
chose to take a stand.___ There was a day when the best of

night; we dreamed of yes - ter - day.___ But
friends of - fered us their hand.___ The

e - ven when the day is dark___ and rain-bows hard to see,___
world can still be beau - ti - ful___ but e - ven when it's gray,___

her - oes walk a - mong___ us and
the sun will shine up - on___ us and

Identify the dynamic markings in "We Remember."
Perform the song, emphasizing the dynamics.

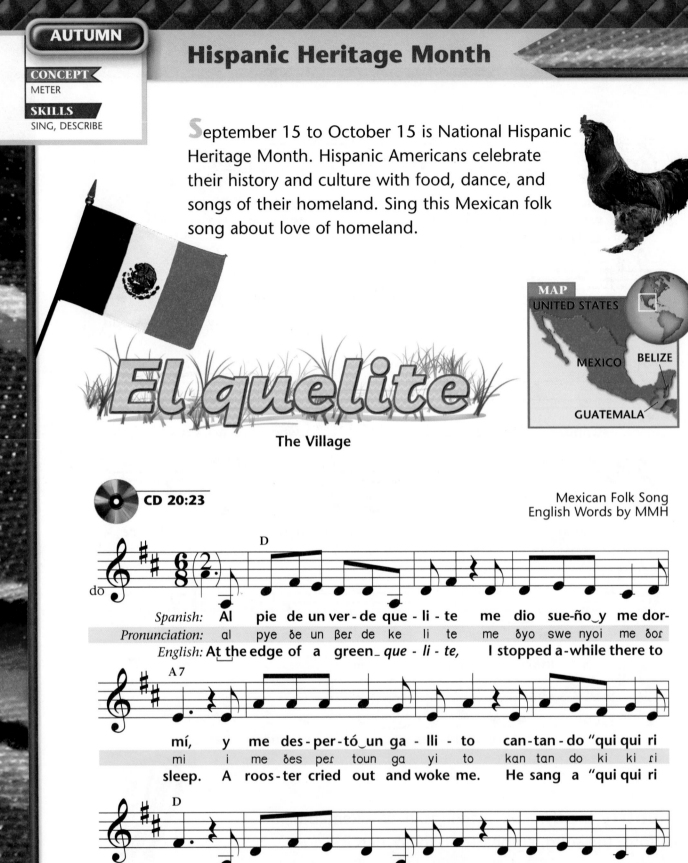

Hispanic Heritage Month

September 15 to October 15 is National Hispanic Heritage Month. Hispanic Americans celebrate their history and culture with food, dance, and songs of their homeland. Sing this Mexican folk song about love of homeland.

El quelite

The Village

CD 20:23

Mexican Folk Song
English Words by MMH

D

Spanish: Al   pie de un ver-de que-li-te   me dio sue-ño y me dor-
Pronunciation: al   pye ðe un ßer de ke li te   me ðyo swe nyoi me ðoɾ
English: **At the edge of a green** *que-li-te,*   **I stopped a-while there to**

A7

mí,   y me des-per-tó un ga-lli-to   can-tan-do "qui qui ri
mi   i me ðes peɾ toun ga yi to   kan tan do ki ki ɾi
sleep.   A roos-ter cried out and woke me.   He sang a "qui qui ri

D

quí." No can-to por-que si pue-da, ni por-que mi voz sea
ki   no kan to poɾ ke si pwe ða ni poɾ ke mi ßos sea
quí."   I don't sing be-cause I'm a-ble, nor be-cause my voice is

buena, can-to por-que ten-go gus-to en mi tie-rra y en la_a-
βwena kan to poɾ ke teng go gus to en mi tye ɾa ien la
good._ I sing be-cause_ I feel joy_ in my land_ and for-eign

je - na. Ma - ña - na, me voy ma - ña - na, ma - ña - na me voy de_a-
xe na ma nya na me βoi ma nya na ma nya na me βoi ðea
lands._ To-mor-row I will be leav-ing, and who can tell where I'll

quí, y_el con-sue-lo que me que-da que se_han de_a-cor-dar de mí.
ki iel kon swe lo ke me ke ða ke sean dea koɾ ðaɾ ðe mi
be? But here is my con-so - la-tion: that some - one re-mem-bers me.

Clap the rhythm of the Spanish verse of "El quelite" along
with the recording.

🔘 **LISTENING** CD 20:27

El tecolote (excerpt) Mexican Folk Song

"El tecolote" ("The Owlet") is a song from the southwest of
Mexico. The song style is called *gusto*.

Identify the group of instruments playing "El tecolote."

See **music.mmhschool.com** to
research Mexican music.

CONCEPT
MELODY
SKILLS
SING, READ

This Danish harvest song tells about the importance of the harvest time for the farmers. The harvest helps them remember the past as well as celebrate the future.

Use hand signs to identify *high do* and *low do* in this song about harvest time in Denmark.

high do   low do

MAP
NORWAY
FINLAND
SWEDEN
DENMARK
RUSSIA

Marken er mejet

Out in the Meadow

CD 20:28

Danish Folk Song
English Version by MMH

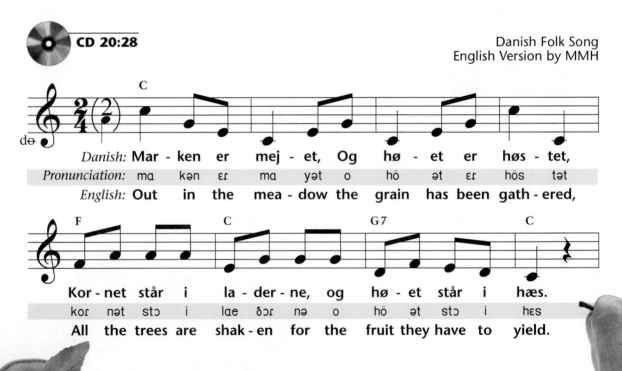

do

Danish: Mar - ken er mej - et, Og hø - et er høs - tet,
Pronunciation: ma kən ɛʁ ma yət o hö ət ɛʁ hös tət
English: Out in the mea - dow the grain has been gath - ered,

Kor - net står i la - der - ne, og hø - et står i hæs.
koɹ nət stɔ i lɑe ðɔɹ nə o hö ət stɔ i hɛs
All the trees are shak - en for the fruit they have to yield.

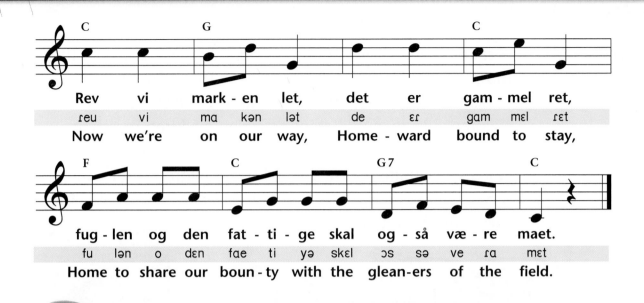

Rev vi mark - en let, det er gam - mel ret,
ɾeu vi mɑ kən lət de ɛɹ gɑm mɛl ɾɜt
Now we're on our way, Home - ward bound to stay,

fug - len og den fat - ti - ge skal og - så væ - re maet.
fu lən o dɛn fɑe ti yə skɛl ɔɜ sə ve ɾɑ mɛt
Home to share our boun - ty with the glean-ers of the field.

Art Gallery

The Harvesters

This painting was created by Pieter Brueghel (1525-1569). It shows people in Northern Europe during wheat harvesting time.

CONCEPT
TONALITY
SKILLS
SING, LISTEN

Tết Trung Thu, or Mid-Autumn Moon Festival, is one of the most popular festivals in Vietnam. Tết Trung Thu means "Children's Festival." Vietnamese families celebrate their children with many different activities. Children march in parades while singing and carrying colorful handmade lanterns. Vietnamese parents tell their children stories and serve them special treats such as *mooncakes*, which are little cakes with bright yellow centers.

Tết Trung

Children's Festival

CD 21:1

Vietnamese Song
Collected and Transcribed by Kathy B. Sorensen
English Words by MMH

Vietnamese: Tết trung thu rước dèn di chơi. Em rước dèn di khắp phố phường.
Pronunciation: tɛt tɾung tu ɾʊk dɛn di choi ɛm ɾuk dɛn di kap fo fʊng
English: 1. At Mid - Au - tumn Fes - ti - val, walk a - round with lan - terns lit.
2. Beau - ti - ful and full the moon, at Mid - Au - tumn Fes - ti - val.

Long vui sướng với— dèn trong tay Em múa— ca trong ánh trăng rằm.
lʌng vuɪ sʊng voɪ dɛn tɾang taɪ ɛm muə ka tɾang ʌn tɾang ɾam
Take them all a - cross the town, Sing-ing— to the au-tumn moon.
Wait - ing for the— moon to rise, I can— hear the sound of drums,

Dèn ỏng sao với dèn cá chám. Dẻn thiên nga với den bướm bướm.
dɛn ʌng sau voɪ dɛn ka cham dɛn tiɛn nga voɪ dɛn bʊm bʊm
Lan-terns all in dif-f'rent shapes, Lan-tern an - gel, lan-tern dream,
Tung yin yin kak tung yin yin, Tung yin yin kak tung yin yin.

366

C   G7   C

em rước dẻn này   dẻn cung trăng.   Dèn xanh   lơ   với   dèn   tim   tim.

ɛm ɾuk dɛn naɪ   nɛn kuŋ tɾaŋ   dɛn sʌn   lə   vɔɪ   dɛn   tim   tim

Lan-tern fish, or   lan-tern star,   Lan-tern swan or   but - ter - fly.

I   can hear the sound of drums,   Tung yin   yin   kak tung yin   yin,

Am   G   C   Am   G7   C

Dèn xanh lam   với   dèn trắng trắng,   trong   ánh   dèn   rực   rở muôn màu.

dɛn sʌn lam vɔɪ   dɛn tɾaŋ tɾaŋ   tɾaŋ   ʌn   dɛn   ɾʊk   ɾʊ mun mɑu

Take   my   lan-tern   to   the   sky;   Take   my   lan-tern   to   the   moon.

Tung   yin   yin   kak   tung   yin   yin.   Wel-come,   la - dy   in   the   moon!

 LISTENING   CD 21:5

Qua Cầ Gió Bay   Vietnamese Folk Song

The title of this song means "Wind on the Bridge." It is traditionally sung during autumn and spring festivals in Vietnam. Children in Vietnam enjoy listening to and singing this song.

CD-ROM

Use *World Instruments* **CD-ROM** to learn more about Southeast Asian instruments.

367

CONCEPT
RHYTHM
SKILLS
SING

Ghosts, goblins, and things that go bump in the night bring thrills and chills to Halloween night. Sing this song about a playful ghost.

The Boogie-Woogie Ghost

CD 21:6

Words and Music Nadine M. Peglar

Verse

C

1. There was a ghost on Hal-low-een, He real-ly made the ghost-ie scene,
2. He'd go out spook-ing late at night, And giv-ing ev-'ry-one a fright,

F   C

He was the Boo-gie-Woo-gie Ghost, He was the ghost-ie with the most,
He knew some wit-ches, two or three, And they would all go on a spree,

G   F

And when the kid-dies came a-round, He'd give out with a ghost-ly sound,
And when the morn-ing came a-round, He'd give one last mys-te-ri-ous sound,

C   F   C   F   1. C   2. C

He'd go,___ "Boo-oo-oo-oo-ooo."   ooo."

Refrain

Though he real - ly was - n't ver - y spook-y, _____

Kids all thought that he was rath - er cool.

E - ven though he was a lit - tle kook - y, _____

He was just a spe - cial _____ ghoul. When you're

out on Hal - low-een And he ap-pears up-on the scene,

Don't give a scream and run a-way, Just ask him if he'll stay and play.

You'll like the Boo-gie-Woo-gie Ghost, He'll be the one you dig the most,

You'll love his Boo - oo - oo-oo - ooo.

Thanksgiving is a time of family gatherings. Family members travel long distances to be with relatives for the holidays.

Sing this traditional Thanksgiving song about being together on Thanksgiving Day.

Use body percussion to accompany this song. Tap your left hand on the desk, then your right hand, then clap your hands together.

Over the River and Through the Wood

CD 21:9

American Folk Melody
Words by Lydia Maria Childs

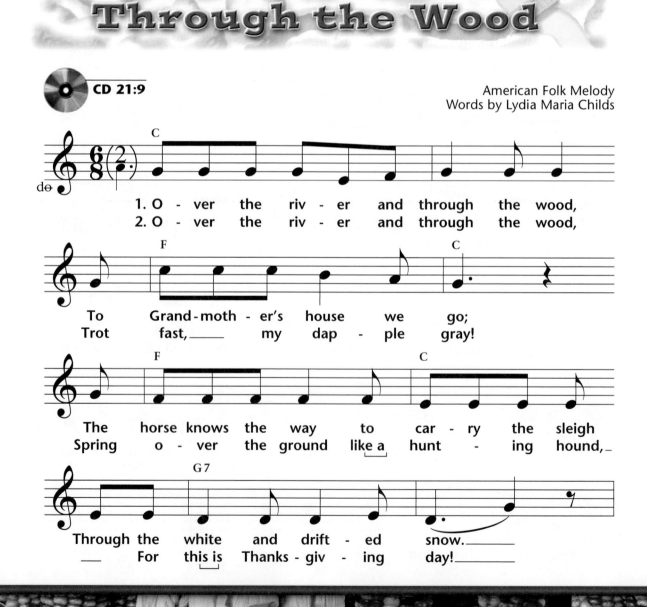

1. O - ver the riv - er and through the wood,
2. O - ver the riv - er and through the wood,

To Grand - moth - er's house we go;
Trot fast,____ my dap - ple gray!

The horse knows the way to car - ry the sleigh
Spring o - ver the ground like a hunt - ing hound, _

Through the white and drift - ed snow.____
_ For this is Thanks - giv - ing day!____

Over the river and through the wood,
Over the river and through the wood,

Oh, how the wind does blow!
Now Grand-moth-er's face I spy!

It stings the toes and bites the nose
Hur - rah for the fun! Is the pud - ding done?

As o - ver the ground we go.
Hur - rah for the pump - kin pie!

Sing this round about the spirit of Thanksgiving Day, standing up each time you sing the word "Thank," and sitting down on the word "Food."

Song of Thanksgiving

CD 21:12

Words and Music by Robert de Frece

Thank you for our man - y bless - ings,

Food and fam - 'ly, friend - ship true.

Seasonal Songs

In winter the days grow shorter and the nights grow longer. The glow of holiday lights coming from the windows warms the winter night.

December Nights, December Lights

CD 21:15

Words and Music by Emily Crocker

Verse

Em   B   Em   Am

1. De - cem - ber days are dark and cold and the
2. De - cem - ber nights are crisp and clear and the
3. De - cem - ber times are hap - py times and they

Em   B   Em   B

snow is grow - ing deep. The trees are bare in the
stars are i - cy cold. From far and near all the
bring a mes - sage true. Good will to all and

Em   Am   B   Em

frost - y air and the world is fast a - sleep. There are
sounds you hear are a prom - ise that's fore - told. There are
peace on earth and a hap - py New Year, too. And

Em   B   Em   Am   Em

can - dles in the win - dow, there are lights up - on the
mer - ry voi - ces sing - ing, there is mus - ic in the
when the snow has gone a - way and the sun shines warm and

Create a piece of artwork depicting the winter scene described in "December Nights, December Lights."

CONCEPT
FORM/STRUCTURE
SKILLS
SING, PLAY

During the eight days of Hanukkah, Jewish people around the world celebrate the victory of a small group of people over a great army. Each night, children eagerly help light the candles of the menorah. Families and friends exchange small gifts, eat special foods, and sing songs that tell the Hanukkah story. Children have fun playing with a spinning top called a *dreidel*.

S'vivon Sov
Dreidel Spin

CD 21:18

Hebrew Folk Song
English Words by Linda Worsley

Play the rhythm patterns to accompany "S'vivon Sov."

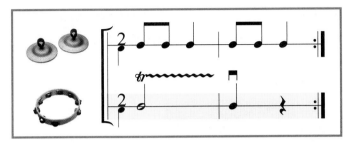

 **Art Gallery**

La Vie

Marc Chagall (1887–1985), often drew subjects based on Jewish life and culture. In this part of his painting *La Vie* (Life), he blends images of animals with people at a celebration.

Las posadas is a Christmas celebration in Mexico and in parts of the southern United States. Families, friends, and neighbors gather to celebrate each night from December 16 through December 24.

Children and adults carry candles and walk behind figures of Mary and Joseph, recreating their journey to Bethlehem. They sing "Para pedir posada" as Mary and Joseph travel from place to place looking for shelter. The first part of this song is a plea, and the second part is an answer. Each time, the answer is that there is "no room" for the pilgrims.

PARA PEDIR POSADA

Looking for Shelter

CD 21:22

Mexican Folk Song
English Version by MMH

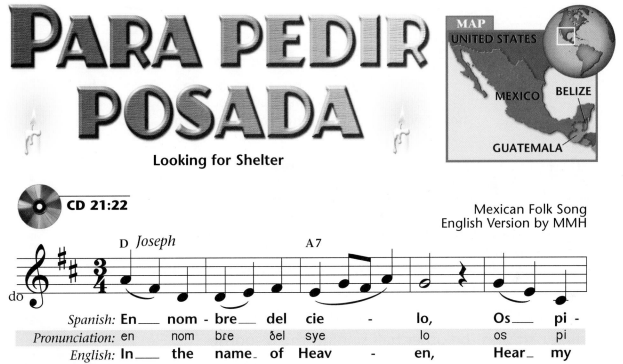

Joseph

Spanish: En_ nom - bre_ del cie - lo, Os_ pi -
Pronunciation: en nom bɾe ðel sye lo os pi
English: In_ the name_ of Heav - en, Hear_ my

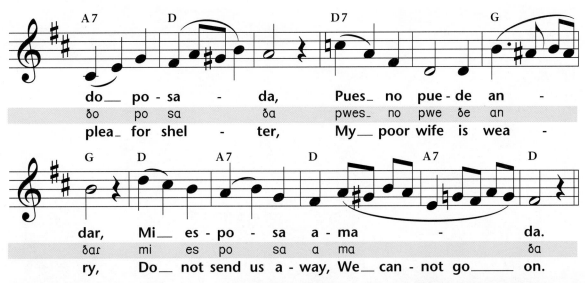

do_ po - sa - da, Pues_ no pue - de an -
ðo po sa ða pwes_ no pwe ðe an
plea_ for shel - ter, My_ poor wife is wea -

dar, Mi es - po - sa a - ma - da.
ðaɾ mi es po sa a ma ða
ry, Do_ not send us a - way, We_ can - not go_ on.

D *Response*   A7

A - quí no__ es me - són, si - gan a - de-
a ki no es me son si gan a ðe
No,__ I have__ no room for__ you here! You must go on,__you

D   D7   G

lan - te, yo__ no pue - do a - brir,
lan te yo no pwe ðo a bɾiɾ
can - not stay, I have no room for you__ to - day!

D   A7   D   A7   D

No__ sea al - gún tu - nan - te.
no sea al gun tu nan te
I do not know who you are, you__ must__ go a - way.

Perform "Para pedir posada" with half of the class singing
the first part and the other half singing the response.

378

After Mary and Joseph reach the place where they are welcomed, everyone sings "Entren, santos peregrinos" (Enter holy pilgrims). Then they celebrate by breaking the *piñata*, a brightly colored papier-mâche figure. The piñata is suspended in the air and is filled with treats. Children take turns breaking the piñata with a stick.

Enter, Holy Pilgrims

CD 21:26

Mexican Folk Song
English Version by MMH

Spanish: En-tren san-tos pe - re - gri - nos, pe - re - gri-nos,— Re - ci-
Pronunciation: en tren san tos pe ɾe gɾi nos pe ɾe gɾi nos ɾe si
English: En - ter in, all ho - ly pil-grims, ho - ly pil - grims.— Wel-come

ban es-te rin - cón, que aun-que es po-bre la mo - ra - da, la mo-
βan es te ɾin koen keaun kes po βɾe la mo ɾa ða la mo
to our hum-ble grove. There is lit - tle we can give you, we can

ra - da,— Os la doy de co - ra - zón.
ɾa ða os la ðoi ðe ko ɾa son
give you,— Still we wel - come you with love.

CONCEPT
RHYTHM

SKILLS
PLAY, SING

This song tells the story of a certain jolly gentleman who works all the year long to bring the gift of joy to children everywhere.

Listen for this rhythm pattern in "Once Upon a Christmastime."

Once Upon a Christmastime

CD 21:30

Words and Music by
Emily Crocker and John Higgins

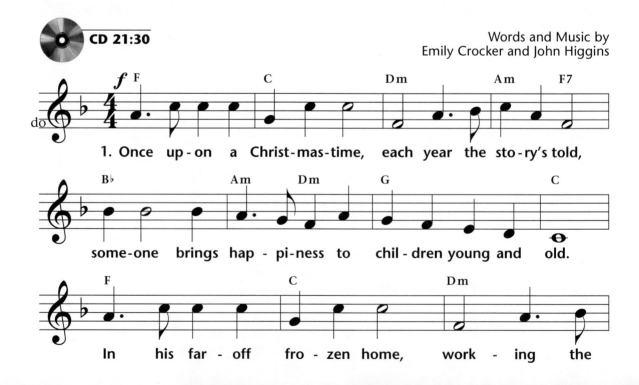

1. Once up-on a Christ-mas-time, each year the sto-ry's told,

some-one brings hap-pi-ness to chil-dren young and old.

In his far-off fro-zen home, work-ing the

whole year through, build - ing toys for girls and boys, he

makes their dreams come true.

2. On and on the sto - ry goes as true as___ true can be,

each year it comes a - gain be - neath the Christ-mas tree.

With - in the heart of ev - 'ry child, a tale that's as

old as time, for hap - py ev - er - af - ter-ing is once up-on a

Christ - mas, once up-on a Christ - mas, a sto - ry-book

Christ - mas, Christ - mas - time.___

To whom will you tell your Christmas wishes?

Jolly Old St. Nicholas

CD 21:33

American Carol

Jol - ly old St. Nich - o - las lean your ear this way.

Don't you tell a sin - gle soul what I'm going to say.

Christ-mas Eve is com - ing soon, now you dear old man,

whis - per what you'll bring to me, tell me if you can.

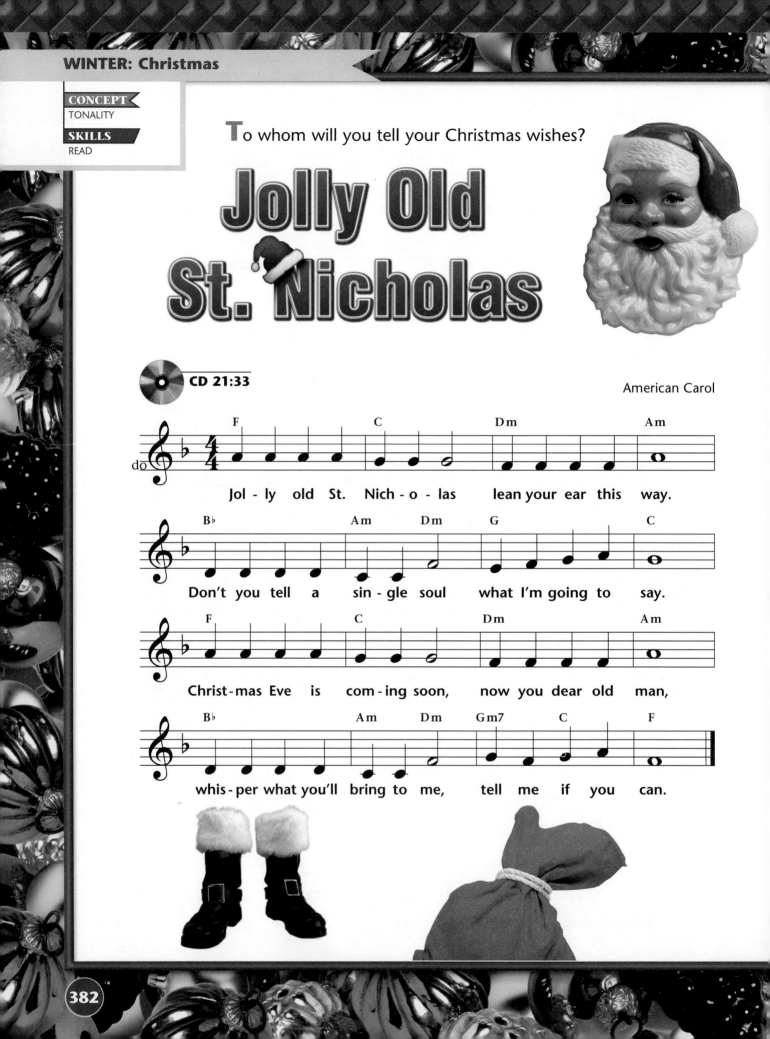

The ideas expressed in this popular Christmas carol come from the Bible. Sing this song and let your joyful feelings show!

Use your arms to follow the melody. Move them down as the pitches go lower, and up as the pitches go higher.

CD 22:1

Music by Lowell Mason
English Poem by Isaac Watts

Joy to the world! the Lord is come.

Let earth re - ceive her King.

Let ev - 'ry heart pre - pare Him room.

And heav'n and na - ture sing, And heav'n and na - ture sing,

And heav'n and heav'n and na - ture sing.

CONCEPT
RHYTHM

SKILLS
READ, LISTEN

The word *Kwanzaa* means "first fruits of the harvest." Kwanzaa is a time when many African American families celebrate their culture, history, and ancestors. This celebration lasts seven days, and uses words from Swahili, an African language.

On one of the days, Kwanzaa celebrates *Nia*, which means "purpose."

CD 22:4

Words and Music by Stan Spottswood

Ni - a stands for pur-pose of our peo-ple, of our fam - i - lies, to make our com-mun-i - ties as great as they can be. We can do this by tak-ing care_ of our homes and com-mun - i - ties, and de - vel-op-ing the skills and the know-ledge of our peo-ple. It's the peo-ple.

Sing Lo Lo Song from Senegal

The English words of this Senegalese song encourage you to dance and have a good time. Performing this song is a way to celebrate the Kwanzaa idea of Umoja, which means unity in Swahili.

CONCEPT
FORM
SKILLS
SING

Martin Luther King, Jr. spoke out for peace and freedom. He believed in peaceful ways of protesting unfair treatment. Dr. King won awards for his actions and ideals about peace and equality for all people. On the third Monday of January we celebrate the life of this very important leader.

In Dr. King's famous "I Have a Dream" speech, he calls for freedom to ring throughout America. He quotes famous words from the Bible, the patriotic song, "My country 'tis of thee, sweet land of liberty…let freedom ring," and from a spiritual, "free at last, free at last, thank God Almighty, I'm free at last."

We Shall Overcome

Musical and Lyrical adaptation by Zilphia Horton, Frank Hamilton, Guy Garawan and Pete Seeger. Inspired by African American Gospel Singing, members of the Food & Tobacco Workers Union, Charleston, SC, and the southern Civil Rights Movement. TRO © Copyright 1960 (Renewed) and 1963 (Renewed) Ludlow Music, Inc., New York, International Copyright Secured. Made In U.S.A. All Rights Reserved Including Public Performance For Profit. Used by Permission. Royalties derived from this composition are being contributed to the We Shall Overcome Fund and The Freedom Movement under the Trusteeship of the Writers.

CD 22:8

African American Spiritual
Adapted by Zilphia Horton, Frank Hamilton,
Guy Caravan and Pete Seeger

1. We shall o - ver - come. ___ We shall o - ver - come. ___ We shall o - ver - come some - day. ___
2. We are not a - fraid. ___ We are not a - fraid. ___ We are not a - fraid to - day. ___
3. Black and white to - geth - er. Black and white to - geth - er. Black and white to - geth - er now. ___
4. We are not a - lone. ___ We are not a - lone. ___ We are not a - lone to - day. ___
5. Whole wide world a - round. ___ Whole wide world a - round. ___ Whole wide world a - round some - day. ___

Oh, ___ deep in my heart, I do be - lieve, we shall o - ver - come some - day.

Valentine's Day is a day to express your feelings for the ones you love. The message of this song is one of friendship. This song is written in a special style of music called the blues, but that doesn't mean it has to be sad!

I Will Be Your Friend

CD 22:11

Words and Music by Guy Davis

Verse

1., 4. If you've got trou-bles and you need a help-ing hand,__
2. If you are hun-gry and you've got no place_ to stay,__
3. If you are lone-ly and you've got no-bod-y_to love,__

If you've got trou-bles and you need a help-ing hand,__
If you are hun-gry and you've got no place_ to stay,__
If you are lone-ly and you've got no bod-y_to love,__

If you've got trou-bles and you need a help-ing hand,__
If you are hun-gry and you've got no place_ to stay,__
If you are lone-ly and you've got no-bod-y_to love,__

__ Come to me, I__ will be your friend.__

Refrain

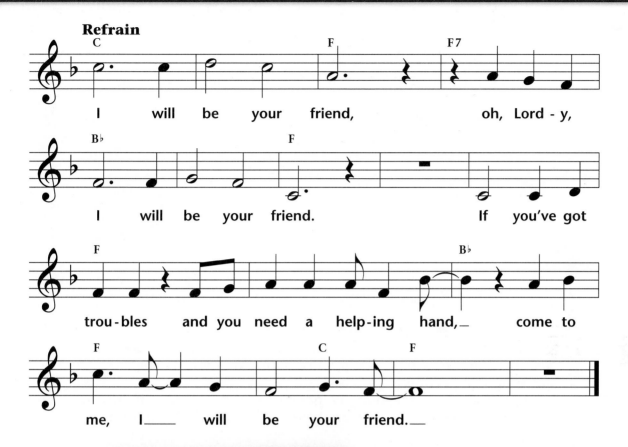

I will be your friend, oh, Lord - y,
I will be your friend. If you've got
trou - bles and you need a help - ing hand, come to
me, I will be your friend.

Write one more verse to "I Will Be Your Friend."

🔘 **LISTENING** ▸ **CD 22:14**

My Friend Mark Kibble and Joel Kibble

Friends are true to each other in good times and in bad.
Listen to this song about friendship, performed by Ray
Charles and the group Take 6. It tells about the meaning of
being a good friend.

CONCEPT
MELODY

SKILLS
READ, SING

Seasonal Songs

When spring arrives, the colors and sounds of the season begin to break through the cold of winter days and nights.

Sing this song about spring in Switzerland.

MAP

SWITZERLAND

ITALY

FRANCE

SPAIN

L'inverno è già passato

Winter Is Over

CD 22:15

Swiss Folk Song
English Words by Linda Worsley

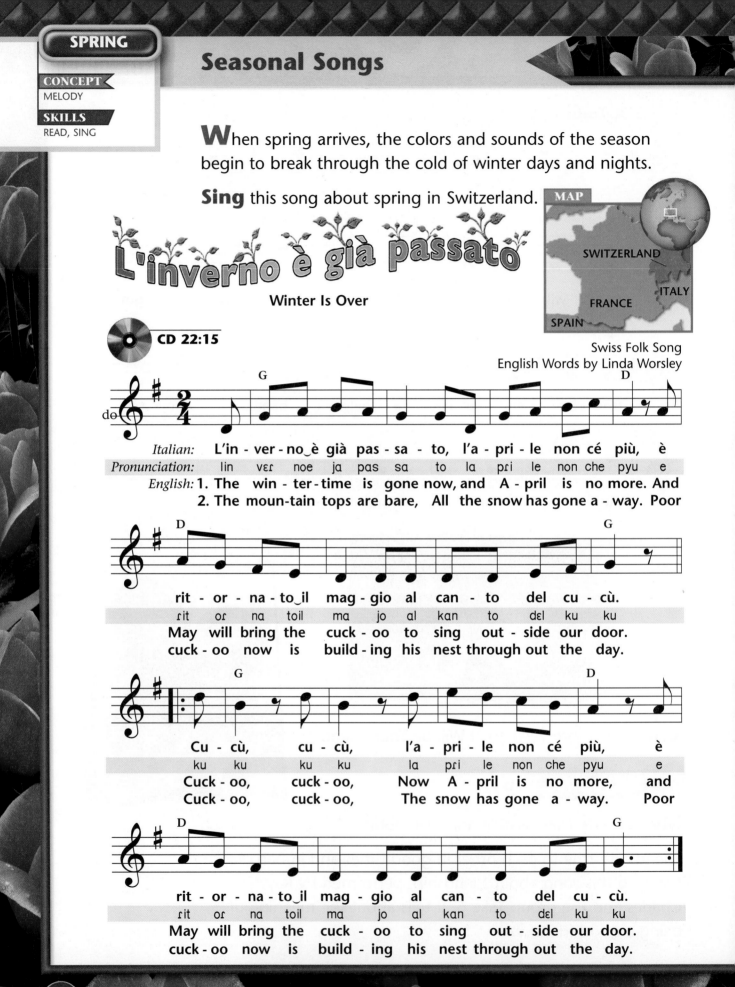

Italian: L'in - ver - no è già pas - sa - to, l'a - pri - le non cé più, è

Pronunciation: lin vɛr noe ja pas sa to la pɾi le non che pyu e

English: 1. The win - ter - time is gone now, and A - pril is no more. And
2. The moun - tain tops are bare, All the snow has gone a - way. Poor

rit - or - na - to il mag - gio al can - to del cu - cù.
ɾit oɾ na toil ma jo al kan to dɛl ku ku
May will bring the cuck - oo to sing out - side our door.
cuck - oo now is build - ing his nest through out the day.

Cu - cù, cu - cù, l'a - pri - le non cé più, è
ku ku ku ku la pɾi le non che pyu e
Cuck - oo, cuck - oo, Now A - pril is no more, and
Cuck - oo, cuck - oo, The snow has gone a - way. Poor

rit - or - na - to il mag - gio al can - to del cu - cù.
ɾit oɾ na toil ma jo al kan to dɛl ku ku
May will bring the cuck - oo to sing out - side our door.
cuck - oo now is build - ing his nest through out the day.

Spring from *The Four Seasons* by Antonio Vivaldi

"Spring" is the first of four concertos for violin from *The Four Seasons*. It has been a favorite ever since it was first performed.

CD-ROM

Use *Orchestral Instruments* CD-ROM to learn more about the violin.

Listening Map for Spring

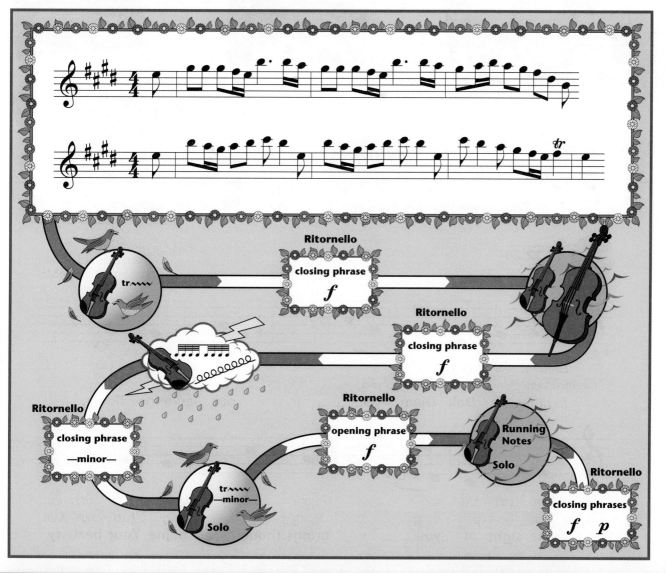

The Laotian New Year is celebrated in April. It is a time of great festivity that lasts for days. On the first day of the new year, people go to the temple and pray for good health and prosperity for the coming year.

For the remaining days of the celebration, people put on a parade with songs and dance.

Dok Djampa

The White Jasmine Flower

MAP
MYANMAR
LAOS
THAILAND
KAMPUCHEA   VIETNAM

CD 22:20

Traditional Laotian
English Words by MMH

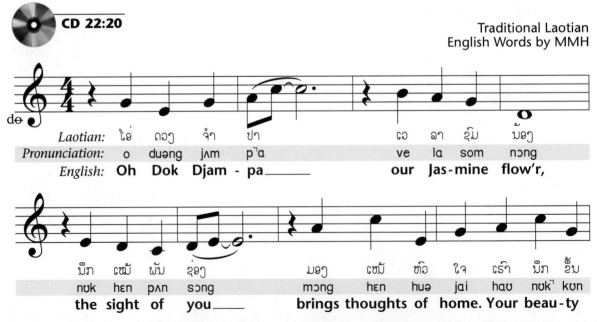

Laotian: ໂອ ດວງ ຈຳ ປາ   ເວ ລາ ຊົມ ນ້ອງ
Pronunciation: o duəng jʌm pʰa   ve la som nɔng
English: Oh Dok Djam - pa_____   our Jas-mine flow'r,

ນຶກ ເຫັນ ພັນ ຊ້ອງ   ມວງ ເຫັນ ຫົວ ໃຈ ເຮົາ ນຶກ ຂຶ້ນ
nʊk hɛn pʌn sɔng   mɔng hɛn huə jai hau nʊk kʊn
the sight of you_____   brings thoughts of home. Your beau-ty

392

The *dok djampa,* a white jasmine flower, is the national flower of Laos. It can be found growing everywhere, from the countryside to the cities. It is often found growing near temples, where its lovely fragrance fills the air. The flower represents sincerity and the joy of life.

Sing this traditional Laotian song.

Use *World Instruments* **CD-ROM** to learn more about Southeast Asian instruments.

On Earth Day we are reminded to look at the world around us and to learn about what needs to be done to protect its beauty. This song reminds us of the Earth's beauty and how important it is to care for our surroundings.

We Are Here

CD 22:24

Words and Music by Sharon Burch

Moth-er Earth says now take good care of me.

Please do not hurt me, Hey, hey-ey-o, Hey-o-hey-o, hey-o.

And Fath-er Sky says now take good care of me.
And all liv-ing crea-tures say take good care of us.

Please do not hurt me.}
Please do not hurt us.} Hey, hey-ey-o, Hey-o, hey-o, hey-o.

And we are here to be our-selves, to

be with one an-oth-er, to be with our sur-round-ings. To

be, to be. And we are here to take
And we are here take to

care of our-selves, to take care of one an-oth-er, to take
love___ our-selves, to love___ one an-oth-er, to

care of our sur-round-ings. Take care to care.
love___ our sur-round-ings. To love, to love, to

love. *Navajo:* **Na-has-dzáán a-nii-la ni-zhó-ní-go shaa hoł-ya**
Pronunciation: na has dzan a ni la nɪ ʒɔ nɪ go sha hoł ya

zhó-ní-go shaa hoł-ya, Hey, hey-ey-o,
ʒɔ nɪ go sha hoł ya hel hel i yo

Hey-o, hey-o, hey-o. Hey, hey-ey-o, Hey-o, hey-o, hey-o.
hel yo hel yo hel yo hel hel i yo hel yo hel yo hel yo

Meet the Musician

The song "We Are Here" was written by
Sharon Burch, a Navajo composer whose
music is based on the songs that her
grandfather, a Navajo medicine man, would
sing during ceremonies. She has performed in
many countries in the world, but always enjoys
returning home to perform for her people.

Seasonal Songs

The ulili, or sandpiper, is a seabird. Ulili is also the Hawaiian name for a bamboo flute which sounds like the sound of the ulili's song—"to-li-li-li-li." The ulili announces the arrival of predators with its call. "ʻUlili E" tells of the musical nature of the ulili bird. This Hawaiian folk song is often performed at Hawaiian Aloha Festivals that begin in August and end in October.

ʻUlili E

The Sandpiper

CD 22:28

Traditional Hawaiian Folk Song
English Text by John Higgins

English: Can you hear the sand-pi-per call a-cross the shore? O lit-tle
Hawaiian: Ho - ne a - na ko le-o e ʻu-li-li e, I ka-hi
Pronunciation: ho ne a nʌ ko le o e ʻu li li e i ka hi

bird dart-ing through the foam-y sea. Yes, ev-er watch-ful is he up-on the
ma-nu no-ho ʻa-e ka-i, Ki-a-ʻi ma ka la-e a ʻo ke-
ma nu no ho ʻa e ka i ki a ʻi ma ka la e a ʻo ke

wa - ter, He makes his home where the sea is al-ways calm.
ka - ha, ʻO-i-a kai u-a la-na ma - li-e.
ka ha ʻo i a kai u a la na ma li e

Sand-pi-per calls) ʻU-li-li e { A-ha-ha-na ʻu-li-li he-he-ne ʻu-
ʻu li li e a ha ha nʌ ʻu li li e he hɛ ne ʻu

Playing the Recorder

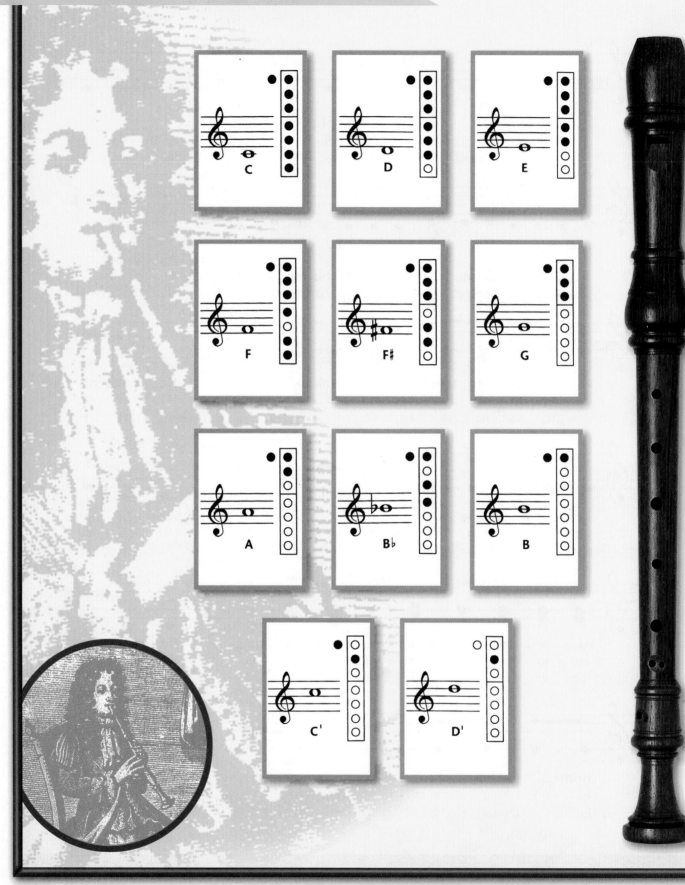

Glossary of Instruments

accordion a hand-held keyboard instrument that is played by pressing keys or buttons while air is forced through the instrument. It is often played while standing, and is held by straps over the shoulders, **CD 24:10**

bagpipe a member of the woodwind family that is played by blowing air through a tube into the bag and then pressing the bag so that the air is forced out through the pipes, **88 CD 24:11**

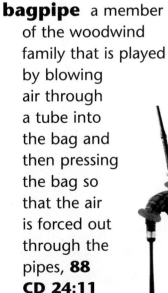

banjo a member of the string family that is played by plucking or strumming the strings, **31 CD 24:20**

bass drum a large member of the percussion family that gives a deep sound when hit, **CD 23:32**

bassoon a member of the woodwind family that is played by blowing into the reed while covering holes along the body with fingers, **CD 23:15**

cello the second-largest member of the string family in an orchestra, which is held between the knees and played by bowing or plucking the strings, **178 CD 23:6**

clarinet a member of the woodwind family that is played by blowing into the mouthpiece while covering holes along the body with fingers, **31 CD 23:12**

conga a percussion instrument used in Latin America that has a low-pitched sound when struck, **CD 24:30**

cymbal A dish-shaped percussion instrument that is often played by hitting one against another to make a clashing sound, **CD 23:37**

djembe a West African drum usually made from pottery or wood that is played with the hands, **CD 24:2**

double bass the largest instrument of the string family in an orchestra, which is held upright and played by bowing or plucking the strings, **CD 23:7**

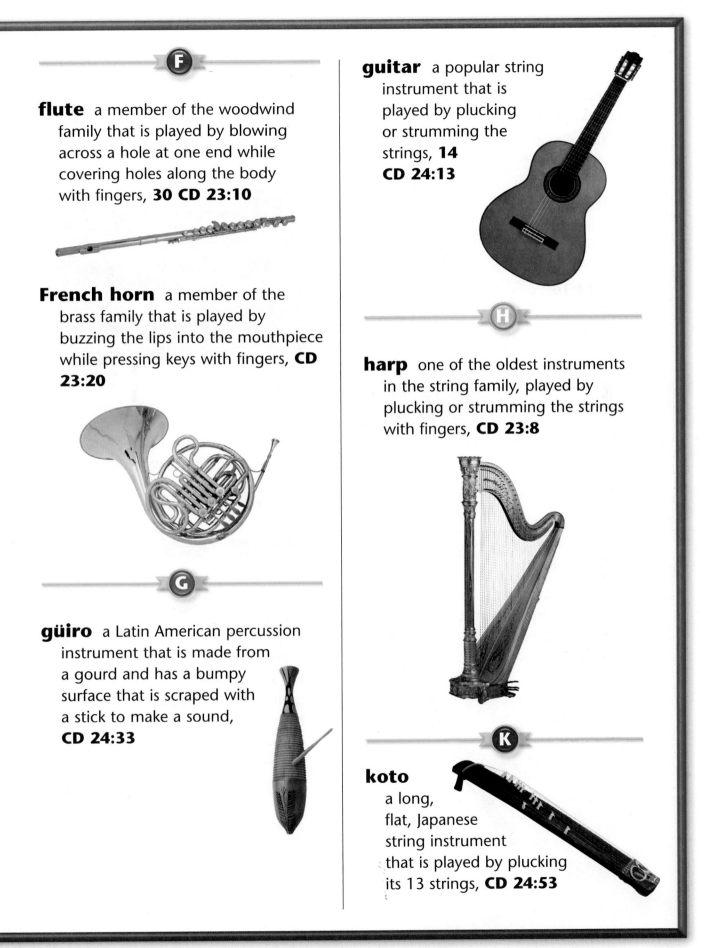

flute a member of the woodwind family that is played by blowing across a hole at one end while covering holes along the body with fingers, **30 CD 23:10**

French horn a member of the brass family that is played by buzzing the lips into the mouthpiece while pressing keys with fingers, **CD 23:20**

güiro a Latin American percussion instrument that is made from a gourd and has a bumpy surface that is scraped with a stick to make a sound, **CD 24:33**

guitar a popular string instrument that is played by plucking or strumming the strings, **14 CD 24:13**

harp one of the oldest instruments in the string family, played by plucking or strumming the strings with fingers, **CD 23:8**

koto a long, flat, Japanese string instrument that is played by plucking its 13 strings, **CD 24:53**

mandolin a member of the string family that is similar to a guitar, but it has a different body shape and 8 metal strings, **CD 24:16**

maracas Latin American percussion instruments played in pairs by shaking when held at the handles, **CD 24:35**

oboe a double-reed woodwind instrument that is played by blowing into the reed while covering holes along the body with fingers, **CD 23:13**

piano a percussion instrument that is played by pressing the keys on the keyboard, **66 CD 23:41**

piccolo one of the smaller members of the woodwind family that is a small flute that plays high pitches, **CD 23:11**

saxophone a member of the woodwind family that is played by blowing into the mouthpiece while pushing the keys along the body with fingers, **CD 23:16**

402

shekere an African percussion instrument that is a hollow gourd covered with a net of beads or seeds and is played by shaking, **CD 24:8**

slit drum
a percussion instrument used in Africa, Asia, and the South Pacific that is formed by hollowing a tree trunk through a slit on one side and played by hitting with sticks, **CD 24:9**

snare drum
a member of the percussion family that is played by hitting the top of the drum with drumsticks to vibrate wires along the bottom, **31 CD 23:35**

spoons a common object used as a percussion instrument by holding two together and hitting them against the body. **14 CD 24:23**

taiko drum
a barrel-shaped Japanese percussion instrument that is played with sticks, or *bachi*, **CD 24:51**

tambourine
a small, hand-held percussion instrument that has metal disks attached loosely around the rim and is played by shaking or hitting it with the hand, **31 CD 23:36**

timpani percussion instruments that are a set of large kettle-shaped drums, played with mallets and tuned to different pitches, **CD 23:26**

trombone a large, low-pitched member of the brass family, which is played by buzzing the lips into the mouthpiece while moving the slide in and out, **CD 23:21**

trumpet the smallest, highest-pitched member of the brass family, which is played by buzzing the lips into the mouthpiece while pressing keys with fingers, **CD 23:18**

tuba the largest, lowest-pitched member of the brass family, which is played by buzzing the lips into the mouthpiece while pressing keys with fingers, **CD 23:22**

viola a member of the string family slightly larger than the violin, which is held under the chin and played by bowing or plucking the strings, **CD 23:5**

violin the smallest member of the string family in an orchestra, which is held under the chin and played by bowing or plucking the strings, **31 CD 23:4**

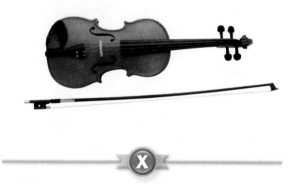

xylophone a percussion instrument that is played by hitting the wooden bars with small wooden hammers, or mallets, **CD 23:30**

Glossary of Terms

A

accent (>) a symbol that shows stress or emphasis on a note or chord, **282**

articulation how notes are played, **208**

augmentation changing a rhythm by making it last twice as long, **216**

B

bassoon a double-reed woodwind instrument that can play very low pitches, **116**

beat the pulse felt in most music, **6**

C

call and response a song form in which a phrase sung by a solo leader is followed by a phrase sung by a group, **70**

calypso a folk music style that was created in the Caribbean islands, **72**

candombe a style of music that was created in Uruguay, typically played for carnivals and festivals, **93**

canon a song form with two or more voices in which the melody is introduced and imitated one or more times, similar to a round, **16**

chord three or more pitches sounded together, **113**

contour the way a melody moves up and down, **12**

D

descant a second melody that is sung above the main melody of the song, **154**

downstage the space on the stage closest to the audience, **291**

duet music written for two performers, **9**

dynamics the loudness or softness of music, **106**

E

eighth notes (♫) musical notes that are half a quarter note, **15**

eighth rest a rest that equals one half a quarter rest.

F

flat (♭) a symbol in the key signature or in front of a note that means the pitch should be sung or played a half step lower, **110**

form the order of phrases or sections, or the plan, of a piece of music, **25**

fusion music musical traditions of more than one culture blended together, including compositions, styles, languages, and instruments, **208**

half note ($\\half$) a symbol for a sound the length of two quarter notes, **15**

harmony two or more pitches sung or played at the same time, **111**

homophony blending two or more lines with the melody that have the same words and rhythm, to be in unison, **218**

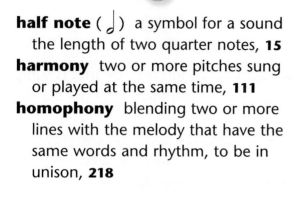

jug a ceramic bottle that is used as an instrument in a jug band, played by buzzing the lips into the opening, **76**

jug band a band that uses simple items as instruments, such as jugs, washboards, and washtubs, **76**

K

key signature the sharps or flats at the beginning of each staff, **110**

L

ledger line a line added above or below the staff, **55**

legato in a smooth and flowing manner, **208**

letter names one way pitches on a staff can be identified, **71**

longways set a dance formation involving several pairs of dancers, the "head couple" at one end of the set and the "foot couple" at the other end, **51**

lullabies quiet songs sung to help babies go to sleep, **18**

major the sound of music that has *do* for its tonal center and uses the pitches of a major scale, **171**

major scale a specific set of eight pitches from *do* to *do*' **180, 186**

melody a series of pitches that moves upward, downward, or stays the same; a tune **11**

meter signature the symbol that tells how many beats are grouped in each measure and what kind of note equals one beat, **8**

minor the sound of music that has *la* for its tonal center and uses the pitches of a minor scale, **171**

minor scale a specific set of eight pitches from *la* to *la*' **186**

O

octave a leap of eight steps between two pitches, **129**

ornaments extra pitches or groups of pitches added to a melody to decorate it, **223**

ostinato a rhythmic or melodic pattern that repeats over and over, **37**

pentatonic scale a scale of five pitches, for example, *do re mi so la*, **21**

phrase a complete musical sentence or idea, **22**

polyphony the overlapping of two or more melodic lines, as in rounds, canons, and descants, **218**

presto very fast, **190**

program music story-telling or image-making music, **116**

quarter note (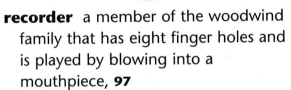) the symbol for a note that equals two eighth notes, **15**

quarter rest ( ) a symbol for a silence the length of a quarter note, **15**

recorder a member of the woodwind family that has eight finger holes and is played by blowing into a mouthpiece, **97**

repeated notes notes sounding on the same pitch, **91**

rhythm the patterns of long and short sounds and silences in music, **15**

rondalla a group of plucked string instruments, **105**

root the pitch on which a chord is built, **143**

round a type of canon; a short song for three or more voices in which each voice begins at a different time, **16**

score written music that shows all the parts to be performed together, **28**

sections groups of related phrases that form a larger unit, **67**

skip one way a melody moves; to move higher or lower by jumping over a pitch, **91**

spiritual a song from the African American tradition that has religious meaning, **65**

staccato in a short and clipped manner, **208**

stage left the space to the left of the actor when facing the audience, **291**

stage right the space to the right of the actor when facing the audience, **291**

step one way a melody moves; to move higher or lower to the next pitch, **91**

syncopation a type of rhythm in which stressed sounds occur between beats instead of on beats, **139**

tempo the speed of the beat, **190**

tempo changes using different tempos to make music more expressive, **191**

theme the main musical idea of a piece, **236**

tie (⌣ or ⌢) a curved line that connects two notes of the same pitch and means that the sound should be held for the length of both notes, **139**

tonal center the home tone or the pitch around which a melody is centered, **21**, **50**

tone color the special sound of each instrument or voice, **28**

triad a chord of three pitches, **148**

U

upstage the space on the stage farthest away from the audience, **291**

V

variation a changed version of a theme or melody, **236**

---

waltz a type of slow dance performed by a couple in which the music has three beats to a measure, **229**

washboard a grooved piece of metal set in a wooden frame that used to be used for scrubbing clothes and is played as an instrument in a jug band by scraping fingernails or fingers in thimbles across the metal piece to create a rhythm, **76**

washtub bass an instrument played in a jug band, built using a metal washtub, a broomstick or garden-tool handle, and some cotton or nylon line and whose pitch can be changed by moving the stick to tighten or loosen the single string, **76**

whole note a note that equals four quarter notes, **127**

woodwind a wind instrument that is or once was made of wood, **60**

Acknowledgments, continued

CREDITS

Illustration Credits: Paul Bachem: 104, 105, 128. Timothy Banks: iv, Spotlight on Concepts (2). Richard Bernal: 46–47. Shennen Bersani: 336. Ka Botzis: 103. Gina Capaldi: 10–11, 358–359. Antonio Castro: vi, Spotlight on Performance (2), 247, 305, 338. Bradley Clark: 168, 169, 178–179, 180–181. Renee Daily: 48–49. Bob Doucet: 312. Louise Ellis: 126–127, 380. Leslie Evans: 226–227. Peter Fasolino: 308–309. Tina Fong: v, Spotlight on Music Reading (2). Jo Gershman: 074–075. Renee Graef: 123. Shelly Hehenberger: vii, Spotlight on Celebrations (2). Jui Ishida: 337. John Kanzler: 30–31, 344. Diana Kizlauskas: 327, 328–329. Nora Koeber: 88–89. Erin Eitter Kono: 368, 385. Fran Lee: 232, 320. Margaret Lindmark: 340. Deborah Maze: 328. Yoshi Miyake: 345, 347. Suzanne Mogensen: 26–27. Cheryl Kirk Noll: 134–135, 136–137. David Opie: 98–99. Donna Perrone: 152–153, 378. Gary Phillips: 192–193. Stacey Schuett: 206–207. Charlie Shaw: 142–143. Janet K. Skiles: 122, 123. Adam Turner: 188–189. Sally Jo Vitsky: 330–331, 332–333. Siri Weber Feeney: 106, 108, 322–323, 324–325. Elizabeth Wolf: 92, 342.

Photography Credits: all photographs are by Macmillan/McGraw-Hill (MMH) except as noted below.

Allan Landau/MMH: cover. iv-vii: trombone. A-H: (bcl tl). 42-43. 51: (tl c br). 58: (bc). 69: (tl tr b). 70: (cl). 71: (cr). 82-83. 116: (tcr). 118: (br). 122-123. 129: (tc). 149: (t). 179. 189: (br). 202-203. 237: (tl tr cl cr). 403: (tcl bl). 404: (tl). Shane Morgan for MMH: 9. 33. 95: (c). 96: (tr). 148: (bcr bc br). 151. 167. 171: (tl tcl tcl tr).

iv-vii: (trumpet, silver drum, decorated drum, French horn) Corbis; (others) PhotoDisc/Getty Images. A: (tr) Corbis; (tcr tc) PhotoDisc/Getty Images. A-H: (bcr) Comstock/Getty Images; (tr) Corbis; (bl tcr) PhotoDisc/Getty Images; (cl tc) Rubberball. C-D: (bkgd) Photolink/Getty Images. G: (cl) Corbis; (tr br) Photolink/Getty Images. G-H: (bkgd) PhotoDisc/Getty Images. H: (bcr) PhotoDisc/Getty Images. 2 3: Bob Daemmrich/PhotoEdit. 4: (l) Bob Daemmrich/PhotoEdit; (br) PhotoDisc/Getty Images. 4-5: (bkgd) Hulton Archive/Getty Images. 5: (tl r) PhotoDisc/Getty Images. 6-7: (r) Ariel Skelley/Corbis; (bkgd) Corel. 8: (br) National Gallery, London, UK/Bridgeman Art Library, © 2011 Estate of Pablo Picasso/Artists Rights Society (ARS), NY. 8-9: (bkgd) Corel. 9: (tr) Photography by Carol Friedman. 10-11: (t) Corel. 12-13: (bkgd) Maury Christian/Corbis Sygma; (t) Corel. 13: (c) Angel Millan/AP Images; (tr) Fox Model 500 English horn, photo courtesy Fox Products Corporation, South Whitley, IN, US. 14: (br) PhotoDisc/Getty Images; (bl) Artville LLC. 14-15: (bkgd) Artville LLC. 16-17: (bkgd). Corel. 17: (cr) Slawsongs. 18-19: Bob Rowan; Progressive Image/Corbis. 20-21: The Newark Museum/Art Resource, NY. 22-23: (bkgd) PhotoDisc/Getty Images. 23: (tr) Corbis; (bl) PhotoDisc/Getty Images; (cr) Redferns/Getty Images. 24: (tr) Patrick Robert/Sygma/Corbis; (bc bl) Roger De La Harpe/Gallo Images/Corbis. 24-25: (bc) David Turnley/Corbis. 26-27: MetaCreations/Kai Power Photos. 28-29: (bkgd) Corel; (t) MetaCreations/Kai Power Photos. 35: Keith Mallett. 36: (c) PhotoDisc/Getty Images. 36-37: (bkgd) PhotoDisc/Getty Images. 38: (t) Fox Model 500 English horn, photo courtesy Fox Products Corporation, South Whitley, IN, US. 44: (l) Comstock Images. 45: (t): PhotoDisc/Getty Images. 48: Marg Hewson. 50-53: Bettmann/Corbis. 54-55: (bkgd) Nathan Benn/Corbis; (t) Corel. 56: (br) Shelley Gazin/Corbis. 56-57: (bkgd c) courtesy Lucasfilm Ltd.; (t) Corel. 58: (bl tl bcl) Corbis; (cr cl) PhotoDisc/Getty Images. 59: Corel. 60: (bl) Kelly-Mooney Photography/Corbis; (br) Roger De La Harpe/Gallo Images/Corbis; (tr). 60-61: (bkgd) Corel. 61: (cr) Archivo Iconografico, S.A/Corbis; (br) Viviane Moos/Corbis; (bl) Liu Liqun/Corbis; (tr) PhotoDisc/Getty Images. 62 63: Bettman/Corbis. 64: (br) Reprinted with permission of ASCAP; (cr) PhotoDisc/Getty Images. 65: Corel. 66-67: (bkgd) Wolfgang Kaehler/Corbis; (t) Corel. 67: (tr) Corbis. 68-69: (bkgd) Israel images/Alamy; (t) Corel. 68: (br) Marc Chagall, Danseuse à la robe fleurie., 1971 © 2011 Artists Rights Society (ARS), New York/ADAGP, Paris/Photo © Christie's Images/The Bridgeman Art Library. 69: (t) Corel. 72-73: (bkgd) David Madison/Getty Images. 73: (br) Betmann/Corbis. 75: (bkgd) Ernesto Gomez. 76: (tr br c) Ernesto Gomez; (c) PhotoDisc/Getty Images; (bl) Photo Spin/Getty Images. 76 77: (bkgd) PhotoDisc/Getty Images. 77: (br bl) Ernesto Gomez; (cl tl) Mark Wagoner Productions. 80: (tr) PhotoDisc/Getty Images. 86-87: Michael Maslan Historic Photographs/Corbis. 90-91: (bkgd) M. Timothy O'Keefe/Photoshot. 91: (cr) Travelsite/Colasanti/DeA Picture Library. 93: (t) Marcelo Hernandez/AP Images; (b) Miguel Rojo/AFP/Getty Images. 96: (br) Dagli Orti/Musée des Beaux Arts Dijon/The Art Archive. 100: Corbis. 101: (t) Julian Coche Mendoza/Arte Maya Tz'utuhil; (r) Dave G. Houser/Corbis. 104: (c) Joe Carini/Pacific Stock; (b) Hinata Haga/HAGA/The Image Works. 105: Paul A. Souders/Corbis. 106-107: PhotoDisc/Getty Images. 108: (c) Bettmann/Corbis; (br) Horace Bristol/Corbis. 108 109: (bkgd) Jeremy Hoare/Life File/Getty Images. 109: (tr) Horace Bristol/Corbis. 110-111: Hugh Beebower/Corbis. 112-113: (bkgd) Richard T. Nowitz/Corbis. 113: (br) Courtesy of Judith Yellin-Ginat. 114: (tr) Billy Rose Theatre Collection, The New York Public Library for the Performing Arts, Astor, Lenox and Tilden Foundations; (l bl) PhotoDisc/Getty Images. 115: (tr) PhotoDisc/Getty Images; (r) MetaCreations/Kai Power Photos. 116: (bcr) Corbis; (tcr, cr, bl, br) PhotoDisc/Getty Images. 117: (c) Fox Model 500 English horn, photo courtesy of Fox Products Corporation, South Whitley, IN, US; (t cl cr br c bl bcr) PhotoDisc/Getty Images. 120: (br) PhotoDisc/Getty Images. 121: (bcr bl) PhotoDisc/Getty Images; (c) C Squared Studios/Getty Images; (tr) courtesy U.S. Army. 124: Carol Rosegg Photography. 125: (tl) Comstock Images; (tr) Corbis. 128: (tr r) PhotoDisc/Getty Images. 128-129: (b) Sergio Pitamitz/Corbis. 130-131: PhotoDisc/Getty Images. 131: (tr) Philadelphia Museum of Art/Corbis. 132-133: Charles & Josette Lenars/Corbis. 134: Wolfgang Kaehler/Wolfgang Kaehler Photography. 138-139: (bkgd) North Wind Picture Archives; (t) SambaPhoto/Julio Bittencourt/Getty Images. 140: (bl) Tiziana and Gianni Baldizzone/Corbis; (br) Hideo Haga/HAGA/The Image Works; (t c) SambaPhoto/Julio Bittencourt/Getty Images. 140-141: (bkgd) Dennis Hallinan/Alamy. 141: (bc) Tiziana and Gianni Baldizzone/Corbis; (bl) Philadelphia Museum of Art/Corbis; (br) North Wind Picture Archives; (t) SambaPhoto/Julio Bittencourt/Getty Image. 143: AP Images. 144: (c) Volker Dornberger/DPA/Landov; (br) R. Booth/Lebrecht Music & Arts Photo Library. 144-145: (bkgd) Corel. 146-147: (t) Corel; (bkgd) Artville LLC. 148-149: PhotoDisc/Getty Images. 150-151: Jeremy Woodhouse/Getty Images. 153: Pool/Kirsty Wigglesworth/Reuters/Corbis. 154-155: Tria Giovan/Corbis. 156-157: (bkgd) Corbis. 157: (bl) Corbis; (br c) PhotoDisc/Getty Images. 158: PhotoDisc/Getty Images. 162: (br) David Hiser/Stone/Getty Images. 162 163: (c) AP Images; (bkgd) Stocktrek/Corbis. 163: (tr) Keren Su/Corbis. 164: (bl) Stocktrek/Corbis; (tr) MetaCreation/Kai Power Photos. 166-167: EPA/Jon Hrusa/AP Images. 168-169: (bkgd) Bo Zaunders/Corbis. 169: (tr) Hamburg Kunsthalle, Hamburg, Germany/Bridgeman Art Library. 170-171: Corbis. 172-173: (bkgd) Corbis. 173: (cr) Bojan Brecelj/Corbis; (r) PhotoDisc/Getty Images. 174: (t) Giraudon/Bridgeman Art Library. 174-175: (bkgd) Corbis. 175: (tr) Giraudon/Bridgeman Art Library. 176: (br) North Wind Picture Archives; (tr) Stapleton Collection, UK/Bridgeman Art Library. 176-177: (bkgd) Corbis. 177: (tl) Lebrecht Music & Arts Photo Library; (br) SuperStock/SuperStock. 178-179: MetaCreations/Kai Power Photos. 180-181: (t) MetaCreations/Kai Power Photos. 181: (br) Erich Hartmann/Magnum Photos. 182-183: (bkgd) Corbis. 183: (tr) Corbis. 184-185: Neil Beer /Corbis. 184: (cl cr bc) Mary Goetze. 186-187: Alain Le Garsmeur/Getty Images. 189: Corbis. 190-191: Robbie Jack/Corbis. 195 (tl) Kelly-Mooney Photography/Corbis; (tr) PhotoDisc/Getty Images. 196-197: (bkgd) J. Michael Short/JMS. 197: (cr) J. Michael Short/JMS; (tr) Multi-Ethnic Cultural and Arts Association. 199: MetaCreations/Kai Power Photos. 200: PhotoDisc/Getty Images. 204: (tr) Reuters/Corbis; (bl) Corbis. 205: Flip Schulke/Corbis. 206-207: Corel. 208-209: (bkgd t) Corel. 208: (cr br) Image Club. 209: (r) Jack Vartoogian/FrontRowPhotos; (br) David Atlas/Retna. 210-211: (t) Corbis; (bkgd) ML Sinibaldi/Corbis. 211: (tr) Dave Bartruff/Corbis. 212: (bl) Dave G. Houser/Corbis; (tr) Morton Beebe/Corbis; (br) PhotoDisc/Getty Images; (br) Image Farm. 212-213: (bkgd) Larry Lee Photography/Corbis; (t) Corbis. 213: (tr) Annebicque Bernard /Corbis/Sygma. 214-215: Terje Rakke/Getty Images. 216: (bl) Bob Nugent; (br tr) PhotoDisc/Getty Images. 216-217: (bkgd) Layne Kennedy/Corbis. 217: (tr br) PhotoDisc/Getty Images. 218-221: Marilyn Root/Photolibrary. 222: (c) Victoria & Albert Museum, London/Art Resource, NY. 222-223: (bkgd) Reunion des Musees Nationaux/Art Resource, NY. 223: (tr) Attar Maher/Corbis/Sygma. 224: Niels Poulsen/Alamy. 255: (t) The Gallery Collection/ Corbis; (b) Ken Walsh/Alamy. 226-227: Corel. 228: (l br) Jack Vartoogian/FrontRowPhotos. 228-229: Corel. 230-231: Jeremy Horner/Corbis; (t) Corel. 232: (tr) Redferns/Getty Images. 232-233: (t) Corel. 233: (tr) Corbis. 234-235: MetaCreations/Kai Power Photos. 236-237: Christine Osborne/Worldwide Picture Library/Alamy. 238: PhotoDisc/Getty Images. 242: Archivo Iconografico, S.A./Corbis. 261: Corel. 262-264: PhotoDisc/Getty Images. 267: PhotoDisc/Getty Images. 268: Corel. 271: PhotoDisc/Getty Images. 276: Corbis. 290: (b) MTI; (cl) PhotoDisc/Getty Images; (cl) Corel. 291: (c) MTI; (cr) Artville LLC. 292: PhotoDisc/Getty Images. 295-297: PhotoDisc/Getty Images. 298: MTI. 300: ImageClub. 303: MTI. 305: (c) MTI; (br) PhotoDisc/Getty Images. 306: Bettmann/Corbis. 307-309: PhotoDisc/Getty Images. 310: (bl) Bettmann/Corbis; (tr) Harold M. Lambert/Getty Images. 311-313: PhotoDisc/Getty Images. 314: Bettmann/Corbis. 315: PhotoDisc/Getty Images. 316: (br tl l bl) PhotoDisc/Getty Images; (tr) Rubberball; (cl) Stockbyte/Getty Images. 317: PhotoDisc/Getty Images. 319: (br) Everett Collection; (tr) PhotoDisc/Getty Images. 321: PhotoDisc/Getty Images. 323: PhotoDisc/Getty Images. 325: PhotoDisc/Getty Images; (b) Barry Lewis/Alamy. 326 327: Photodisc/Getty Images. 328: Logan Mock-Bunting/Getty Images. 329 331 333: PhotoDisc/Getty Images. 335: (t) Ariel Skelley/Corbis; (tr) PhotoDisc/Getty Images. 337: PhotoDisc/Getty Images. 339 341: PhotoDisc/Getty Images. 343: (br) Terry Cryer/Corbis; (tr) Corel. 345: Corel. 347 349: Corel. 351: (b) Galen Rowell/Corbis; (tr) Corel. 354-355: PhotoDisc/Getty Images. 356: (tr) The Granger Collection, New York. 356-357: (flags, bunting, red hat, bow) PhotoDisc/Getty Images; (star, white hat, bell) Image Club. 358 361: PhotoDisc/Getty Images. 362: (tl tr) PhotoDisc/Getty Images. 363: PhotoDisc/Getty Images. 364: (tl br bl) PhotoDisc/Getty Images. 364-365: (bkgd) MetaCreations/Kai Power Photos. 365: (b) Bridgeman-Giraudon/Art Resource. 367: (cl) Reuters/Corbis; (cr) Philippe Giraud/Corbis. 368-369: PhotoDisc/Getty Images. 370-371: (bkgd) PhotoDisc/Getty Images; (bkgd) ImageClub. 370: (tr tl) PhotoDisc/Getty Images. 372-373: (bkgd) Corbis; (yellow light, red light, green light, blue light, bulb cord) PhotoDisc/Getty Images. 373: (br) Artville LLC. 374 375: (bkgd) PhotoDisc/Getty Images; (bkgd) Image Club. 374: (tl) Image Club. 375: (tr) MetaCreations/Kai Power Photos; (b) Marc Chagall, La Vie, 1964 © 2011 Artists Rights Society (ARS), New York/ADAGP, Paris. 376: (cl) AP Images; (br) Keith Dannemiller/Corbis; (cr) Corbis; (bl) PhotoDisc/Getty Images. 380-381: PhotoDisc/Getty Images. 382-383: (bkgd) PhotoDisc/Getty Images; (bkgd) Image Club. 382: (bl) Pat LaCroix/Getty Images; (tr br) PhotoDisc/Getty Images. 383: Corel. 384: (tl) Comstock Images; (tr) PhotoDisc/Getty Images. 385: (tr) Ariel Skelley/Corbis; (tl) Richard Lord/PhotoEdit. 386-387: PhotoDisc/Getty Images. 386: (br) Flip Schulke/Corbis; (cr) Hulton Archive/Getty Images; (bl) Hulton Archive/Getty Images. 389: (bl) Corbis; (br) PhotoDisc/Getty Images. 390-391: Corbis. 392-393: (bkgd) PhotoDisc/Getty Images. 392: (c) Garden City Telegram/AP Images; (cr) Alison Wright/Corbis; (cl) Nevada Wier/Corbis. 393: (br) Corbis. 394-395: Corbis. 395: (br) Photo by John Running courtesy Canyon Records. 396-397: PhotoDisc/Getty Images. 398: Bettmann/Corbis. 399: Photodisc/Getty Images. 400: (br) Jules Frazier/Getty Images; (cl cr) PhotoDisc/Getty Images. 401: (tl br) PhotoDisc/Getty Images. 402-404: PhotoDisc/Getty Images.

All attempts have been made to provide complete and correct credits by the time of publications.

Classified Index

CHORAL SONGS

Arroyito serrano
(Little Mountain Stream), **340**
At the Hop, **306**
Circle of Song, **330**
Don't Let the Music Stop, **334**
Down at the Twist and Shout,
308
E nānā kākou i nā manu (Let's
Watch the Birds), **338**
Eagle, **337**
Hitori, **345**
Kettle Valley Line, The, **348**
La Yunsita, **350**
Little David Play on Your Harp,
323
Loco-Motion, The, **312**
New Day, The, **316**
Ogguere, **327**
Over the Sea to Skye, **344**
Owl and the Cuckoo, The, **337**
Swing, The, **320**
This Train, **343**
Twist and Shout, **314**
Wake Up Canon, **326**
Walking in the Air, **317**
We Got the Beat, **310**

FOLK AND TRADITIONAL

African

Allundé, Alluia, **34**
Dima, **265**
New Africa (listening), **209**
Sansa kroma (Little Hawk), **166**
Sing Lo-Lo (listening), **385**
Take Time in Life, **156**
Vinqo (listening), **24**

African American

Big Bunch, a Little Bunch, **267**
Chicka-hanka, **138**
Goodbye My Riley O, **257**
Hold My Mule, **249**
How Long the Train Been
Gone?, **264**

Little David Play on Your Harp,
323
'Most Done Ling'rin' Here, **65**
Oh, Won't You Sit Down?, **70**
Old Ark's A-Moverin', **130**
Old Aunt Dinah, **245**
Old House, **282**
This Train, **343**
This Train (listening), **343**
Train Is A-Coming, **270**
We Shall Overcome, **386**

American *see also* African
American; Native American;
Puerto Rican
America, **354**
Bell Doth Toll, The, **276**
Buckeye Jim, **136**
Built My Lady a Fine Brick
House, **252**
Cedar Swamp, **50**
Circle of Song, **330**
Cotton-Eye Joe, **52**
Derby Ram, The
(Ozark version), **259**
E nānā kākou i nā manu (Let's
Watch the Birds), **338**
Eagle, **337**
Early in the Morning at Eight
O'Clock, **59**
Eight Bells, **281**
Frog Went A-Courtin', **46**
Girl I Left Behind, **249**
Goodbye Brother, **273**
Grandma's Feather Bed, **E**
Green Gravel, **247**
Heave-Ho Me Laddies, **258**
Hold My Mule, **248**
Hop Up and Jump Up, **271**
How Long the Train Been
Gone?, **264**
Hush, Little Baby (listening), **9**
I'll Rise When the Rooster
Crows, **36**
It Rained a Mist, **262**
Johnson Boys, **233**
Jolly Old St. Nicholas, **382**
Li'l 'Liza Jane, **20**

Long-Legged Sailor, **243**
Love Somebody, **94**
My Home's in Montana, **274**
Night Herding Song, **110**
Old Joe Clark, **74**
Old Paint, **275**
Over the River and Through
the Wood, **370**
Owl and the Cuckoo, The, **337**
Page's Train, **246**
Pat Works on the Railway, **86**
Push Boat Song, **266**
Ridin' of a Goat, Leadin'
of a Sheep, **251**
Row, Row, Row Your Boat, **268**
Sail Away, Ladies (listening), **55**
Sail Away, Ladies, **54**
Sandy McNab, **142**
Sea Shell, **245**
Shenandoah, **C**
Star-Spangled Banner, The,
356
Swapping Song, **253**
Wake Up Canon, **326**
Walk in the Parlor, **226**
Who's Got the Fishpole?, **261**
Yankee Doodle, **154**

American Indian
see Native American

Argentinian *see also*
Hispanic
Arroyito serrano, **340**
¿Quién es ese pajarito?
(Who Is That Little Bird?), **284**

Canadian
America, My Homeland, **358**
Chumbara, **172**
Kettle Valley Line, The, **348**
Old Carrion Crow, The, **192**

Caribbean
Day-O (listening), **72**
Jamaica Farewell (listening), **73**
Water Come a Me Eye, **90**

Chinese
Bamboo Flute, **134**

Congolese *see also* African
Dima, **265**

Cuban *see also* Hispanic
El manisero (Peanut Vendor), **106**
Ogguere, **327**

Danish
Marken er mejet
    (Out in the Meadow), **365**

Dutch
Sarasponda, **210**
Twee emmertjes (listening), **212**

English
Chairs to Mend, **272**
Derby Ram, The,
    (Ozark version) **259**
Old Aunt Dinah, **245**
Oliver Cromwell, **269**
Walking in the Air, **317**

French
Frère Jacques
    (Are You Sleeping?), **260**

Gaelic
Morning Has Broken, **22**
Morning Has Broken
    (listening), **23**

German
Himmel und Erde
    (Music Alone Shall Live), **280**

Ghanaian (Akan) *see also*
    African
Sansa kroma, **166**

Guatemalan *see also*
    Hispanic
La sanjuanerita
    (The Girl from San Juan), **100**

Hawaiian
E nānā kākou i nā manu (Let's
    Watch the Birds), **338**
`Ulili E (The Sandpiper), **396**

Hebrew, Israeli, Jewish
Achshav (Now), **112**
Erev Shel Shoshanim
    (listening), **68**

S'vivon Sov (Dreidel Spin), **374**
Zum Gali Gali, **255**

Hispanic
A la nanita nana
    (A Little Lullaby), **230**
A la puerta del cielo
    (At the Gates of Heaven), **12**
Arroyito serrano
    (Little Mountain Stream), **340**
Caballito blanco
    (Little White Pony), **278**
El barquito (The Tiny Boat), **214**
El coquí (The Frog), **178**
El manisero (Peanut Vendor), **106**
El quelite (The Village), **362**
El tecolote (excerpt)
    (listening), **361**
Entren santos peregrinos
    (Enter, Holy Pilgrims), **379**
Festival Dance (listening), **140**
Hojas de té (Tea Leaves)
    (speech piece), **256**
La Otra España (listening), **64**
La Otra España
    (The Other Spain), **62**
La sanjuanerita
    (The Girl from San Juan), **100**
La Yunsita, **350**
Las mañanitas (listening), **197**
Las mañanitas
    (The Morning Song), **194**
Molinillo de café
    (Little Coffee Mill), **250**
Ogguere, **327**
Para pedir posada, **376**
¿Quién es ese pajarito?
    (Who Is That Little Bird?), **284**

Irish
Macnamara's Band, **88**
Oro My Bodeen, **279**
When I Was Young, **187**

Italian
Farfallina (Butterfly), **244**

Jamaican *see also*
    Caribbean
Day-O (listening), **72**

Jamaica Farewell (listening), **73**
Water Come a Me Eye, **90**

Japanese
Ame fure (Rain), **26**
Hitori, **345**

Korean
Ban Dal (listening), **184**

Laotian
Dok Djampa (The White
    Jasmine Flower), **392**

Lebanese
Hala lala layya, **222**

Liberian *see also* African
Take Time in Life, **156**

Mexican *see also* Hispanic
Caballito blanco
    (Little White Pony), **278**
El quelite (The Village), **362**
El tecolote (listening), **361**
Entren santos peregrinos
    (Enter, Holy Pilgrims), **379**
Hojas de té (Tea Leaves)
    (speech piece), **256**
Las mañanitas (listening), **197**
Las mañanitas
    (The Morning Song), **194**
Molinillo de café (Little Coffee
    Mill) (speech piece), **250**
Para pedir posada, **376**

Native American
Hopi
    Bu-Vah (Sleep), **18**
    Bu-Vah (listening), **19**
Navajo
    We Are Here, **394**

Norwegian
Nokken Danser (listening), **168**

Panamanian *see also*
    Hispanic
El barquito (The Tiny Boat), **214**

Peruvian *see also* Hispanic
Festival Dance (listening), **140**
La Yunsita, **350**

Philippines
Sitsiritsit, **102**
Tinikling (listening), **105**

Puerto Rican *see also*
Hispanic
A la nanita nana, **230**
El coquí (The Frog), **178**

Russian
Beryoza (The Birch Tree), **286**
Korobushka, **285**
Katyusha, **188**
Porushka-Paranya (listening), **208**

Senegalese *see also* African
New Africa (listening), **209**
Sing Lo-Lo (listening), **385**

Scottish
Over the Sea to Skye, **344**

Spanish *see also* Hispanic
A la puerta del cielo, **12**

Swiss
L'inverno è già passato, **390**

South African *see also*
African
Vinqo (listening), **24**

Vietnamese
Qua Câu Gió Bay (listening), **367**
Tết Trung, **366**

Welsh
All Through the Night, **277**

West African *see also*
African
New Africa (listening), **209**
Sansa kroma, **166**

HOLIDAYS, SEASONAL, PATRIOTIC

Autumn
Marken er mejet
(Out in the Meadow), **365**
Tết Trung (Children's Festival), **366**

Christmas
A la nanita nana
(A Little Lullaby), **230**
Entren santos peregrinos
(Enter, Holy Pilgrims), **379**
Jolly Old St. Nicholas, **382**
Joy to the World, **383**
Once Upon a Christmastime, **380**
Para pedir posada, **376**

Earth Day *see also* Spring
We Are Here, **394**
Just One Planet, **164**

Halloween *see also* Autumn
Boogie-Woogie Ghost, The, **368**

Hanukkah
December Nights, December Lights, **372**
S'vivon Sov (Dreidel Spin), **374**

Kwanzaa
Nia (Purpose), **384**

Martin Luther King, Jr., Day
We Shall Overcome, **386**
What Can One Little Person Do?, **204**

Patriotic
America, **354**
Patriotic Medley, **G**
Stars and Stripes Forever, The (listening), **355**
Star-Spangled Banner, The, **356**
This Land Is Your Land, **146**
We Remember, **360**
Yankee Doodle, **154**

Spring
`Ulili E (The Sandpiper), **396**
Dok Djampa (The White Jasmine Flower), **392**
L'inverno è già passato, **390**
Spring, from *The Four Seasons* (listening), **391**

St. Patrick's Day
Macnamara's Band, **88**

Thanksgiving *see also* Autumn
Over the River and Through the Wood, **370**
Song of Thanksgiving, **371**

Valentine's Day
I Will Be Your Friend, **388**
My Friend (listening), **389**
Love Somebody, **94**

Winter *see also* Christmas; Hanukkah; Kwanzaa
December Nights, December Lights, **372**

YOUR BROADWAY MUSICAL

Annie Junior
I Think I'm Gonna Like It Here, **299**
It's the Hard-Knock Life, **293**
N.Y.C., **302**
Tomorrow, **295**
You're Never Fully Dressed Without a Smile, **304**

INDEX OF POETRY

Corre el rio (Haiku) by
P. Vasquez, **183**
Dream Dust by L. Hughes, **235**
Hojas de té (Tea Leaves)
(speech piece)
(Mexican Folk), **256**
Jolly Old St. Nicholas
(Traditional American), **382**
Journey, A (speech piece), **14**
Mighty River (speech piece) by
W. Brecht, **217**

Alphabetical Index

Modern Dragon, A (speech piece) by R. B. Bennett, **98**

Molinillo de café (Little Coffee Mill) (speech piece) (Mexican Folk), **250**

One Song, America, Before I Go (excerpt) by W. Whitman, **147**

Rain Haiku by M. A. Mohanraj, **27**

Trains at Night by F. M. Post, **246**

Whispers by M. C. Livingston, **95**

Woodpecker, The (speech piece) by E. M. Roberts, **48**

💿 INDEX OF LISTENING SELECTIONS

Adagio (excerpt) from *Concierto de Aranjuez* by J. Rodrigo, **13**

Al Hebben de Princen haren by J. Van Eyck, **225**

All Through the Night (Welsh Folk Song), **277**

Arroyito serrano by C. Guastavino, **341**

Augie's Great Municipal Band (excerpt) from *Star Wars Episode 1: The Phantom Menace* by J. Williams, **56**

Autumn Music, First Movement (excerpt) by J. Higdon, **121**

Badinerie from *Suite in B Minor* by J.S. Bach, **61**

Ban Dal by Y. Kyekyoung, **184**

Big Bunch of Roses by J.W. Work III, **267**

Big Turtle—Fanfare from *The South China Sea*, by G. Ligeti, **201**

Boléro (excerpt) by M. Ravel, **41**

Brooklyn Jugs by Brooklyn Jugs, **77**

Bu-Vah (Hopi Lullaby), **19**

Canon in D by J. Pachelbel, **17**

Carillon from *L'Arlesienne, Suite No. 1*, by G. Bizet, **244**

Cattle from *The Plow That Broke the Plains* by V. Thomson, **274**

Children's Chorus from *Hansel and Gretel* by E. Humperdinck, **280**

Concertino for Marimba, Op. 21, First Movement ("Vigorous") by P. Creston, **120**

Contredanse (excerpt) from *Les Indes galantes* by J. P. Rameau, **93**

Dance No. 4 (excerpt) by P. Glass, **144**

Dance of the Mirlitons from *The Nutcracker* by P. Tchaikovsky, **173**

Day-O (excerpt) by H. Belafonte, I. Burgie, and W. Attaway, **72**

Debka Kurdit (Yemeni folk dance), **236**

East St. Louis Toodle-Oo by D. Ellington, **232**

El tecolote (Mexican Folk Song), **361**

Erev Shel Shoshanim by J. Hadar and M. Dor, **68**

Festival Dance (Peruvian Folk Melody), **140**

Galop (excerpt) from *The Comedians* by D. Kabalevsky, **254**

Guadalcanal March from *Victory at Sea* by R. Rodgers, **108**

Guantanamera by J.F. Dias, **228**

Hush, Little Baby (American Folk Song), **9**

In the Mood by J. Garland, **143**

Infernal Dance of King Kashchei from *Firebird Suite* by I. Stravinsky, **191**

Jamaica Farewell by I. Burgie, **73**

La canarie from *Dances from Terpsichore* by M. Praetorius, **176**

La otra España by J. C. Calderón, **64**

Las mañanitas (Mexican song), **197**

Magic Flute, The, (Overture) by W. A. Mozart, **252**

Milan (Meeting of the Two Rivers) (excerpt) by K. Kale, **208**

Miniwanka (or The Moments of Water) by R. M. Schafer, **28**

Morning Has Broken (Traditional Gaelic Melody), **23**

Musette from *Notebook for Anna Magdalena Bach* by J. S. Bach, **261**

My Friend by M. Kibble and J. Kibble, **389**

New Africa by Youssou N'Dour and Habib Faye, **209**

Night of the Mockingbird by J. Huling, **153**

Nokken Danser (Norwegian folk melody), **168**

Ogguere (Afro-Cuban lullaby), **329**

Oito Batutas by Pixinguinha, **128**

One Note Samba by A. C. Jobim, **92**

Parade in the Parlor (North Carolina folk melody), **229**

Porushka-Paranya (Russian folk song), **208**

Vivo from Pulcinella Suite by I. Stravinsky, **201**

Qua Cà Gió Bay
(Vietnamese Folk Song), **367**
Quintet, Op. 43 (Menuet)
(excerpt) by C. Nielsen, **121**
Refavela by G. Gil, **209**
Repicados sobre Madera
(excerpt) (Uruguayan
Candombe), **93**
Russian Sailors' Dance from *The
Red Poppy* by R. Glière, **266**
Sail Away (Mountain Dance), **55**
Salsa in the Parlor (North
Carolina folk melody), **229**
Scheherazade by N. Rimsky-
Korsakov, **161**
Serenade No. 10 in B Flat
Major, K. 361 ("Gran
Partita"), Theme and
Variations (excerpt) by W. A.
Mozart, **235**
Sing Lo-Lo from *Afrika Wassa* by
V. Diop, **385**
Sonata for Cello and Piano, Op.
40 Second Movement by D.
Shostakovich, **40**
Sonata for Flute and Piano,
Third Movement by F.
Poulenc, **200**
Sonata for Piano No. 2 in D
Minor, Vivace (excerpt) by S.
Prokofiev, **181**
Sonatina for Three Timpani and
Piano, First Movement
(excerpt) by A. Tcherepnin, **81**
Sorcerer's Apprentice, The
(excerpt) by P. Dukas, **116**
Spinning Wheel by D. Clayton-
Thomas, **211**
Spring (Allegro) from *The Four
Seasons* by A. Vivaldi, **391**
Stars and Stripes Forever, The,
by J. P. Sousa, **355**
Summer (Allegro non Molto)
(excerpt) from *The Four
Seasons*, **161**
Summertime from *Porgy and
Bess* by G. and I. Gershwin,
160

Symphony No. 4, Fourth
Movement by P. Tchaikovsky,
287
Symphony No. 7 in A Major,
Second Movement (excerpt)
by L. van Beethoven, **242**
Symphony No. 73 ("La Chase")
("The Hunt"), Fourth
Movement by F. J. Haydn,
263
Take Five (excerpt) by P.
Desmond, **41**
This Train (African American
Spiritual), **343**
Tinikling (national dance of the
Philippines), **105**
Tragic Story, A by B. Britten,
190
Turandot from *Symphonic
Metamorphosis* (excerpt) by P.
Hindemith, **81**
Twee emmertjes
(traditional spinning song),
212
Vinqo (Zulu song), **24**
Walking in the Air by H. Blake,
319
Waltz in the Parlor (North
Carolina folk melody), **229**
What Did You Do Today at
Jeffrey's House? by P.
Schickele, **80**

Global Voices

Ban Dal (Korean Hand-
Clapping Game), **184**
Tinikling (Filipino Dance), **105**
Twee emmertjes
(traditional spinning song),
212
Vinqo (Zulu/Xhosa Song), **24**

Interviews

Brooklyn Jugs, **77**
Criddle, Lauren
(From the Top), **160**
Feder, Abraham
(From the Top), **40**
Nissman, Barbara, **181**
Ross, David (From the Top),
200
Turner, Catherine
(From the Top), **80**
Vasan, Neil (From the Top),
120

INDEX OF SONGS AND SPEECH PIECES

A la nanita nana
(A Little Lullaby), **230**
A la puerta del cielo (At the
Gate of Heaven), **12**
Achshav (Now), **112**
All Through the Night, **277**
Allundé, Alluia, **34**
Ame fure (Rain), **26**
America, **354**
America, My Homeland, **358**
Are You Sleeping?
(Frère Jacques), **260**
Arroyito serrano
(Little Mountain Stream),
340
At the Gate of Heaven
(A la puerta del cielo), **12**
At the Hop, **306**
Bamboo Flute, **134**
Bamboo, **218**
Bell Doth Toll, The, **276**
Beryoza (The Birch Tree), **286**
Big Bunch, a Little Bunch, **267**
Birch Tree, The (Beryoza), **286**
Boogie-Woogie Ghost, The,
368
Buckeye Jim, **136**
Built My Lady a Fine Brick
House, **252**
Butterfly (Farfallina), **244**
Bu-Vah (Sleep), **18**
Caballito blanco
(Little White Pony), **278**
Cedar Swamp, **50**

Chairs to Mend, **272**

Chicka Hanka, **138**

Children's Festival (Tết Trung), **366**

Chumbara, **172**

Circle of Song, **330**

Cotton-Eye Joe, **52, 53**

December Nights, December Lights, **372**

Derby Ram, The, **259**

Dima, **265**

Dok Djampa (The White Jasmine Flower), **392**

Don't Let the Music Stop, **334**

Down at the Twist and Shout, **308**

Dreidel Spin (S'vivon Sov), **374**

E nānā kākou i nā manu (Let's Watch the Birds), **338**

Eagle, **337**

Early in the Morning at Eight O'Clock, **59**

Eight Bells, **281**

El barquito (The Tiny Boat), **214**

El coquí (The Frog), **178**

El manisero (Peanut Vendor), **106**

El quelite (The Village), **362**

Enter, Holy Pilgrims (Entren santos peregrinos), **379**

Entren santos peregrinos (Enter, Holy Pilgrims), **379**

Farfallina (Butterfly), **244**

Follow Your Dream, **234**

Frère Jacques (Are You Sleeping?), **260**

Frog, The (El coquí), **178**

Frog Went A-Courtin', **46**

Girl from San Juan, The (La sanjuanerita), **100**

Girl I Left Behind Me, The, **249**

Goodbye Brother, **273**

Goodbye, My Riley O, **257**

Grandma's Feather Bed, **E**

Green Gravel, **247**

Hala lala layya, **222**

Happiness, **124**

Happy Talk, **84**

Heave-Ho, Me Laddies, **258**

Hey, Look Me Over, **114**

Himmel und Erde (Music Alone Shall Live), **280**

Hine Ma Tov (How Good It Is), **66**

Hitori, **345**

Hojas de té (Tea Leaves) (speech piece), **256**

Hold My Mule, **248**

Hop Up and Jump Up, **271**

How Good It Is (Hine Ma Tov), **66**

How Long the Train Been Gone?, **264**

I Heard a Mockingbird, **150**

I Think I'm Gonna Like It Here, **299**

I Will Be Your Friend, **388**

I'll Rise When the Rooster Crows, **36**

It Rained a Mist, **262**

It's the Hard-Knock Life, **293**

Johnson Boys, **233**

Jolly Old St. Nicholas, **382**

Journey, A (speech piece), **14**

Joy to the World, **383**

Just One Planet, **164**

Katyusha, **188**

Kettle Valley Line, The, **348**

Korobushka, **285**

L'inverno è già passato (Winter Is Over), **390**

La otra España (The Other Spain), **62**

La sanjuanerita (The Girl from San Juan), **100**

La Yunsita, **350**

Las mañanitas (The Morning Song), **194**

Let's Watch the Birds (E nānā kākou i nā manu), **338**

Li'l 'Liza Jane, **20**

Little Coffee Mill (Molinillo de café) (speech piece), **250**

Little David Play on Your Harp, **323**

Little Hawk (Sansa kroma), **166**

Little Lullaby, A (A la nanita nana), **230**

Little Mountain Stream (Arroyito serrano), **340**

Little White Pony (Caballito blanco), **278**

Loco-Motion, The, **312**

Long-Legged Sailor, **243**

Looking for Shelter (Para pedir posada), **377**

Love Somebody, **94**

Macnamara's Band, **88**

Marken er mejet (Out in the Meadow), **365**

Mighty River (speech piece), **217**

Modern Dragon, A (speech piece), **98**

Molinillo de café (Little Coffee Mill) (speech piece), **250**

Morning Has Broken, **22**

Morning Song, The (Las mañanitas), **194**

'Most Done Ling'rin' Here, **65**

Music Alone Shall Live (Himmel und Erde), **280**

My Home's in Montana, **274**

My Town, My World, **6**

New Day, The, **316**

Nia (Purpose), **384**

Night Herding Song, **110**

Now (Achshav), **112**

N.Y.C., **302**

Octopus's Garden, **30**

Ogguere, **327**

Oh, Won't You Sit Down?, **70**

Old Abram Brown, **32**

Old Ark's A-Moverin', **130**

Old Aunt Dinah, **245**

Old Carrion Crow, The, **192**

Old House, **282**

Old Joe Clark, **74**

Old Paint, **275**

Oliver Cromwell, **269**

Once Upon a Christmastime, **380**

Oro, My Bodeen, **279**

Other Spain, The (La otra España), **62**

Out in the Meadow (Marken er mejet), **365**

Over the Rainbow, **126**

Over the River and Through the Wood, **370**
Over the Sea to Skye, **344**
Owl and the Cuckoo, The, **337**
Page's Train, **246**
Para pedir posada (Looking for Shelter), **377**
Pat Works on the Railway, **86**
Patriotic Medley, **H**
Peace Round, **16**
Peanut Vendor (El manisero), **106**
Peasant's Dancing Day, **132**
Please, Mr. Postman, **44**
Purpose (Nia), **384**
Push Boat Song, **266**
¿Quién es ese pajarito? (Who Is That Little Bird?), **284**
Rain (Ame fure), **26**
Ridin' of a Goat, Leadin' of a Sheep, **251**
Rise Up, O Flame, **283**
Roll on, Columbia, **182**
Row, Row, Row Your Boat, **268**
S'vivon Sov (Dreidel Spin), **374**
Sail Away, Ladies, **54**
Sandpiper, The ('Ulili E), **396**
Sandy McNab, **142**
Sansa kroma (Little Hawk), **166**
Sarasponda, **210**

Sea Shell, **245**
Shabat Shalom, **170**
Shenandoah, **D**
Sing Alleluia, Allelu, **220**
Sing of America (speech piece), **359**
Sitsiritsit, **102**
Sky Dances, **206**
Sleep (Bu-Vah), **18**
Something for Me, Something for You, **4**
Somos el barco (We Are the Boat), **10**
Song of Thanksgiving, **371**
Star-Spangled Banner, The, **356**
Step Into the Spotlight, **A**
Swapping Song, **253**
Swing, The, **320**
Take Time in Life, **156**
Tea Leaves (Hojas de té) (speech piece), **256**
Têt Trung (Children's Festival), **366**
This Land Is Your Land, **146**
This Train, **343**
Tiny Boat, The (El barquito), **214**
Tomorrow, **295**
Train Is A-Coming, **270**
Twist and Shout, **314**
'Ulili E (The Sandpiper), **396**

Village, The (El quelite), **362**
Viva la musica, **174**
Wake Up Canon, **326**
Walk in the Parlor, **226**
Walking in the Air, **317**
Water Come a Me Eye, **90**
We Are Here, **394**
We Are the Boat (Somos el barco), **10**
We Got the Beat, **310**
We Remember, **360**
We Shall Overcome, **387**
What Can One Little Person Do?, **204**
When I Was Young, **187**
White Jasmine Flower, The (Dok Djampa), **392**
Who Is That Little Bird? (¿Quién es ese pajarito?), **284**
Who's Got a Fishpole?, **261**
Winter Is Over (L'inverno è già passato), **390**
Woodpecker, The (speech piece), **48**
Yankee Doodle, **154**
You're Never Fully Dressed Without a Smile, **304**
Zum gali gali, **255**

Pronunciation Key

Simplified International Phonetic Alphabet
VOWELS

ɑ	father	o	obey	æ	cat	ɔ	paw
e	ape	u	moon	ε	pet	ʊ	put
i	bee	ʌ	up	ɪ	it	ə	ago

SPECIAL SOUNDS

β — say *b* without touching lips together; *Spanish* nueve, haba

ç — hue; *German* ich

ð — the; *Spanish* todo

ɬ — put tongue in position for *l* and say *sh*

ņ — sound n as individual syllable

ö — form [o] with lips and say [e]; *French* adieu, *German* schön

œ — form [ɔ] with lips and say [ε]; *French* coeur, *German* plötzlich

ɾ — flipped r; butter or r native to language

ɼ — rolled r; *Spanish* perro

ǂ — click tongue on the ridge behind teeth; *Zulu* ngcwele

ü — form [u] with lips and say [i]; *French* tu, *German* grün

ʊ̈ — form [ʊ] with lips and say [ɪ]

x — blow strong current of air with back of tongue up; *German* Bach, *Hebrew* Hanukkah, *Spanish* bajo

ʒ — pleasure

ˈ — glottal stop, as in the exclamation "uh oh!" [ˈʌ ˈo]

~ — nasalized vowel, such as *French* bon [bõ]

˺ — end consonants *k, p,* and *t* without puff of air, such as sky (no puff of air after *k*), as opposed to kite (puff of air after *k*)

OTHER CONSONANTS PRONOUNCED SIMILAR TO ENGLISH

ch	cheese	ny	onion; *Spanish* niño
dy	adieu	sh	shine
g	go	sk	sky
ng	sing	th	think

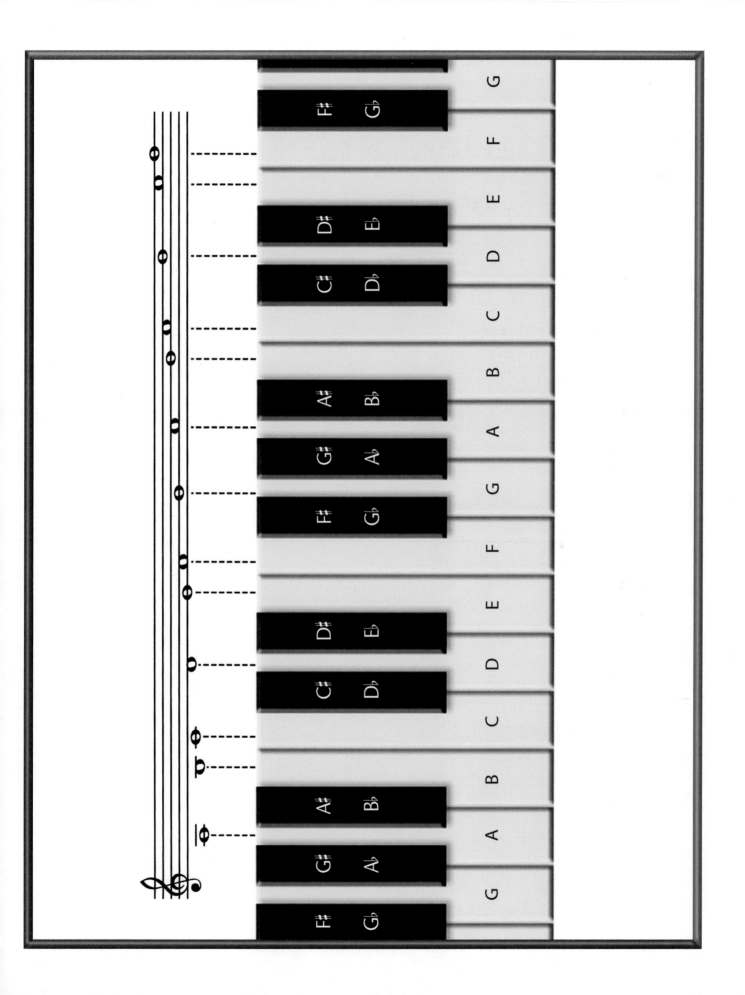